PLATO ON PUNISHMENT

PLATO

ON PUNISHMENT

MARY MARGARET MACKENZIE

UNIVERSITY OF CALIFORNIA PRESS

Berkeley ◆ *Los Angeles* ◆ *London*

FOR MY PARENTS

UNIVERSITY OF CALIFORNIA PRESS
BERKELEY AND LOS ANGELES, CALIFORNIA

UNIVERSITY OF CALIFORNIA PRESS, LTD.
LONDON, ENGLAND

© 1981 BY
THE REGENTS OF THE UNIVERSITY OF CALIFORNIA

PRINTED IN THE UNITED STATES OF AMERICA

1 2 3 4 5 6 7 8 9

Library of Congress Cataloging in Publication Data

Mackenzie, Mary Margaret.
  Plato on punishment.

  A revision of the author's thesis, Cambridge.
  Bibliography: p.
  Includes indexes.
  1. Plato—Ethics.   2. Ethics.   3. Punishment.
4. Values.   I. Title.
B398.E8M3   1981   364.6'01   80-6065
ISBN 0-520-04169-0

CONTENTS

ACKNOWLEDGMENTS

This book is the beneficiary of support, advice, criticism and discussion from many people. Colleagues and students have provided a persistent stimulus, especially by requiring me to defend my ideas against their attack. Those whom I have not acknowledged severally will, I hope, accept my thanks here.

In particular, I have profited from conversations and seminars with Myles Burnyeat, Geoffrey Lloyd, Martha Nussbaum and G.E.L. Owen, who have provided a climate of philosophical excitement and meticulous enquiry both in Cambridge and at Harvard. They, A.W.H. Adkins, and Gerasimos Santas have read and provided valuable comments on drafts of *Plato on Punishment*; my warm thanks to them for the liberal gift of their time and the assistance of their encouragement and advice. Malcolm Schofield was equally generous, and he has been tireless as a supervisor, constant as a friend. I owe him a great deal.

An early version of this work (entitled "Plato's Theory of Punishment and its Antecedents") formed my doctoral dissertation at the University of Cambridge. Parts of Chapter 6 appeared in *Philosophy and Literature* (Spring 1978); I am grateful to the editor for permission to reprint that article here.

Grant Barnes of the University of California Press has been helpful and supportive throughout; to him too, I am very grateful. I should also like to thank Sheila Levine, Susan Peters, Rebecca Stein, and Leonie Gordon for their editorial assistance. Helen Gibson typed the manuscript with exemplary patience and skill. I thank her.

Gavin, my husband, has sustained me throughout; my debt to him goes far beyond the scope of an acknowledgement. Finally, the book is dedicated to my parents, in deep gratitude.

INTRODUCTION

Why punish? The question burns because punishments hurt. So either they are wrong, or they need justifying. Whether we inflict the punishment or suffer it, then, we need either to give or to receive a moral account of why it is taking place. And, as crimes are a commonplace, so the justification of their punishments should be frequently heard.

This book is an essay in the philosophy of punishment, a discussion, from several aspects, of the problems inherent in justifying penal institutions. Thus it is in part exegetic; but in part it is contentious, not least because the issue is a controversial one.

There is a dilemma. On the one hand, it is impossible to produce a theory of punishment that is coherent, consistent, and free from moral outrage. This I argue in Part I. On the other hand, to practice punishment appears to be irresistible, once men become organised into social groups. This I argue in Part II. Part III then presents this dilemma in operation, as the problems of theory meet head-on the pressures of tradition in the penology of Plato.

As my title bears witness, the discussion of Plato—Part III—is the core of the book. For Plato's account of punishment is important both historically and philosophically. Historically we have here the first fully argued penology of the classical tradition. It is a part of a complete moral theory, derivative from (Chapter 9) and finding its strength in that moral theory (Chapter 12). But philosophically its importance is greater still. For within Plato's moral theory, his penology is philosophically very strong, proof against many of the objections to be levelled against his modern counterparts. And this reveals the cost of a humanitarian theory of punishment; such a theory must be underwritten with a moral theory extreme in its metaphysical commitment. But unhappily even this is not enough to insure Plato against the demands of a tradition based on considerations of justice (Chapter 13).

The first and second parts of the book are, like the third, self-contained. But they are intended also to complement each other and to illuminate the penological issues discussed in the final part.

Part I is an analysis of what punishment is and how it may be justified. It offers an account of three major theories of punishment—retribution, utilitarianism and reform—and shows how they compare with one another. This comparison, however, is the sting in the tail. Different theories of punishment cannot be held conjointly because they conflict. But they cannot be held separately, either, or they risk being violent or unintelligible. Violence is what theories of punishment guard against, and if a theory is incomprehensible, it is no theory at all. So the argument of Part I concludes by reiterating the question: Why punish?

Part II offers an historical answer. Going back to the earliest Greek literature, it shows the moral background of the institution of punishment as it developed in the archaic and classical periods. Justice emerges as the major feature of moral reasoning at this time. But here again there lurks controversy. For I argue, from the evidence of Homer's *Iliad*, that there were, first of all, no punishments; there were not even any crimes. To draw this conclusion is to invite two challenges. The first is scholarly, for this kind of interpretation of Homer is by no means universally accepted. The second is psychological, for to imagine a society so different, both morally and legally, from our own is to strain the suspension of disbelief to its limits.

Thus in Part II the Homeric evidence is examined in considerable detail, in order to satisfy the scholarly opponent and the sceptic. The evidence of the later archaic and classical periods is less problematic, because it begins to look familiar. Consequently I have felt justified in treating that in a more cavalier fashion. In particular I have not repeatedly stressed the lapse of time between one author and another discussed in the same section, for my objective has been to establish what types of moral argument were current by the time of Socrates.

In the matter of Greek, I have not assumed that the reader will be fluent. I have transliterated some words where a translation would prejudice my argument. And I beg for patience from my Greekless reader, who will find that some translation or explanation is forthcoming in the end.

The exegetical parts of the book are intended to clarify areas which would be obscure to the non-specialist. Specialists—philosophers, classicists, lawyers, or historians of ideas—will, I trust, be indulgent where their own specialisation is discussed. For it is to draw together philosophy, law and the history of ideas in the classical topic of Plato's penology that I have written this book.

PART
I

THEORIES OF PUNISHMENT

CHAPTER

1

WHAT IS A PUNISHMENT?

Henry Lightfingers is in a department store one day. He is overcome by the desire to possess a shiny, expensive wristwatch. He steals one from the counter, knowing that stealing is illegal, and knowing that he will be punished if he is caught. The store-detective sees him at it, follows him from the shop, and arrests him. In due course, Henry comes before the courts, is found guilty of larceny, and is sentenced to six months' imprisonment. He serves his sentence, but he hates it in prison.

The sad story of Henry Lightfingers is the history of a crime and a punishment. In its detail, it illustrates what we, conforming members of society, and Henry, our criminal fellow, consider to underpin the notion of punishment. For without these detailed conditions, either we would deny that a punishment has taken place at all, or Henry would appeal against his conviction or against his sentence. There are two grounds, therefore, upon which the description of this affair as a punishment can be rebutted. The first is logical, that in some sense the word is improperly used; the second is moral, that in some respect the penalty is improperly applied.[1]

1. A.M. Quinton, "On Punishment," in H.B. Acton, ed., *The Philosophy of Punishment* (London: Macmillan, 1969), argues that the moral account of a punishment is separable from its logical content, to the effect that retributivism (logic) and utilitarianism (morals) may combine in the justification of a penal system. Several difficulties attach to this argument; cf. Chs. 3, 4 and 5 below. In the present chapter it is made clear, contra Quinton, that, to describe an action as a punishment, we at times invoke moral, as well as logical considerations. So it is not possible to make the clear-cut distinction upon which Quinton's argument relies. The difficulty is avoided by two other writers who advance a similar solution to the clash of retributivism with utility, since they avoid the morals/logic antithesis.

a. THE CRIME

Henry did take the wristwatch, and he did know that stealing wrist-watches is illegal. Thus Henry is the author of the action under scrutiny, which is a crime because it is illegal. The reason that he is punished is that he has committed a crime; he is sentenced to six months *for larceny*. The description of a sentence passed by the courts must contain information about the offence. If Henry's story began with his appearance in court and failed to mention the crime he had committed, or even that he had committed a crime at all, we would feel uneasily that the story was either incomplete or surreal. The incompleteness of the story would be a matter of logic. "Is this a punishment at all?" we would ask. Surrealism, on the other hand, exploits our sense of moral outrage, that Henry is not punished for a crime, and that therefore his punishment is unfair. Thus the commission of a crime is a necessary condition of our describing this transaction as a punishment.[2]

But what is a crime? A crime may be illegal, or immoral, or both. In either case, the crime is committed in disobedience to a known set of rules. In the most basic instance, these rules are laid down by the criminal law; thus the primary sense of 'crime' is 'illegal act'.[3] Derivatively, an immoral (and not illegal) act may be described as a crime. "It is a crime to charge high prices for bread": here 'crime' is hyperbole, and normal usage would expect a moral, rather than a legal, wording, such as "It is wicked to charge high prices for bread." Moreover, what is moral may not overlap with what is legal. For we can hardly suppose that laws are prescriptions for the perfect moral order, and, further, it can cogently be argued that some of morality should be a matter for personal choice, positively outside the jurisdiction of any court.

The set of rules must be public[4] (known or knowable, since ignorance of the law is no defence). To this end, the rules should be previously instituted and publicised; the offender should not be liable under some new or private statute. Otherwise, either the offender may argue that

---

J. Rawls, "Two Concepts of Rules", in P. Foot, ed., *Theories of Ethics* (Oxford: O.U.P., 1967), replaces it with a distinction between the rule (morals, utilitarianism) and the case (logic, retributivism), whereas H.L.A. Hart, "Prolegomenon to the Principles of Punishment," in *Punishment and Responsibility* (Oxford: Clarendon, 1968), offers "general justifying aim" versus "distribution." But see d. below and Ch. 3.c.

2. Cf. J.I. Mabbott, "Punishment," in H.B. Acton, ed., *The Philosophy of Punishment* (London: Macmillan, 1969).

3. "A 'criminal' means a man who has broken a law, not a bad man; an 'innocent' man is a man who has not broken the law in connection with which he is being punished, although he may be a bad man and have broken other laws" (Mabbott, "Punishment," p. 41). Cf. Hart, "Legal Responsibility and Excuses," in *Punishment and Responsibility*, p. 37.

4. Cf. Rawls, *A Theory of Justice*, (Oxford: Clarendon, 1972), p. 56.

he acted in good faith and should not be punished (it is unfair) or we might object that he has not committed a crime at all (his action is improperly described as a crime).

That an action is called criminal is a sign that it is subject to general social disapproval. This, I suggest, is because,[5] considered from the point of view of the original legislator,[6] it injures those whose interests the law is designed to preserve and protect.[7] To this extent a legal code, possibly unlike its moral counterpart, is teleological. There is something prudentially undesirable about the crime or its effects, so it is proscribed. Consequently the penal reasoning will not be "You ought not to do this because you will be punished," wherein the independent offensiveness of the crime is obscured, and the argument becomes random, if not vicious. Nor will it be "You ought not to do this (simply because it is wrong, no consequential reason given), and if you do, you will be punished," as the deontologist would require. Rather it will be "You ought not to do this (because it is harmful, either directly or indirectly, and for that reason it is forbidden), and if you do then punishment will follow."

The legislator must, then, decide which acts are criminal before embarking upon a general justification of the punishment for those acts.[8]

b. THE CRIMINAL

Punishment is not of the innocent. Henry cannot complain, at least without perjury, that the crime is not his, for he is the criminal. A plea of 'alibi', however, if accepted, would exempt him from conviction and thence from punishment. Thus, if what happens to him is to be described legitimately as a punishment, he must be the perpetrator of the crime.

5. Cf., e.g., Quinton, "On Punishment", p. 63: "Considerations of utility, then, are alone relevant to the determination of what in general, what *kinds* of action, to punish."

6. Cf. Rawls, "Two Concepts," p. 108. I do not wish to make mileage from the notion of the original legislator; it serves merely to remind us that the legal system may be seen as purposive, as having general aims which individual statutes are designed to promote.

7. This description will apply to legal codes of societies with either a wide or a narrow franchise.

8. Here Hart is nearly, but not quite, right. He emphasises the distinction between "the primary objective of the law in encouraging or discouraging certain kinds of behaviour, and its merely ancillary sanction of remedial steps" ("Prolegomenon," p. 7). But the weasel lurks in the notion of encouragement and discouragement. The distinction should properly be made between the law's declaring certain acts to be criminal, and the means which are instrumental to maintaining that prescription, of which encouragement and discouragement will be the first steps. On this account, punishment should be thought of as a denunciation separate from the declarations embodied in the legal code—although this is what Hart denies.

This condition holds for reasons both of logic and of fairness. Consider the case where the accused is convicted of a crime of which he is innocent. If the judge knows that he is innocent but punishes him nevertheless, we should call this victimisation, not punishment.[9] If, however, the judge believes the criminal to be guilty and sentences him in good faith, we will exclaim against the sentence on the grounds that it is unfair. In both cases, were the truth to be made public, we should expect the sentence to be withdrawn.

In general, morality demands that the crime should be freely committed,[10] not under duress or misapprehension, so that responsibility may be properly ascribed to the offender. A penalty is exacted from an agent who has disobeyed the law, of his own free will. Under such circumstances, punishment may be justified; if the offender had no control over his act,[11] or if he has not committed the offence at all, the punishment will again be said to be a victimisation.

Logically, we may distinguish between responsibility and culpability. In general, according as a man is responsible, so he is culpable (subject to punishment and blame). 'Responsibility', however, describes the relation between the agent and his act,[12] while 'culpability' refers to the relation between the responsible man and our reactions. So modern legal theory supposes that responsibility and culpability are co-extensive.[13] But some accounts of responsibility do not presuppose culpability, as I shall argue.[14]

However, three factors render the notion of responsibility opaque[15] and cast doubt upon the straightforward relation between the agent and his act.

The first is a question of metaphysics. If determinism is true, can we make any sense of the condition that the agent acted freely? A strong

9. The charge of victimisation may be a moral objection, but it need not be. For example, a strict utilitarian who did not find victimisation objectionable might nevertheless argue that this case is not to be *described* as a punishment. Such an argument is the source of the "definitional stop" (Hart, "Prolegomenon," p. 6).

10. Cf. Aristotle, *E.N.* 1109b35.

11. Cf. Hart, "Legal Responsibility and Excuses," p. 105.

12. Cf. J. Feinberg, "Action and Responsibility," in *Doing and Deserving* (Princeton: Princeton U.P., 1970).

13. Cf. H. Gross, *A Theory of Criminal Justice* (Oxford: O.U.P., 1979), Ch.3. I have profited greatly from discussion with Professor Gross.

14. Neither ancient Greeks, in general, nor Plato, in particular, did so. Cf. Chs. 6, 7 and 9.

15. N.b., of course, the valuable discussion of excuses and responsibility provoked by J.L. Austin's "A Plea for Excuses," in A.R. White, ed., *The Philosophy of Action* (Oxford: O.U.P., 1968), and expanded, e.g., by Hart, "The Ascription of Rights and Responsibility," *Proc. Ar. Soc.* (1948–49):171–194; P.T. Geach, "Ascriptivism," *Ph. Rev.* (1960):221–225, and Feinberg, "Action and Responsibility."

deterministic thesis claims that none of us control what we do, in the sense that external causes (and thereafter internal ones) operate to determine our behaviour. Consequently, there can be no significant difference between the agent who acts under compulsion (he is not liable to punishment) and the agent who acts freely, under the duress of the totality of causes (he is liable to punishment).[16] In short, determinism suggests that the guilty are innocent, in the sense that what they do is beyond their control.

The second is a question of moral psychology.[17] Henry is adjudged guilty, not insane. But how do we know that all guilt is not a symptom of insanity? Some would argue that all crimes are committed under conditions of limited control.[18] Henry, for example, was 'overcome by desire' to possess the wristwatch. That he was overcome might suggest that he had no control over his actions. Or a forensic psychiatrist might claim that Henry is abnormally attracted to shiny things—he is in fact a millionaire, has no need to steal wristwatches, and in any case has ten others at home that were legally come by. Nevertheless he is possessed by the magpie instinct of the kleptomaniac and finds the impulse towards shiny objects irresistible. For this reason should he be absolved from responsibility? Thus our uncertainty about the facts of psychology, no less than our metaphysical doubts, must cloud our ascriptions of responsibility.

The third question is one of the legal relation between an agent and his act. Although the straightforward case is one where the criminal himself physically commits the crime, there are others where, either morally or legally, the ascription of responsibility is indirect. Imagine, for example, that Henry had trained his dog to steal the coveted wristwatch. We should be indignant, not at the dog's (well-trained and obedient) action in stealing the watch, but at Henry's instigation of the crime. For in such a case, he would be morally, though not physically, responsible. The English laws of strict liability[19] enshrine a further, and often more dubious, sense of extended responsibility. Here the crime has not been committed by the responsible person, who may not even

16. Cf. Hart, "Legal Responsibility," p. 96.

17. This is a central issue to the present study. I shall argue below that the penologist's account of moral psychology must determine his general theoretical direction, Ch. 3.a; Ch. 4.b; Ch. 5.f and g; Ch. 10.

18. An argument outlined, for example, by J. Hospers, "What Means This Freedom?" in S. Hook, ed., *Determinism and Freedom* (New York: Collier, 1961), p. 131. Some, however, resist the implication of exculpation from a deterministic moral psychology; cf., e.g., A. Wertheimer: "Even if much crime can be explained (in some social scientific sense) by its underlying causes, it simply does not follow that the criminal is not to blame" ("Punishing the Innocent: Unintentionally," *Inquiry* [1977]:62–63). The generality of this claim obscures its speciousness.

19. Cf. Gross, *Theory of Criminal Justice*, Ch. 8, §3.

know of the offence. The law demands, however, that this person be punished as responsible, even though our moral sense may revolt against so tenuous an extension of responsibility.

The general principle, therefore, is that we should punish those who are responsible for offences. However, we may feel that any ascription of responsibility is metaphysically or psychologically suspect. Alternatively, we may find that legal ascriptions of responsibility go far beyond not only the physical relation between the act and its agent but also the moral relation that we would allow between the crime and the person whom we call responsible.

c. THE PUNISHMENT

Henry hates it in prison; he knows in advance that he will hate it in prison, and he expects that anyone else in their right mind will feel the same. For the punishment must be unpleasant; it must involve suffering of some kind for its victim.[20] And, for this reason, morally it needs to be justified.[21]

What is more, this suffering must be in some sense supererogatory. For a punishment is not a payment.[22] Both may involve suffering or deprivation, inasmuch as to pay means to give up the price. To this extent, both will be undesirable. However, the contract to pay is willingly entered into, whereas punishment is inflicted against the will, if not the expectations, of the criminal. Thus the criminal should not reason (although sometimes no doubt he does) that the punishment is a 'fair price to pay' for the crime and therefore worth undergoing, even though, while he risks the punishment,[23] he may accept that, considered as a penalty rather than as a price, it is fair for that offence. If a punishment is not a payment, then the transactions of punishment are not those of commerce; witness the fact that a punishment may be exacted in the absence of a payee.

A punishment must be deliberately carried out. If an agent's wrongful act happens to bring in its train unpleasant consequences to himself, we should not strictly say that he is being punished.[24] Indeed, we might

20. Cf. the psychologist's adoption of the term "punishment" for an unpleasant response; R.M. Church, "The Varied Effects of Punishment on Behaviour," in R.H Walters *et al.*, eds., *Punishment* (London: Penguin, 1972), p. 19.

21. Although, as we shall see, even the conferring of benefits may need justification; cf. Ch. 5.c; Ch. 12.e.

22. Cf. Hart, "Prolegomenon," p. 6; Feinberg, "The Expressive Function of Punishment," in *Doing and Deserving*, p. 96.

23. Cf. A. von Hirsch, *Doing Justice* (New York: Hill & Wang, 1976), p. 63.

24. Although sometimes this situation is persuasively described as a punishment, possibly drawing on the notions expanded below, n. 26, that these unpleasant consequences

punish him as well, without feeling that he has been unfairly subject to double jeopardy.[25] Yet the same suffering that follows as a natural consequence of an action may also be inflicted deliberately, in order to achieve punishment or revenge. Both occurrences may be adduced to dissuade the criminal from crime. The only true distinguishing mark lies in the fact that misfortune is not produced by an external agency, whereas punishment is governed by human will.[26]

Henry would be indignant if his 'punishment' were to take place at the hands of the store-detective. This, he would complain, would be improper and unfair; it would be revenge rather than punishment.[27] For Henry looks to an authority to punish him. But what constitutes an authority?

The authority must, of course, be powerful enough to exact the punishment. Mere strength, however, is not enough to distinguish the penal authority from the agent of revenge.[28] For although punishment and revenge may have the same purpose, namely, to react against an injury, the agent of revenge tends to be an individual acting to recover his own loss, or to exact his own vengeance. The penal authority, on the other hand, may be expected to be impersonal and impartial, for we should feel that the interests of fairness can only be served if no one who is the immediate victim of an offence is vested with the authority to punish for that offence.[29]

Nevertheless, we may still envisage an authority capable of bias or a dispassionate avenger. To complement the notions of power and impar-

---

are in fact inflicted deliberately, by some supernatural (causal) agency. Cf. J. Teichman, "Punishment and Remorse," *Philosophy* (1973): 335, on natural punishment versus punishment proper.

25. Notice that here again considerations of logic and of fairness operate in harness.

26. In some situations, however, the agent of punishment and the source of a fortuitous sequence may be thought to be identical—particularly where cause and effect may be explained in terms of the operation of gods—in Judaeo-Christian, as well as in Greek, culture. In contexts of divine activity, a caveat should be entered, therefore, against too readily declaring a transaction to be a punishment. We should look, maybe, to the characterisation of the god concerned—is he portrayed vividly as a personality, and hence as a penal agent, or mentioned conventionally, as the causal origin?

27. Where revenge is characterised as a transaction taking place between individuals.

28. Although the psychologists confuse this issue, cf. B.F. Skinner, "Punishment: a Questionable Technique," in R.H. Walters *et al.*, eds., *Punishment*, p. 23.

29. The exception will presumably be offences against society, where society, the victim, is also the penal agent. We may suppose that impartiality, or at least distance, is achieved here by the notion that society is the victim only by analogy. The direct victim may be an individual or a group, both members of the society, but the offence is classified as being generally injurious and thus 'anti-social'. An offence against the state is different again; the goods of the state are so described for lack of any alternative collective term for the owner. Here again, the state is a victim only indirectly.

tiality, the penal procedure must be institutionalised[30] so that the authority is exercised by statute. This means that the authority will be recognised as such by those subject to it, including the unfortunate prisoner at the bar. Only under such conditions may we avoid the complaint, either from the offender or from the observer, that the punishment has been improperly carried out.

The importance of the statute is felt in all the circumstances of the punishment. For the law tells us not only who will punish but also for what offences and within what limits of severity in each case.[31] The expectations that we have as a result are grounds for complaint against improper punishments. For if the guidelines for sentencing laid down by the law are not followed, either the observer (maybe in the case of too slight a penalty) or the criminal himself (if the penalty is too severe) will appeal against the sentence. Furthermore, a new or private punishment (revenge, in the latter case) should not suddenly apply to a crime already committed and tried, just as a man's actions should not, after they have been performed, be made criminal under some new or private statute. Thus the sequence of punishment upon crime should be random in neither occurrence nor severity. As both fairness and expediency require,[32] the punishment should be predictable from the public statute book.

A punishment, therefore, is suffering deliberately inflicted by a penal authority upon a criminal for his crime, insofar as he is responsible for that crime.

d. JUSTIFICATION

Why punish at all? The question of the justification of punishment is a complex one. In an influential article, Hart has suggested:

What we should look for are answers to a number of different questions, such as: What justifies the general practice of punishment? To whom may punishment be applied? How severely may we punish?[33]

---

30. In fact, revenge can also be institutionalised; in some societies revenge is the accepted method of dealing with an offence. Perhaps the best known examples are to be found in the feuds or vendettas of tribal societies. See, for example, Max Gluckman, *Politics, Law and Ritual in Tribal Society* (Oxford: Blackwell, 1965), especially Chs. 3 and 5. When revenge is accepted, however, the agent lacks impartiality and, it could be argued, the institution lacks power—for which reason it delegates penal authority. The example serves only to indicate that impartiality and institutionalisation should be adopted as complementary criteria in the exercise of distinguishing punishment from revenge.

31. Mabbott, "Punishment," p. 49 discusses the relative merits of fixed and variable penalty systems. Cf. also von Hirsch, *Doing Justice*, pp. 98 ff.

32. To ensure effective deterrence.

33. "Prolegomenon," p. 3.

We should distinguish, Hart argues, between the 'general justifying aim' of punishment and the principles of its distribution, which cover both liability (who is to be punished) and allocation (how severely they are to be punished).[34] A punishment, therefore, may be justified in two *different* ways: either according to its general aim, or according to how it is to be distributed.[35] Quinton and Rawls, similarly, differentiate the rule (why punish) from the case (who is to be punished) in their attempts to effect a reconciliation between utilitarianism and retribution.[36]

The logic of this distinction remains unclear. Rawls and Quinton, on the one hand, maintain that the antithesis of the rule and the case is co-extensive with the antithesis of morals and logic. Hence justice is a matter of logic and definition, and determines the case, while the rule may be governed by considerations other than justice, such as utility. Against this I have suggested that in the definition of punishment considerations both of morals and of logic enter; thus logic alone cannot explain away the insistent claims of justice. Hart, on the other hand, fails to explain the logical relation of these various aspects of justification.[37]

34. "Allocation" is von Hirsch's term, *Doing Justice*, p. 36.

35. Hart appears to be attracted towards a utilitarian general aim, with punishments distributed according to criteria of justice (retribution). The specific case, utilitarianism combined with retribution, will be taken further below (Chs. 3 and 4).

36. Quinton, "On Punishment" and Rawls, "Two Concepts." Their answer to the problem of victimisation—it is a matter of definition that punishment is just—is vulnerable to Hart's "definitional stop" criticism, "Prolegomenon," pp. 5–6. For they attempt to cut off further argument by claiming the privilege of a 'definition'.

37. Hart believes that "retribution in general aim entails retribution in distribution" (p. 9), whereas a principle of distribution "may qualify the pursuit of our general aim, and is not deducible from it" (p. 25). His position appears to be this: sometimes the general aim implies the principle of distribution (namely, when and only when the general aim is retributive). At other times, the general aim is different from, but restricted by, the principle of distribution. In this case, there is no logical relation between general aim and distributive principle (when the general aim is other than retributive, and requires some qualification by the claims of justice). Such an assertion would be 'perfectly consistent' (p. 9).

If this is true, it is certainly not verifiable directly from the distinction between general aim and distributive principle. What is more, we should expect any relation between the two (however they are filled out as retributive, utilitarian, etc.) that is claimed to be logical, also to be constant. Inconstancy will admit the possibility of conflict—as Hart himself comes close to admitting: "a compromise between *partly discrepant* principles" (p. 10, my emphasis). Thus if he is anxious to rebut the charge of conflict levelled against a theory of punishment which combines utilitarianism with retributivism, Hart, like Quinton and Rawls, will fail if he relies on this logical analysis.

Furthermore, Hart's evidence suggests a compromise dictated by the exigencies of circumstance rather than a fully reconciled theory. For he demonstrates no more than that someone can hold two different principles affecting the practice of punishment without being aware that he is being inconsistent. Some systems of law, for example, in Nazi Germany, have been known to embody the most outrageous unfairness, while still maintaining

The danger which all three writers are trying—albeit unsuccessfully—to avoid is that conflict may arise when two principles of action are held conjointly. There will be no conflict if either the principles govern different non-conflicting actions or if they govern the same action and their priority is previously determined.[38] In the latter case the prior principle must be satisfied or impossible to satisfy before the secondary principle may be considered. Thus they are rank-ordered to preclude conflict. If, however, we need to perform a single action and our principles governing that action conflict and are not rank-ordered, we run into difficulties in deciding what to do. Similarly, a moral theory which contains two principles of equal priority liable to conflict may be thought to be intolerable or ineffective.

But why should conflict matter? In the case of an individual's acts conflict undeniably occurs, and that may be thought to be a sign of the healthy rationality of that individual's moral sensitivity. He will not be bigoted in favour of a single principle to override all the rest and will be prepared to give thoughtful consideration to various moral claims. What is more, his dilemma does not entail that he will not act at all. He may, for example, decide in favour of one principle this time and resolve to compensate by observing the other on some future occasion.[39] His moral conflict is resoluble in a rational way. And, it may be argued, a moral theory which is prone to conflict may also be determined, when it comes to cases, by a system of checks and balances. Such a system would be desirable inasmuch as it avoids the bleakness of bigotry that could result from the prevalence of a single principle, and it would allow for the rich complexity of competing moral claims.[40] So is there any reason why a penal system should not, in exactly this way, contain provisions for observing two quite different notions—for example, utility and justice?

The answer to this question is yes, by reason of two characteristics peculiar to punishment: constraints placed upon penal institutions by those who, in whatever capacity, are subject to them.

Suppose, first of all, that the problem of conflict is treated in a man-

---

the fair principle that only the guilty should be punished. This example does little more than tell us that Nazi legislators were only unfair some of the time—and hence that they were inconsistent. In other words, that some principles are held conjointly does not entail that they are held consistently.

38. Cf. Rawls, *A Theory of Justice*, p. 43.

39. Cf. B.A.O. Williams, "Ethical Consistency" in Williams, ed., *Problems of the Self* (Cambridge: C.U.P., 1973).

40. Cf. I. Berlin, "Equality," in Berlin, ed., *Concepts and Categories* (London: Hogarth, 1978), pp. 90 ff.; Rawls, *Theory of Justice*, pp. 34 ff.; Feinberg, "Rawls and Intuitionism," in N. Daniels, ed., *Reading Rawls* (Oxford: Blackwell, 1975).

ner analogous to the decisions of individuals. That is, each judge is given a generous instruction to observe justice and utility in sentencing, and the rest is left to his discretion. Now, it may happen that such a judge may decide the first motoring offence to come before him in observance of the principle of justice, and so he may exact a large fine. But then, balancing the alternatives, a further motoring offence receives a sentence of life imprisonment for reasons of utility. The judge has behaved rationally in resolving the two principles, and he has, by distributing sentences in this way, fairly observed them both. However, such a system of punishment is severely disruptive because it makes punishments unpredictable. How are we to know, before the event, which principle is to operate in our case—will it be life or a fine? It is such unpredictability that systematised punishments are supposed to guard against. Moreover, the criminals who have been sentenced, particularly those who have received sentences more severe than they might have expected, will be disturbed and litigious as a result of what has happened to them.

The response, of course, is to propose a less fanciful way of dealing with punishments, which might both accommodate the two conflicting principles and provide predictability. A detailed penal code, where punishments are laid down before the offences occur, might observe both principles in a balanced way and guarantee predictability. But such a system will not do either. Suppose that here again one type of motoring offence received a fine and another (possibly a more preventable type) was subject to life imprisonment. Such a system, wherein similar offences receive, by statute, dissimilar punishments, is equally disruptive. It violates the demand for parity of treatment, the requirement that similar offences be treated in a similar way. And that requirement matters.[41] Indeed, we should cling to it, I suggest, despite the system, whose problems would then be revealed in three practical ways.

First, and most important, my hypothetical system would lead to a radical revision of what we think of as criminal. The offence that receives a minor sentence would come to be regarded as minor, whereas its seriously treated counterpart would come to be thought of as grave. This would be the effect of disparate treatment of similar cases, and it would result in the alteration of our moral beliefs to fit the penal code. And in that eventuality, the multiple objective of the code would no longer be fulfilled, since all offences would now be thought of as receiving a just (or a useful) sentence. This, if not disruptive, would be self-

---

41. Although Berlin, "Equality," presents a persuasive case for parity not being our sole moral interest, he nevertheless concedes that it is important. My argument relies on the belief that parity is a principle to which we are considerably—possibly even irrationally—attached.

defeating. Second, this system would be disruptive of our expectations in an indirect way, since the precise specification of the crime—hard to ascertain before the event—would determine whether our sentence would be lenient or severe. Third, such a system would be legally disruptive, provoking a stream of appeals against the precise charge under which the offender received so harsh a sentence.

Accordingly, the possibility of direct moral conflict may be incorporated into a penal system in two ways: either by leaving the decision to the judge or by embodying the conflict in a penal code. But the two requirements—that punishments should be predictable and that they should avoid disparity of treatment—render these systems intolerable. They become no longer a just or useful political institution but a directly disruptive influence upon society.

Hart, Quinton and Rawls attempt an indirect solution to the problem. Thus they hope to avoid the impasse that may be generated by moral conflict, while enjoying the benefit of recognising moral complexity. They suggest that in the case of a theory of punishment, two principles may be offered to govern two different things: in one case the act of punishment, and in the other its justification.[42]

This view of penology must be false. The purpose of a theory of punishment is to justify either a single action or a series of actions which compose the practice or institution. Now, Rawls may be right in differentiating the institution from the individual actions that may be subsumed under it.[43] Nevertheless, once the threat of punishment needs to be implemented, the institution comes up with a single act of punishment. And in order for this act to take place at all, it must not be simultaneously forbidden and enjoined. Furthermore, if the practice is to be composed of a series of punishments, there must be some consistency between one instance and the next, in order that our expectations may not be outraged.

So, of each act of punishment, we may and should ask not only "Why is this man singled out for punishment?" (distribution, the case) but also "What do we hope to achieve by punishing him in this way?" (general justifying aim, the rule). In short, our various considerations, both gen-

---

42. Cf. A.G.N. Flew, "The Justification of Punishment," in Acton, ed., *The Philosophy of Punishment*, p. 88: "The term 'justification' is multiply relational." Yes, but this does not allow several conflicting justifications for the many dimensions of a single act. It means simply that in finalising a justification we must consider the various levels upon which it may operate.

43. This is his defence, I take it, of rule-utilitarianism in the face of the difficulties advanced by the act-utilitarian. Cf. below, Ch. 4.a; J.J.C. Smart and B.A.O. Williams, *Utilitarianism, For and Against* (Cambridge: C.U.P., 1973), pp. 9 ff.

eral and distributive, rule and case, meet in the individual punishment and must not, for that punishment to take place at all, conflict.

Nevertheless, Hart is surely right to argue that there are three different areas to consider when we theorise about punishment: the general aim, the liability and the allocation. But the various claims of each must be considered and reconciled before the theory of punishment can become operative.

CHAPTER

2

RESTITUTION

Restitution is a penal system operated on a *quid pro quo* basis. It assumes that the principles of commerce are good ones, whereby any gain should be paid for, any loss repaired. And a crime, it is supposed, is an unfinished commercial exchange; it constitutes a gain to the criminal that has not been paid for and an uncompensated loss suffered by the victim. According to the principles of equity, however, the victim has a right to payment or reparation.[1] The object of restitution, therefore, is to observe that right and to ensure that payment is made. The penalty is thus rendered direct from criminal to victim, and, it is hoped, the *status quo* is restored.[2]

The great advantage of a restitutive theory is that it considers the crime alone and need make no allowances for the responsibility of the criminal.[3] For it is the effect of his act upon his victim, not his intentions towards the victim, that restitution aims to cancel out. Such an account of punishment, therefore, avoids the thin ice of moral psychology.

The simplicity of the restitutive approach, however, is deceptive. We might grant that commerce is equitable, providing us with a right way

1. Cf. Mabbott, "Punishment," p. 42.
2. Cf. Aristotle's account of corrective justice, *E.N.* 1131b25 ff, and von Hirsch's (inaccurate) description of Kant's *lex talionis*, which, von Hirsch claims, is restorative, not retributive, and looks to the effect of the crime rather than the desert of the offender. But note von Hirsch's shift from considering the offence (the offender vis-à-vis his victim, where restitution would be appropriate) to considering the offender (vis-à-vis other law-abiding and restrained members of society, where restitution is inappropriate); *Doing Justice*, pp. 47 ff. Cf. Ch. 3.c.
3. Cf. Aristotle *E.N.* 1132a4, although Aristotle allows, 1132b21 ff., that the status of agent and patient will affect the amount of damage done.

to govern certain exchanges. But is it proper to think of crimes and punishments as commercial? Restitution assumes that a crime is nothing more nor less than a gain to the criminal, a loss to the victim, an imbalance which can be cancelled by compensation. Certainly in some cases this process is simple: larceny, for example, can be restored in kind or in coin. But even in cases of larceny, and more strikingly in cases where the injury is to the person, rather than the property, of the victim, compensation is no easy matter.

It may well be that the victim of a crime always sustains some unseen grievance. The victims of a burglary, for example, feel not only the loss of their goods but also the violation of their privacy. Is this sense of violation properly to be described as a gain to the burglar? Even if it can be thought of in this way, is the victim's grievance alleviated, as if it had never been felt, by the criminal's paying of compensation? And even if we suppose that the victim could be satisfied thus, we may be unable to measure the amount of distress that he has suffered or the amount of compensation that he requires. At the same time, we cannot be sure that we are simply cancelling the unwarranted gain of the criminal and not penalising him too little or too much—either of which would be inequitable.

In short, and despite the pious hope of modern courts, it may be impossible to make commensurable the suffering of the victim and the compensation paid. Given these imponderables, restitution simply does not work, or it does so only in the limited number of cases in which the injury can be clearly and completely determined, and the compensation matched.

Restitution behaves like commerce. Thus there must be a payee, both in normal commerce and in restitutive punishment. This may not be typical of punishments,[4] for the notion of a penalty does not entail the existence of a recipient, although, at the same time, the presence of a payee does not exclude the possibility of a punishment taking place. Nevertheless, the commercial analogue does cast doubt upon the claim of a theory of restitution to be a theory of punishment.[5] I have argued that a punishment should not operate like a payment, that a criminal should not regard it as a fair price to pay for the gain he receives from the crime. For example, we should prevent the trainrobbers from reasoning that during their long stays in prison they are "earning" the unrecovered loot. Yet a restitutive system actively promotes this attitude in

4. Cf. Ch. 1.c.
5. Feinberg, "The Expressive Function of Punishment," p. 105, would argue that restitution lacks the condemnatory function essential to punishment, providing only "retroactive licensing fees" for the offences with which it deals.

the criminal, since such a system establishes equitable payment for loss. Thus the larcenist instigates a compulsory purchase, and his 'punishment' is merely the completion of the transaction.

This may be the right way to think of crimes and punishments, especially if determinism is true. But thinking this way is not thinking about crimes and punishments at all, but rather about goods and payments.[6] The association with commerce lays a restitutive theory open to attack on both philosophical and practical grounds. For any condemnatory or even discouraging effect that punishments may be thought to have will vanish, and criminals may instead feel encouraged, like their capitalist counterparts, to engage in their nefarious activities. If the compensation is right, this may be unobjectionable.

The difficulty, then, will be that such right compensation may not, even cannot, be achieved by our present, or even any, system of punishment. The danger for the restitutive theorist, therefore, is that he 'institution-begs'; he supposes, unwarrantably, that the institution of punishment will in fact have the restitutive effect that he claims to justify it. Whereas the proper procedure would be to deny the system of punishment altogether and set up a new institution of compensation to take its place.[7]

6. Hence, as Mabbott, "Punishment," observes, the victim has no "right to punish" correlative to his "right to reparation." Cf. Ch. 1.c. But cf. H. Morris' reformulation of the idea of the "right to be punished" of the criminal, "Persons and Punishment," *The Monist* (1968): 475 ff.

7. Although I shall argue, Ch. 5.h and Ch. 12.f, that the problem of begging the institution works on two levels:

a. the penologist assumes that punishment is a necessary institution and then attempts to justify it, begging the question whether punishment is the most effective way to promote the end he adduces;

b. the penologist replaces punishment by an alternative institution, in which case he begs the question whether *punishment* is not, in itself, an important institution, whatever its justification.

Level *a* is a matter of thoughtlessness; *b* will occur when the radical and thoughtful penologist ignores a fundamental, if emotional, function that can be performed by punishment alone.

CHAPTER
3

RETRIBUTION

a. DESERT

Retributivists believe that punishment should take place just in case the criminal deserves it. So the desert of the criminal is thought to be both a necessary and a sufficient condition for his being punished.[1] This explains not only the general justifying aim of retribution—"We punish criminals because they deserve it"—but also its distribution—"This man is subject to punishment because he deserves it, while that man must not be punished because he does not deserve it" *and* "This amount of punishment is appropriate to that desert."[2]

Why we punish, whom we punish, and how severely we punish are all determined by the single principle of desert, which, because it is single, precludes conflict, when we come to consider a particular case.[3] Indeed, what we deserve may not even be a punishment; it may equally be a reward.[4] There may be no system for allocating rewards in the same way as punishments. Nevertheless, we associate reward with

1. Those who try to combine utilitarianism with retributivism must, of course, deny that desert is both necessary and sufficient, in order to leave room for utility to operate. Thus Quinton, "On Punishment," pp. 56–57, holds that desert is only necessary; contrast Mabbott, "Punishment," p. 40. Quinton's denial of the sufficiency of desert opens the door to conflict and dilemma.

2. Cf. Ch. 1.d. Hart, Quinton and Rawls again want to compromise by admitting desert as a distributive principle to *determine* liability, but only to *limit* amount (Hart, "Prolegomenon;" Quinton, "Punishment"; Rawls, "Two Concepts"). In this way they hope to guard against victimisation, but, as I argue here, they misuse the concept of desert.

3. Cf. Ch. 1.d.

4. Cf., e.g., Feinberg, "Justice and Personal Desert," in *Doing and Deserving*, on "polar desert."

the right kind of behaviour, just as we anticipate punishment for the wrong.[5] But what do we mean when we speak of a man's desert?

First, we look to what he has done (his acts) or to what he has been (his disposition) in the past.[6] His desert cannot be decided from a prediction of what he will do or from an assessment of what he might have done. But it can be determined by what he intended, but failed, to do. In the case of punishment, the condition that punishments belong to crimes requires that we look at what the criminal has done. His disposition will then affect his culpability (second stipulation).

Second, we stipulate that he should be responsible for the action that creates his desert.[7] Usually, according as he is responsible, he deserves praise or blame (he is culpable).[8] And a man does not deserve praise or blame for an accidental occurrence in which he was involved; however, he does deserve praise or blame for an accident which he actively prevents. So his responsibility is not simply a matter of what happens, the harm or good done, but of what happens as a result of his intentional activity.[9]

If, when a man deserves a punishment, he is rewarded, his desert is violated. Maybe that is all there is to it. He deserves either a reward or a punishment, and so long as he gets the right one, the measure of the reward or the punishment may be determined by other factors than desert. Desert governs more than that, however. The man executed because he is guilty of petty theft may be said to have been punished undeservedly. And the man convicted of murder may deserve more than a short prison term. In general, the idea of desert requires not only that a man be punished, but also that his punishment fit his crime.

5. "He deserves a reward for that" suggests not necessarily that there is a system, complementary to the penal system, for allocating rewards but that such a system is not incompatible with our retributive notions of punishment.

6. Cf., e.g., von Hirsch, *Doing Justice*, pp. 84, 102, 125; Mabbott, "Punishment," p. 39; and Feinberg, "Justice and Personal Desert," p. 58:

"If a person is deserving of some sort of treatment, he must, necessarily, be so *in virtue* of some possessed characteristic or prior activity. It is because no-one can deserve anything unless there is some basis or ostensible occasion for the desert that judgments of desert carry with them a commitment to the giving of reasons."

7. Cf. von Hirsch, *Doing Justice*, p. 80. And compare Aristotle, *E.N.* 1113b25; P. Strawson, "Freedom and Resentment," in Strawson, ed., *Studies in the Philosophy of Thought and Action* (London: O.U.P., 1968); and W.K. Frankena, *Ethics* (Englewood Cliffs: Prentice-Hall, 1963), p. 58, all of whom argue that the fact that we have a notion of desert which is determined by responsibility militates against our accepting the truth of determinism. But contrast the notion of desert required by the *lex talionis*, below, d.

8. Cf. Ch. 1.b.

9. But then, of course, there are problems about what constitutes intentional activity; cf., e.g., G.E.M. Anscombe, *Intention* (Ithaca: Cornell U.P., 1976); Austin, "Three Ways of Spilling Ink," *Ph. Rev.* (1966):427–440.

So how exactly does desert measure the punishment? It may be that it provides broad parameters within which the precise sentence may be justified by other factors.[10] Or it may be that desert is, ideally, a precise measure. Thus either desert is itself vague, or it is precise but, due to human frailty, difficult to capture, thus giving the appearance of imprecision.

Now desert does distinguish between two widely differing punishments. But on the parameter interpretation, it also distinguishes between two similar punishments, when these occur at the borderline: this one is outside the spectrum of what is deserved in this case, that one is just within. On this view, desert can sometimes operate with precision, in order to delineate the parameters at all. So why should it not always be equally exact? There is nothing intrinsic to the concept of desert to suggest that it is sometimes vague, sometimes precise.[11] Rather, it is our own ignorance that leads to adoption of the parameter view.

Both conditions of desert—the act and the responsibility—may be elusive: how exclusively was the act the cause of the harm, and how far was the act intentional?[12] Moreover, our assessments will be blurred by the incompleteness of our understanding. Consequently we may be unable to determine the precise measure of a man's desert. It does not follow from this, however, that his desert is indeterminate.[13] There is a fact of the matter, even though we may never be in a position to know it. The act is completed and the effect is caused; these are determinate, and the agent participates in them so much and no more. His true desert,[14] therefore, is neither imprecise nor vague; nor can it be defined as rough parameters within which variation is of no account. Ideally, the correlate punishment should be precisely matched to this desert.[15] Un-

10. This is the fundamental mistake of *Doing Justice*. Von Hirsch and his colleagues suppose that desert supplies the rough guidelines of how much we should punish, within which punishment may be determined by deterrent considerations; cf., e.g., p. 93. The mistake lies not only in understanding desert as an indeterminate measure but also in the possibilities of conflict allowed by the admission of deterrence.

11. It is interesting, and supportive of my view of desert, that the word 'just', in one of its usages as a particle, indicates a precise measurement: 'just so' equals 'exactly so'. Cf. also the philosophical usage 'just if', 'just because'.

12. For examples: to what extent did the action of the driver of the getaway car contribute to the harm of the bank robbery? How far may we ascribe intentionality in the *crime passionel* committed by someone crazed with jealousy?

13. Contrast Teichman, "Punishment and Remorse," p. 337, who is, in fact, making the point below, that the correlation between precise desert and the appropriate punishment is confused by those—fallible, subjective and ignorant—who make it.

14. I do not wish to claim that 'true desert' has somehow metaphysical force; I want to emphasise, however, that there is a hiatus between desert as it could, ideally, be read off from act plus responsibility, and desert as it is actually assessed by fallible judges.

15. Cf. Hegel, *Philosophy of Right* trans. T.M. Knox (Oxford, Clarendon, 1942), p. 137,

fortunately for the retributivist the very humanity of the judge precludes such accuracy.

For a man to have a desert means that he deserves *something*, that in view of his past actions we ought to treat him in a particular way. But is it true that "a person's desert of X is always a reason for giving X to him, but not always a conclusive reason. . . . Considerations irrelevant to his desert can have overriding cogency in establishing how he ought to be treated in balance"?[16] To the retributivist this is false—desert necessitates the appropriate treatment. "This man deserves that punishment" may be translated into the moral imperative "This man ought to receive that punishment."[17]

b. JUSTICE

The problem, then, is to explain the obligation thus laid upon us. Does the criminal have a *right* to be punished? At first sight this seems an incongruous notion,[18] particularly if we reflect on the antithesis of punishment, reward. For, unlike punishment, reward is not systematised or institutionalised. So the good man has no right to reward, corollary to some right of the bad man to be punished, for rights such as these do not exist.

Nevertheless, the issue of rights is relevant here. Each member of a community has the right to preserve his position, his privacy, his property. And his expectations are that if he behaves in a certain way he will be allowed to maintain those rights, or even to improve them. At the same time, he may consider himself to have a right of redress against unwarranted infringement of his position, his privacy, his property. Or

---

quoted (though rejected) by C.W.K. Mundle, "Punishment and Desert," in Acton, ed., *The Philosophy of Punishment*, p. 72: "Injustice is done at once if there is one lash too many, or one dollar or one cent too many *or too few*" (my emphasis). This suggests that desert is not merely a factor providing the upper limit of the punishment; contrast the views cited above, n. 2.

16. Feinberg, "Justice and Personal Desert," p. 60.

17. "Ought" here signifies a moral imperative, not the 'ought' that is the conclusion of a piece of prudential reasoning, where 'ought' equals 'in my interests'.

18. S.I. Benn, "An Approach to the Problems of Punishment," *Philosophy* (1958):329, attacks Bosanquet's idea of the rights of the offender, arguing that this is a violation of the normal meaning of rights. Cf. Quinton, "On Punishment," p. 57: "It is an odd sort of right whose holders would strenuously resist its recognition." But n.b., of course, Morris' argument that the criminal has a right to be treated as a person, and therefore to be punished, not treated, "Persons and Punishment," p. 479: "There is some plausibility in the exaggerated claim that in choosing to do an act violative of the rules, an individual has chosen to be punished." This account of choice violates, of course, the condition that the content of a choice is subject to referential opacity; cf. W.V.O. Quine, "Reference and Modality," in L. Linsky, ed., *Reference and Modality* (Oxford: O.U.P., 1971).

he may think that the institutions of the community have a duty to punish (not necessarily with a view to restitution) whoever thus infringes
upon him. The offender, however, does not have a duty or a right to be
punished, although he should expect it. Yet he will not expect, and indeed will exclaim vigorously against, any attempt to exact more than the
deserved punishment for what he has done; therefore his desert constitutes his right not to be victimised, exploited or manipulated.

That he will be punished is thus a consequence of the right of the
victim to redress, or of the duty of the society to punish. That he will
not be punished in excess is a consequence of his own right not to be
victimised. His deserving punishment (and the severity of that punishment) arises from this complex of rights and duties.

It is natural to describe this complex as a system of justice. Why
should my property be defended? Because it is unjust to invade it. Why
does the criminal deserve this punishment? Because this punishment is
just, as both he and society recognise. This appeal to justice invokes the
distributive norms according to which the society is organised, whereby
one man's rights create another's restrictions, expectations and duties.

Distributive justice, the just state of affairs, is complemented by retributive justice.[19] But retribution is neither the same thing as nor the converse of distribution.[20] Rather, the just state of affairs is the *focus* of the
just punishment.[21] And, at the risk of archaism, we should say that the
just man is he who preserves, promotes or observes the just state of
affairs, whereas his unjust counterpart is the criminal with whom just
punishment must deal.

The primary purpose of retribution seems to be to reaffirm the just
state of affairs, threatened by an unjust act. This 'expressive punishment'[22] is a complex act both to denounce the crime and to dissociate
the society from complicity in it.[23]

19. But see von Hirsch on just punishment in the just society, and his comments on
Marx' restriction that punishment can only be fair when the society is already organised in
a just way (*Doing Justice*, pp. 143ff.). There is some evidence, however, that Marx would
reject these distributive notions altogether; see *Critique of the Gotha Programme*, in R.C.
Tucker, ed., *The Marx-Engels Reader* (New York: Norton, 1972), p. 388.

20. Cf. Rawls, *A Theory of Justice*, p. 314. Rawls argues this on the grounds that his
version of distribution is made not on the basis of moral worth (desert) but from the
position of ignorance which is the major part of the technical substructure of his theory.
Although he is right in claiming that retribution and distribution are not converses, he is
wrong, in my view, to disallow the function of retribution in distribution. Compare Aristotle, *E.N.* 1130b30 ff.; Sidgwick, *Methods of Ethics* (London: Macmillan, 1907), p. 273. Cf.
Ch. 13.c.

21. Cf. G.E.L. Owen, "Logic and Metaphysics in Some Earlier Works of Aristotle," in
J. Barnes *et al.*, eds., *Articles on Aristotle*, Vol. 3 (London: Duckworth, 1979).

22. Cf. Feinberg, "The Expressive Function of Punishment."

23. *Ibid.*, pp. 101 ff., explains this as a threefold function: authoritative disavowal

Punishment is a conventional device for the expression of attitudes of resentment and indignation, and of judgments of disapproval and reprobation, on the part either of the punishing authority himself or of those "in whose name" the punishment is inflicted. Punishment, in short, has a *symbolic significance* largely missing from other kinds of penalties.[24]

Because it offers a legalistic denunciation of the crime, the sentencing of the criminal expresses our resentment that the just state of affairs has been disturbed.[25] We feel resentment because we identify with the distributive justice in which we share, and a retributive punishment is a violent expression of our disapproval, which may, to an extent, alleviate our distress at the disruption. But the purpose of the punishment is not to lift our distress. Under other theories punishment may be seen as instrumental—the means, perhaps, to the deterrence of criminals, or the restitution of a wrong. Retribution, by contrast, is an end in itself, the very act of denunciation.[26]

c. RETRIBUTION AND OTHER THEORIES

Retribution differs from restitution.[27] The latter looks solely to the harm done to the victim; it takes from the criminal and gives to the victim whatever will cancel out that harm. Considerations of desert, however, clearly exclude so straightforward a procedure. For retribution concentrates upon the criminal, not upon his victim. His desert is assessed not only according to the harm done, but also—and perhaps largely—according to his responsibility for it. Consequently, the punishment demanded to effect proper restitution may either exceed or fall short of the punishment required on a desert basis. The restitutive theory, therefore, is potentially in conflict with the retributive theory, inasmuch as each may demand quite different punishments to satisfy their dominant principles and may, furthermore, repudiate the punishment laid down by the other as violating those principles.

(condemning the act and disavowing complicity in it); symbolic nonacquiescence (openly declaring the act to be wrong); and vindication of the law (vindicating or reaffirming the statute forbidding the act).

24. *Ibid.*, p. 98 (his emphasis).

25. Cf. Strawson, "Freedom and Resentment."

26. To denounce and not primarily to discourage, as Hart would have it, "Prolegomenon," pp. 6–7. Cf. Ch. 1, n. 9; Mabbott, "Punishment."

27. Cf. Mabbott, "Punishment," p. 42; Sidgwick, *Methods of Ethics*, p. 282. This distinction is obscured by von Hirsch's discussion of Kant, *Doing Justice*, pp. 47 ff., 160–161, where he makes the operation of the *lex talionis* look like the commercial exchanges of restitution. Kant's own explication of the *lex talionis* (*Metaphysical Elements of Justice* [New York: Library of Liberal Arts, 1965], pp. 99 ff.), however, refers to *equalling* the injury rather than paying for it. Cf. Ch. 2, n. 2; below, d.

Imagine that a drunk heaves a brick through a shop-window and damages the goods on display. Restitution will demand that the drunk be forced to compensate all the damage done. Retribution, on the other hand, will offer a low estimate of such a man's desert, arguing, perhaps, that he should spend a mere night in the cells for his just deserts to be met. The damage to the store may be rectified by non-penal means— perhaps by the insurance company—whereas an equivalent large fine exacted from the drunk may well be regarded as grossly unfair.

From this comparison it is clear that the retributive principle does not have the instrumental approach to the purposes of punishment that is exemplified by a theory of restitution. And indeed, whenever the punishment is justified in terms of a further, useful or desirable effect beyond the very justice of the punishment itself, a case can be made for potential conflict with the requisites of desert.

Some have attempted to justify severe retributive punishments by the satisfaction that the victim derives therefrom.[28] The victim is grieved by the crime. Particularly in cases of non-material damage, this grievance is not readily reparable in coin, but, it is hoped, the sight of the criminal's suffering assuages the victim's grief.[29]

Now it may be that the punishment does have this satisfying effect on the original victim. We cannot be sure, however, that either the precisely deserved punishment will be severe enough to satisfy the victim, or the full, deserved punishment will have been carried out by the time the victim is satisfied. It all depends on the vindictiveness of the victim. There is no necessary correlation between desert and satisfaction. The principle that the victim should be satisfied, therefore, is sufficient neither to explain nor to justify a retributive theory, wherein desert must have priority in deciding the nature and the severity of the punishment.

Retribution may, nonetheless, have some contingent effect of alleviating distress. For not only the victim but also the observer is morally outraged by the crime. It may then be that the violent denunciation embodied in the punishment will lift this sense of outrage. As long as this effect is seen as merely incidental to the main retributive purpose— the denunciation itself—then there is no danger of conflict.

It is often argued that retribution is justified because it deters the criminal from repeating his offence.[30] But there is no guarantee that the

28. A line tried, and rejected, by T. Honderich, *Punishment, its Supposed Justifications* (London: Penguin, 1971), p. 28.

29. See the impassioned plea of the mother of a child murdered by Myra Hindley, against Hindley's being released early from prison on parole, *The Times* (London), 3rd Jan. 1978, p. 11.

30. This, for example, seems to lie at the heart of von Hirsch's combination of desert with deterrence. Cf. also M. Ginsberg, "The Nature of Responsibility," in Ginsberg, ed., *On the Diversity of Morals* (London: Mercury, 1962), p. 93.

punishment the criminal deserves will in fact be deterrent; it may be greater or less than what will effectively deter him or others. In general, a deterrent theory of punishment is utilitarian and makes demands, in the interests of the maximisation of benefit, which run counter to the requirements of justice.[31] As a result, the two theories cannot be run in harness with equal priority, without the risk of conflict.[32]

Yet here again a retributive punishment may have a subsidiary effect. The pronouncement "You will get what you deserve" may well discourage, if not deter. The punisher declares the crime to be wrong, and, at the same time, the criminal comes to realise that he did wrong.[33] Thereafter he may be dissuaded from repeating the offence. If this is the case, two further conditions hold. First, deterrence of this kind is parasitic on retribution, for the effect is obtained by, and contingent upon, the fulfilling of the central tenet of the retributive theory. Second, deterrence is still not what is *meant* by retributivism. For the requirement that the desert of the criminal must be met is independent of and prior to the hope that he or others will be deterred from crime. Deterrence, of this parasitic kind, is subsidiary and incidental to retribution.

Despite these additional effects of retribution—the satisfaction of a sense of outrage and the deterrence from further crime—retributivism is a self-contained theory, viewing punishment as an end in itself, rather than as instrumental to further ends. This characterisation of retribution means that it does not beg the institution, but confronts it straightly as intrinsically justifiable.[34] This does not mean, however, that retribution appears merely in the definition of punishment, which may then be justified by appeal to other principles such as utilitarianism.[35] In the first place, as I have argued, such a procedure is liable to generate conflict; in the second place, the definitional function of retribution is dubious,[36] not least because some theories of punishment ignore desert altogether.[37]

The fundamental mistake, however, of this view of retribution as

31. But see Ch. 4.d.

32. Nor must retribution and deterrence be conflated, despite Hart: the law declares certain actions to be criminal "to announce to society that these actions are not to be done and to secure that fewer of them are done" ("Prolegomenon," pp. 6–7); cf. above, n. 25; Ch. 1, n. 9.

33. Ginsberg, "Nature of Responsibility," p. 93.

34. Cf. Ch. 2 and Ch. 4.c; Ch. 5.h, and Ch. 12.f, and Ch. 13.

35. As Quinton et al. maintain, cf. above, nn. 1 and 2; Ch. 1.d; Ch. 4.d.

36. Cf. Ch. 1.d.

37. E.g., strict utilitarianism, Ch. 4.g, and reform, Ch. 5.g, operate according to criteria of efficiency to their ends, or need of the offender. It may, of course, be objected to either theory that they are for this reason deficiently theories of punishment; this is true particularly of reform. If they are theories of punishment, then they institution-beg.

merely the logical part of a complex theory of punishment is to ignore the character of a retributive theory, essentially at odds with the utilitarian alternative. The theory is not formulated as a tautology, as some have believed.[38] But retributivism is a deontological theory,[39] different in its logical behaviour from its teleological counterpart.

A teleological theory would consider the punishment as the means to some good, either general or individual.[40] But the obligation laid upon us by "This is a just punishment" asserts the independent moral value of the punishment itself, considered apart from, and even to the frustration of, some prudential value to be derived from its effects. Consequently, although a teleological theory may cite some beneficial effect of the institution in its justification, a deontological theory has recourse to a moral imperative and gives the false impression that the appeal to justice is part of the definition rather than the centre of the justification. In a teleological theory we may ask of each action in a sequence "why?" until we reach an answer that is considered prudentially sufficient. This answer must explain the desirability characteristic of the action[41] or train of actions so that further explanation is unnecessary and even impossible. In a deontological theory, on the other hand, the "why?" questions terminate in a judgment which is considered to be morally sufficient—maybe from an intuitionist point of view.[42] So the declaration that punishment according to deserts is just is sufficient to explain, within the terms of deontological theories, why retribution is justified.[43]

Several objections may be levelled against retributive punishment. They fall largely under two headings: the first charges that the theory makes no sense; the second complains that it is morally intolerable.

d. RETRIBUTIVISM MAKES NO SENSE

Retributivism, I have suggested, is a deontological theory. The teleologist may immediately declare that deontological theories are in general nonsensical. For either such theories invoke a multiplicity of principles,

38. Benn, "Approach," p. 327. The assertion, "It is just that the guilty suffer," would "only reiterate the principle to be justified—for 'it is fitting [just]' means only that it ought to be the case, which is precisely the point at issue."

39. Cf. Kant, *Metaphysical Elements*, p. 100.

40. Whose good marks the difference between utilitarian and humanitarian theories of punishment, cf. Chs. 4 and 5.

41. Cf. Anscombe, *Intention*, pp. 70 ff.

42. Cf. Rawls' discussion of intuitionism, *Theory of Justice*, pp. 34 ff.

43. Contrast Rawls' attempt to answer deontological questions in a teleological way. The people in the original position behind the veil of ignorance make a prudential calculation and come up with the account of justice that will be the least risky. Cf. Sidgwick, *Methods of Ethics*, p. 440.

leading inevitably to conflict,[44] or they employ a moral imperative whose derivation is suspect.[45] A theory of retribution is not liable to generate conflict because it contains a single principle only, the principle of justice. Yet the teleologist is right to inquire about the source of this principle.

Maybe our ideas of justice are derived from the prudential necessities of community life[46]—justice is that order which best protects and preserves the society.[47] Here, however, the deontological theory has turned into a teleological one, since the moral imperative is based upon the prudential considerations of maintaining the social order for the good of all members. As a consequence of this covertly teleological view, the retributivist is committed to the specious and institution-begging[48] claim that society needs, for its preservation, a system of just punishments. But it is certainly possible that just punishments do not have this effect. In this case, the retributivist must abandon his apparently deontological theory and pursue his true objective according to the dictates no longer of justice but of utility. And as a utilitarian, he will confront other difficulties.

Alternatively, 'justice' may have an independent moral importance, aside from its prudential effects. But then, if not from these prudential considerations, whence comes this idea of justice? At this juncture, the deontologist might argue that there are matters of value apart from matters of fact. After all, we make judgements of fact *and* judgements of value.[49] It is fallacious, he would say,[50] to suppose that judgements of value can be derived from facts. No, what our values are, and how important they are, we must intuit,[51] but we ignore or deny such intuited principles at our moral peril.[52]

44. Cf. Frankena, *Ethics*, p. 23 on Ross' distinction between actual duty and *prima facie* duty.

45. Cf., e.g., the objection of Sidgwick, *Methods of Ethics*, p. 420.

46. Cf. P. Foot, "Moral Beliefs," in Foot, ed., *Theories of Ethics* (Oxford: O.U.P., 1967), p. 92: "It is surely clear that moral virtues must be connected with human good and harm. . . ."

47. This may be an explanation based on nature or on convention. The former supposes that the (naturally occurring) rules of justice do in fact order our society well; the latter that the way in which our society is well-ordered is what we call, by convention, justice. Cf. Callicles in Plato's *Gorgias*, 483a ff.; the naturalism of the Athenians, Thucydides, I.76 ff., V.87 ff. Cf. Ch. 8.b.

48. Cf. Ch. 2, n. 7.

49. Cf., e.g., R.M. Hare, *The Language of Morals* (Oxford: O.U.P., 1952), Ch. 7. But see Rawls, *Theory of Justice*, pp. 404 ff.

50. The naturalistic fallacy; but cf. Frankena, "The Naturalistic Fallacy," in Foot, ed., *Theories of Ethics*.

51. This is a conclusion that Rawls tries to avoid; cf. above, n. 42.

52. Although what our moral *peril* is, if it is not teleological, is open to question. The

The sceptic must counter that we do not know what intuition is, how it works, or even whether there is such a thing. Thus the deontological argument collapses into a dubious process for deriving these supposedly independent moral principles. And so we must be suspicious of the priority, claimed by the retributivist, of justice over utility.

This is not the only area where the retributivist calls upon ideas that are vague or opaque. That 'desert' is a notion that makes sense has been variously asserted[53] and denied.[54] Critics argue that 'desert' boils down to the contested moral imperative.[55] "It is just that he should get what he deserves" may be cashed as "It is just that he should get what is just for him," and we are no further forward. The 'desert' terminology appears to explain the notion of justice and, further, to enable us to make some real assessment of what the punishment should be. But this appearance is a false one.

Against this, the retributivist will argue that 'desert' is not derived from 'justice', but rather from two matters of fact—the past act and the offender's responsibility for it. Desert, therefore, is independent of the matter of value which is the appeal to justice.[56]

Then arises a further difficulty that retribution makes no practical sense. Retribution aims to match the desert of the criminal with the penalty to be exacted from him. But how is this correlation to be made? First, the retributivist begs the question that crime and the suffering that is punishment are commensurable, that the punishment can indeed fit the crime. Second, the assessment of desert is fraught with ignorance which renders it indeterminate. The danger, therefore, is that in a retributive system, put into practice, the principle of justice will constantly be violated. Pervaded by human fallibility the retributive process will miss the mark more often than hit it and will thus be the embodiment of injustice.

Kant attempted to ensure that the punishment fit the crime by advo-

---

prudential approach is betrayed in the argument (typical, for example, of Plato) that we will end up bad men, which is a bad thing.

53. E.g., by von Hirsch, although here the argument is vitiated by the supposition that the individual's desert is not susceptible to precise or exact measurement. Cf. above, a. Cf. also Mundle, "Punishment and Desert"; Feinberg, "Justice and Personal Desert."

54. E.g., extensively, by Honderich, *Punishment*, pp. 26 ff.

55. Cf. n. 38 above.

56. Equally, to avoid the naturalistic fallacy, justice must not be merely derivative from desert. Cf. Hare, *Language of Morals*, Ch. 5; Compare J. Searle, "How to Derive 'Ought' From 'Is'," in Foot, ed., *Theories of Ethics*. The retributivist might offer, as evidence of the independence of desert from justice, the fact that we might conceivably say "It is *not* just that men should be punished as they deserve," although this remark would not display a retributive approach.

cating the *lex talionis*.[57] In this system the match is made exactly, even simplistically: an eye for an eye, a life for a life. To the *lex talionis* there are two immediate objections. First, it leaves us in a puzzle about why some actions are classified as criminal at all. If to rob someone of an eye is objectionable and hence criminal, what exempts the punishment from being criminal also? Or, conversely, if the punishment is acceptable and authorised, why should the crime not be so? Unsatisfactorily, the advocate of the *lex talionis* must have recourse to the definitional stop: the crime is defined as illegal, while the punishment is prescribed by the law and is thus, by definition, authorised. Second, the *lex talionis* raises, rather than solves, problems in our understanding of desert. For here, desert is read off directly from the act and apparently takes no account of responsibility. Consequently, no distinction will be made for the purposes of punishment between accidents and deliberate actions, or between negligence and premeditated malice. This we find intolerable.[58]

Apart from the *lex talionis*, retributivism presupposes that we can understand and determine the criminal's responsibility.[59] But can we? A great deal of modern controversy centres upon the question of how we attribute responsibility. Suppose, on the one hand, that determinism is true, that we do not cause our actions *ab initio*, and therefore that we are not in control of those actions. This is incompatible with retributivism, where the criminal's control is a deciding factor in his desert. On the other hand, even if we reject determinism, the extent to which the causes of the criminal's action lie within the criminal himself is obscure.[60] His action may be pathological, or socially conditioned. Again our ignorance inhibits us, this time in analysing intention. Philosophers from Plato onwards have debated the problem of intentionality, and the debate continues. The retributivist obstinately assumes that there are fully intentional actions, and that we can distinguish one level of intentionality from another and hence the desert of one man from the desert of another.

There are, therefore, three areas where the charge of incoherence or obscurantism can be levelled against the retributivist. First, we may object that his notion of justice is doubtful. Second, we may argue that desert is imponderable, and therefore crime and punishment are incommensurable. And third, we may be sceptical that the question of the responsibility of the criminal can be settled.

57. *Metaphysical Elements*, pp. 101, 104.

58. Why? Because it is unjust. Here we must make concessions to the deontologist.

59. Other theories, by contrast, might only require that he can be influenced by the punishment.

60. Cf. Ginsberg, "Nature of Responsibility," p. 88; B. Wootton, *Crime and the Criminal Law* (London: Stevens & Sons, 1963).

e. RETRIBUTIVISM IS INTOLERABLE

Retribution is often thought to embody a vindictiveness or violence that is morally unacceptable.[61]

The old conviction still lingers in the popular view of Criminal Justice: it seems still to be widely held that Justice requires pain to be inflicted on a man who has done wrong, even if no benefit result either to him or to others from the pain. Personally I am so far from holding this view that I have an instinctive and strong moral aversion to it. . . .[62]

In an attempt to defuse this objection, von Hirsch offsets the principle of desert against the principle of "parsimony in inflicting pain,"[63] but here again he risks conflict. The retributivist has two answers to the charge of vindictiveness. The first is to admit it and to insist that considerations of justice are and should be prior to the principle of parsimony in inflicting pain. Thus there is no injustice involved in the violence of retributive punishment.[64] The second answer, offered by Feinberg,[65] suggests that punishment, to fill its expressive function, need not be vindictive, nor as painful as rival theories might require it to be. The more grave the crime, the more severe should be the denunciation, but not necessarily the more painful the punishment.[66]

The objection that punishment is painful, however, is one that may properly be levelled at it under any theory. For, by definition, punishment is painful. Certainly, we need strong reasons to justify the infliction of any suffering on anyone. But these reasons are required by the utilitarian or the reformist no less than the retributivist. As long as the institution of punishment is itself accepted without question,[67] the charge of violence must necessarily be shelved.

To sum up, a retributive theory of punishment declares that punishment is just and should be carried out whenever it is deserved. Such punishments are thought to have moral value independent of the possible benefit they may supply to the criminal or to society as a whole. The charge of violence, levelled against retributive theory, seems to be endemic to theorising about punishment. Retributivism is particularly open to criticism, however, on the grounds that its central notions are opaque or incoherent. Our ignorance conceals the truth about desert, about moral responsibility, and, fundamentally, about justice.

61. Ammunition for the deontologist here again; cf. above, n. 57.
62. Sidgwick, *Methods of Ethics*, p. 281.
63. *Doing Justice*, p. 86.
64. Cf. Bosanquet, quoted by Ginsberg, "Nature of Responsibility," p. 84.
65. "The Expressive Function of Punishment," p. 118.
66. The pain may be physical or mental—the humiliation, perhaps, of a public condemnation.
67. This, of course, is institution-begging.

CHAPTER

4

THE UTILITARIAN APPROACH

If a deontological theory is found wanting, the alternative is a teleological theory. Here primacy is given not to the moral imperative to punish but to the benefit that may be derived from penalising the criminal.[1] Teleological theories may be thought to operate either according to principles of benevolence (the benefit of others) or of egoism (the benefit to ourselves).[2] The principle of benevolence, as manifested in punishments,[3] is complex in turn. For the legislator may consider two different areas of benefit when he establishes a punishment: either the benefit accruing to society in general or the benefit accruing to the criminal himself.[4] The difference, of course, lies between the majority, as yet non-criminal, who are potential criminals or potential victims, and the minority, the criminals themselves.[5]

If the penologist is concerned to maximise benefit, so that he is considering the majority,[6] then he is a utilitarian. If, on the other hand, he

1. Cf. Ginsberg, "The Nature of Responsibility," p. 83.

2. Cf. Frankena, *Ethics*, pp. 13 ff.; Rawls, *A Theory of Justice*, pp. 25 ff.; Sidgwick, *Methods of Ethics*, p. 431, discusses the egoism of the principle of benevolence in utilitarianism.

3. I am unable to conceive of a purely egoistic theory of punishment, inasmuch as a theory of punishment, by definition, operates within a group. But cf. Ch. 7.g.

4. It might be argued, though oddly, that the criminal, as a member of society, partakes of the benefit accruing to the society. But that he is punished is obviously a harm, not a benefit, to himself and it would require considerable proof to demonstrate that he derives a greater benefit indirectly from the effect of his punishment on the society as a whole.

5. The fact that the criminals are in the minority is suggested by two considerations: first, otherwise the law would itself be changed by the criminal majority; second, in the case of individual penal transactions the criminal is usually single, ranged against the multitude of society—crimes are 'anti-social'.

6. But see below, d.

focusses his attention on the individual criminal, I call him a *humani-tarian*.[7] These two approaches to the focus of punishment give rise to two distinct types of theory.

a. PUNISHMENT AND THE PRINCIPLE OF UTILITY

By Utilitarianism is here meant the ethical theory that the conduct which, under any given circumstances, is objectively right, is that which will produce the greatest amount of happiness on the whole; that is, taking into account all whose happiness is affected by the conduct.[8]

Sidgwick argues that in our behaviour—for example, when we justify and carry out the practice of punishment—we should seek to promote the greatest good for the greatest number or the least harm to the greatest number.[9] This principle, utilitarians claim,[10] is a single one, which thus precludes conflict; it is a principle of "generalised benevolence, that is the disposition to seek happiness, or . . . good consequences for all mankind. . . ."[11]

Within utilitarianism we should distinguish between two types of theory:

1. Act-utilitarianism[12] argues that each individual decision should be made *ad hoc*, favouring whatever action will produce the greatest good in the particular case.

2. Rule-utilitarianism[13] supposes that individual actions should be dictated by rules derived from the principle of utility, and therefore particular acts are only indirectly utilitarian.

Two different accounts of the rules may be given.[14] On the one hand, some regard them as 'rules of thumb',[15] generalising the best course of action under various circumstances, which is a shorthand version of 1.[16]

7. Because his concerns tend to be humane; cf. Ch. 5.

8. Sidgwick, *Methods of Ethics*, p. 411.

9. Various versions of what is the good have been put forward; contrast the hedonism of Bentham with the idealism of Moore.

10. Cf., e.g., Smart and Williams, *Utilitarianism*, p. 12.

11. *Ibid.*, p. 7.

12. 'Extreme utilitarianism', Smart in "Extreme and Restricted Utilitarianism" in Foot, ed., *Theories of Ethics*; cf. Sidgwick, *Methods of Ethics*, pp. 429 ff.

13. 'Restricted utilitarianism', Smart in "Extreme and Restricted Utilitarianism"; cf. J.O. Urmson on Mill, "The Interpretation of the Moral Philosophy of J.S. Mill." in Foot, ed., *Theories of Ethics*.

14. Thanks to Rawls, "Two Concepts of Rules," pp. 157ff.

15. Sidgwick, *Methods of Ethics*, p. 448, on "justice as a guide to different kinds of utilities."

16. "But is it not monstrous to suppose that if we have worked out the consequences and if we have perfect faith in the impartiality of our calculations, and if we know that in this instance to break [the rule] will have better results than to keep it, we should neverthe-

On the other hand, some regard the rules as of independent importance,[17] outlining practices[18] which are themselves for the best. Individual actions are recommended if they conform to the practice. If they deviate from the rule, they will tend to distort the practice and will be thought a disutility. The rule thus intervenes between considerations of utility and individual practical decisions.

Consider the apparent clarity and simplicity of utilitarian theory compared to retributivism. The person who offers a utilitarian account of some aspect of our public or private behaviour has no recourse to opaque notions such as justice or desert.[19] Nor, apparently, need he consider the complexities of moral psychology or responsibility. For the principle of utility demands only the maximisation of good or the minimisation of harm over the greatest number of people. It makes no stipulations as to who these people should be, whether they should deserve the good they receive, or whether they are responsible for being considered among the candidates for the receipt of good.

The justification of punishment, on utilitarian lines, is straightforward. For, without dispute,[20] a crime is considered to be a harm, and the principle of utility demands that these harms should be reduced as much as possible. Punishment, therefore, should have a triple function: *to deter* potential criminals from committing crimes, *to protect* the potential victims of crimes from becoming actual victims, and *to prevent* criminals from committing the crimes they have in mind.

Deterrence works by threat and by example. The law institutes, by statute, the threat that behaviour of a particular kind will be punished. Then it punishes those who indulge in that behaviour, that everyone should see that the threat is no empty one. A deterrent punishment, therefore, exploits our fear of physical or mental suffering. When we are tempted to commit a crime, we will weigh the temptation against

---

less obey the rule?" (Smart "Extreme and Restricted," p. 176); cf. Smart and Williams, *Utilitarianism*, pp. 10 ff.

17. Rawls himelf, for example—at least in "Two Concepts." Possibly Sidgwick also, *Methods of Ethics*, p. 458, on laws. He speaks of maintaining the *rules*.

18. Although I have argued, Ch. 1.d, that to regard punishment as a practice separate from its individual cases is a mistake. Cf. also Smart:

"The rule does not give us a reason for acting so much as an indication of the probable actions of others, which helps us to find out what would be our own most rational course of action" ("Extreme and Retricted Utilitarianism," p. 181).

Cf. Ch. 1.c, and below, g, on expectations.

19. Cf. Feinberg, "Justice and Personal Desert," p. 81.

20. There may be difficulties about what is a real benefit, what a real harm. Cf. Plato, *Gorgias*, 464 ff. But the penologist tends to assume that crimes are harmful to their victims, and we should accept that assumption except in the most cavilling of moods. For which, cf. below, g.

our fear of punishment and, it is hoped, refrain from the crime. The threat will be directed against the general public; against those predisposed to commit crimes in particular; and, more particularly still, against the criminal who has actually committed the offence, in the hope that he will not repeat it.

If the principle of utility argues that the general aim of punishment should be to deter, then liability to punishment and the amount of the punishment should be precisely determined by whatever will be effective to that end. This does not entail that everyone who commits a crime will necessarily be punished for it. Nor does it require that the punishment match in severity the gravity of the crime. The focus is rather upon the fear generated by the threat or the infliction of suffering.

There are, however, two provisos to be entered here. First, utility does restrict who is liable to punishment. The effectiveness of the threat relies largely upon the publicity of its exemplification. If it becomes widely known that someone who did commit the crime was not punished for it, the statute is liable to be held in contempt as ineffective, and the threat will no longer operate. *Prima facie*, therefore, *all those who* are known to have committed a particular crime should be punished, in order to uphold the law. Contrariwise, those who are to be deterred must suppose that the criminal who is punished did in fact commit the crime; otherwise they will not consider the threat to apply to the crime in question. Consequently, *only those who* are known to have committed the crime should be punished for it. Furthermore, since it is intentional criminal activity that we hope to deter (acknowledging that accidents cannot be legislated against), the criminal should be thought to have committed the crime on purpose. So effective deterrence appears to demand that, at least in conditions of complete publicity, committing a crime intentionally is both a necessary and a sufficient condition for incurring the punishment.

Second, utility also imposes some restraint upon the severity of the punishment. For in making the utilitarian calculus, the judge must consider not only the benefit of preventing the crime, but also the harm in the punishment itself. It is not necessarily the case, for example, that the evil of a single capital sentence is outweighed by the good of the thousand thefts it prevents. In other words, excessive punishment may be effective to deter, but it may also violate the utilitarian principle that we should maximise benefit or minimise harm—in which case it should not be carried out. Hence, in laying down a utilitarian penal system, the legislator must "weigh the 'costs' of punishing against the deterrent returns of the penalty."[21]

21. Von Hirsch, *Doing Justice*, p. 64.

The plain formulation of the deterrent theory seems to give carte blanche for any punishment of anyone as long as it generates fear. But the principle of utility itself acts as a brake upon the penal authorities, both in the matter of who is liable to punishment (criminals only) and in the matter of how much they should be punished (as little as possible).

In addition to deterrence, utilitarian punishment may both prevent the repetition of the crime and protect the society, by one and the same penal act. For example, the incarceration of the habitual thief will both protect the public at large from his depredations and prevent him from renewing the offence, while at the same time others are discouraged from emulating him. Here the potential harm done by the criminal is thought to be greater, and spread over a larger number of individuals, than the harm done to him by his punishment. The calculus of utility, therefore, offsets the thinly spread benefit to many against the great harm to one, and comes up with the answer that the action is justified.[22]

Considered from the point of view of society, the purpose of punishment is to protect,[23] and thus who should be punished and how much will be determined by the requirements of what will be effective protection. This may mean the permanent incarceration of the criminal. For if the calculus justifies his incarceration for a short period, it will justify it for a series of short periods, and hence permanently, unless we suppose that after some (short) period the criminal is deterred and may safely be released.

From the point of view of the criminal, the punishment is preventive. Again, there is no reason why the individual punishment should not be permanent, unless we suppose that after a time the criminal becomes less likely, through deterrence, to go back to his old ways. This segregation of the criminal from society ('predictive restraint'[24]) supposes that the criminal's past behaviour is an indicator of his future behaviour, and that segregation is the least harmful means of restricting his future activities.

All of these purposes of punishment—to deter, to protect and to prevent—are closely associated. They should be distinguished, however, from the different teleological purpose of the theory of restitution, which is not utilitarian at all. For restitution goes no way towards increasing benefit, for many or for one; it simply aims to cancel out harm. Thus not only does restitution take place between individuals rather

22. Distinguish here between the act-utilitarian, who would argue for the punishment in this case, without setting a precedent, and the rule-utilitarian, who would argue for this punishment in this and every case, even if exceptionally the calculus suggests that particular punishments will be a disutility.

23. Wertheimer's "social quarantine" of the offender, "Punishing the Innocent."

24. Von Hirsch, *Doing Justice*, pp. 19 ff.

than in the wider social context (the greatest number) of the utilitarian, but also it is a finite transaction, the cancellation of harm, no more, no less.

The theory of retribution argued that crimes cause us to feel moral (rather than prudential) distress. Punishment, the expression of our distress, is then morally justified by the fact that we do, naturally, have these feelings of resentment and gratitude, or impulses to praise or blame.[25] The utilitarian, in reply, offers an instrumental explanation of these phenomena[26] and a consequential argument for perpetuating them. To be punished can make the criminal realise that he did wrong; and he may, as a result, be dissuaded from repeating the offence.

The purpose of the punishment is to create in the criminal recognition of guilt and to explain to him vividly through his own suffering that he did wrong and that he should not do so. The expressive function of punishment, therefore, is not merely to denounce, but to deter.[27] Equally our attitudes of resentment and gratitude, and our activities of praise and blame, are not naturally occurring emotions, but deliberately conjured up to make the object of our resentment or our gratitude refrain from, or repeat, the behaviour in question.[28]

The definition of punishment stipulated that the criminal be responsible for the crime, and, as I suggested, the lay observers of the punishment will concur with this requirement. But the utilitarian will not consider the abstract and difficult question of whether this man is responsible and need not take into account the issues of determinism and social or psychological conditioning. He will ask, rather, whether this man is likely to respond (by being himself deterred afterwards or by being suitably affected to provide an object lesson) to the punishment suggested for him.[29] Inasmuch as he will respond, then he is liable to punishment, whereas his unresponsive fellow will not be so liable, since here the immediate harm is offset by no beneficial consequences. The former, therefore, is thought to be responsible, the latter irresponsible.[30]

The act-utilitarian will quite consistently reply that the notion of *the* responsibility is a piece of metaphysical nonsense, and should be replaced by "Whom would it be useful to blame?"[31]

25. Cf. Strawson, "Freedom and Resentment."
26. Cf. Sidgwick, *Methods of Ethics*, p. 449.
27. Contrast Ch. 3.b,c.
28. Cf., e.g., Feinberg, "Action and Responsibility," p. 127.
29. Smart, "Extreme and Restricted Utilitarianism," p. 182 on "praiseworthy"; Sidgwick, *Methods of Ethics*, p. 428.
30. Cf. Ginsberg, "Nature of Responsibility," p. 85–86; Hart, "Legal Responsibility and Excuses," p. 40.
31. Smart and Williams, *Utilitarianism*, p. 54.

b. THE CALCULUS OF UTILITY

This apparently simple theory of punishment, however, confronts several practical difficulties. The utilitarian advocate of punishment must assume that it does in fact deter or prevent future crimes.

The utilitarian position commits one, as the absolute positions do not, to a factual inquiry as to the effects on society of the use of the . . . penalty. . . .[32]

However, considerable doubts have been raised by modern sociologists as to whether punishments, even extremely severe ones, do indeed deter.[33] Two problems are involved here.

The first concerns how to predict the frightening effect of the statute upon the potential criminal. One man may be frightened of suffering and so be deterred. But another man may consider the punishment a fair price to pay for the profits of the crime, so he will go ahead and commit it. Then the deterrent statute will lose its justification; indeed, the evil of the subsequent punishment is then a disutility, inasmuch as it is never balanced by a corresponding benefit to others. A third man may be attracted by the penalty and actively encouraged to commit the crime.[34] In this extreme case, the utilitarian calculus must be turned on its head. But for each of these men we need an impossibly accurate prediction of their response[35] in order to justify the risk we take when we inflict suffering upon them. Similarly, our preventive punishments rely on the confident prediction that this man is recidivist, that man not, and we are in considerable danger of inflicting unnecessary pain on the one-time offender.[36] Our difficulty here, therefore, is our ignorance both in general, and in the individual case, of the psychology of the criminal—what is likely to motivate him, and what he is likely to do.

The second problem is whether we can do the utility calculus at all. Suppose we prescribe very severe punishments for every offence, relying on their deterrent effect in order to justify their infliction in the few exemplary cases. Can we be sure that the pain caused to the exemplar is outweighed by the benefit to others of prevention or deterrence? Here we are let down by our inability to calculate the relative benefit and harm of penal procedures, to assess the harm they do and the harm they prevent, and to determine whether indeed these harms and benefits are commensurable.

32. Hart, "Murder and the Principles of Punishment," in Hart, *Punishment and Responsibility*, p. 73.

33. Cf., e.g., Hart, "Murder," pp. 65 ff.; von Hirsch, *Doing Justice*, pp. 37 ff.

34. Cf. Hart, "Murder," p. 88, on the psychology of the murderer.

35. The individualism of this factor encourages an act-utilitarian approach to the imposition of a punishment.

36. Cf. von Hirsch, *Doing Justice*, pp. 21 ff., on the risk of "false positives" in predictive restraint.

The utilitarian is betrayed, on the one hand, by his ignorance of the moral psychology of the criminal, which makes him unable to predict what will deter and whom to restrain. On the other hand, he is unable to meet the demands of his own philosophy to do a cost-accounting of benefits and harms which are imponderable and may even be incommensurable.

c. BEGGING THE INSTITUTION

Why should it be punishments that deter? Are punishments best fitted to do the job of deterrence?

An act-utilitarian theory of punishment asserts that whenever a particular punishment is likely to have a useful deterrent effect, it should be carried out. A rule-utilitarian theory of punishment institutes a penal system either because the practice of punishment produces benefits on the whole, or because the existence of the institution is itself beneficial.

The act-utilitarian, however—and the rule-utilitarian who advocates rules of thumb[37]—has not proposed an institution of punishment at all. For if the consequence of suffering upon crime is random, and if it will take place only after an *ad hoc* decision has been made that it will be an overall benefit, then there is no statute, no system, and no institution of punishment. Indeed, under act-utilitarian auspices, the criminal will frequently claim that he is suffering against his expectations. In the long term his and our accurate view of what are crimes, let alone what should follow them, will be eroded.

Guarding against this dilapidation of the moral structure, some rule-utilitarians[38] argue that punishments should be institutionalised, and that what utility recommends is the institution, rather than the particular cases where it is brought into effect. This is to assume that some practice, near enough to the familiar to be called 'punishment,' does in fact have the beneficial effect that utility requires. This is more serious than to claim that fear deters. It is to say that, even under ideal conditions,[39] the institution that we know as punishment is the right one to achieve utilitarian ends. It is, therefore, a weakness of this theory that it institution-begs, instead of adopting a radical and critical approach to the systems that are supposed to provide the greatest benefit for the greatest number.

---

37. Cf. above, a. This type of rule-utilitarian is really an act-utilitarian.

38. This, I take it, lies at the root of Rawls' advocacy of *practices* in "Two Concepts."

39. Contrast Plato's presentation of the ideal state in the *Republic*, where he seems to suppose that under ideal conditions (in the ideal state) there will be no need for any punishments at all. See Ch. 11.c.

d. UTILITY AND JUSTICE

Utilitarianism is deceptively simple. It purports to offer a single standard[40] for assessing and then comparing the value of alternative courses of action. Difficulties in decision-making are thus confined to the practical problems of making such a calculus which, once made, will tell us directly which course of action to adopt.

However, the principle of utility is not as simple as its exponents claim. Benevolence will require us to maximise benefit, but not necessarily to distribute the benefit over the greatest number. Strictly, benevolence cannot distinguish between the case where one man is supremely happy at the cost of the misery of others[41] and the case where, producing the same net happiness, many are moderately content. Yet we,[42] including the utilitarians amongst us,[43] tend to feel that rights are being violated[44] or some primary value overlooked unless the wider distribution of benefit is preferred.

In order to be sure that the benefit is spread over many, the principle that we should maximise the good may be supplemented by a distributive maxim, whereby of two courses of action which offer equal utility, preference is given to that which benefits more people. Or the calculus itself may take account of the good of a fair distribution in assessing the utility of each course of action.[45] Thus either there are two principles—benevolence and justice—in utilitarianism, or else justice is among those goods which constitute happiness.

However, in the latter case, there seems to be no prudential or teleological reason why justice is constitutive of happiness. Thus the calculus is liable to break down under the task of measuring incommensurables—justice, for example, weighed against pleasure. In the former case, the utilitarian loses the advantage of his singular principle. And in either case, he makes a greater concession to the deontologist than he would like. For by allowing the appeal to justice he admits, at one and the same time, the cogency of deontological theories of justice and the reality of the imperative that we should preserve the just state of affairs for intuitive or moral rather than prudential reasons.[46]

40. But see Smart and Williams, *Utilitarianism*, p. 137.

41. Although beware here of benevolence slipping over into (non-utilitarian) egoism, should that one be oneself.

42. As Rawls observes, *A Theory of Justice*, p. 26.

43. See the Benthamite maxims, "The greatest good of the greatest number," and, "Every man to count for one, no man to count for more than one": cf. Sidgwick, *Methods of Ethics*, p. 432.

44. "The individual has a valid claim not to be made the instrument of society's welfare unless he has broken its laws" (Hart, "Murder," p. 82). Cf. von Hirsch, *Doing Justice*, p. 50.

45. Cf. Smart and Williams, *Utilitarianism*, p. 71.

46. Cf. Ch. 3.c.

Alternatively, the utilitarian may repudiate the appeal to justice. He has, therefore, no grounds for preferring "the greatest good of the greatest number" over "the greatest good" *tout court*. But then we, whom he needs to convince, persist in our anxiety for a just distribution, and the utilitarian theory is threatened not by internal incoherence but by its failure to persuade. The utilitarian may believe in it, but do we?

e. VICTIMISATION AND EXPLOITATION

A utilitarian theory of punishment confronts these general difficulties. If we punish simply in order to maximise benefit, there is nothing to prevent serious cases of victimisation of the innocent or exploitation of the guilty. For the principle of utility does not legislate against the following possibilities:

1. A has committed no crime at all. Nevertheless, it is thought that his punishment may have a deterrent effect,[47] perhaps because others think that he has committed the crime. On strict utilitarian lines, therefore, the general good is to be served by his being punished; so he is punished.

2. B is a recidivist who has committed crimes, but not this one. Nevertheless, perhaps for preventive reasons, it is thought useful to punish B for this crime; so he is punished.

3. C actually committed this crime. He is only partly responsible for it because he was coerced. Yet punishment may still deter him from repeating the offence (next time, for example, he may offer greater resistance to coercion); therefore he is responsible in the instrumental sense.[48] Again, utility demands that he be punished; so he is punished.

Within a retributive system, A, B and C would be said to have been victimised or exploited.[49] For in each case the responsibility, and hence the culpability, of the offender is limited.[50] To punish him as if this were not so would be unjust. So the utilitarian faces a series of problems about the rights and responsibility of the minority—the criminal himself. First, does utility alone justify the random imposition of suffering on individuals which is resisted by our other feelings of justice? In other

47. Cf. von Hirsch, *Doing Justice*, p. 25; Quinton, "On Punishment," p. 55; H.J. McCloskey, "A Note on Utilitarian Punishment," *Mind* (1963):599.

48. Cf. above, a.

49. Although the victimisation objection is usually considered in the context of the punishment of the innocent, it has perhaps greater force in the examples of the mildly guilty (B and C), who are excusable for one reason or another; cf. Austin, "A Plea for Excuses," and "Three Ways of Spilling Ink." Here the title of "punishment" may not be suspect, but the propriety of its exaction is. Thus the exploitation of the guilty cannot be avoided by the definitional stop.

50. Cf. Ch. 3.a. Cf. Rawls, "Two Concepts," p. 149.

words, is it true, and if so is it acceptable, that utilitarianism allows or requires the victimisation of the innocent (A)? Second, in the cases of those who are not innocent but are only mildly guilty (B and C), should utility overrule what we still suppose to be the right even of a criminal to be exempt from punishment for the crime? Third, does the utilitarian not ignore traditional accounts of liability—that the offender committed the offence[51]—and look, rather, to the offender's disposition to offend (B) which may not yet have manifested itself in any offence? Fourth, is the forward-looking utilitarian explanation of responsibility, namely, the offender's susceptibility to be influenced by the punishment, sufficient for what retributivists regard as essentially a retrospective issue, namely, the relation between the criminal (C) and his crime?

Utilitarianism may take three different forms in order to account for these difficulties.

f. INDIRECT UTILITARIANISM

Some have argued that victimisations are *de facto* excluded either by the calculus of utility[52] or by the publicity of the rules in a utilitarian system.[53]

First, the sum of misery caused by the victimisation itself and by the threat it poses of further victimisations *is bound*,[54] it is thought, to outweigh the sum of benefit derived from the deterrent effects of the punishment; therefore utility forbids victimisation. In extreme cases—for example, if the victim is executed although the crimes which are prevented are either minor or rare—this must surely be true. But there seems to be no clear reason why utility will *necessarily* produce this result.[55] For example, perhaps only a single victimisation is needed to prevent widespread and grave violence, in which case it is certainly not obvious that the victimisation is a greater harm than the harm it prevents. But even in such a case, the fact that we still speak of victimisation or sacrifice suggests that we are still reluctant to countenance it.

Second, utilitarians claim that the publicity necessary in order for deterrence to work excludes cases of victimisation.[56] We, the potential

51. Cf. Ch. 1.a.

52. Cf. Hart, "Murder," p. 76, Sidgwick, *Methods of Ethics*, p. 446.

53. Smart and Williams, *Utilitarianism*, p. 70, and Mabbott's objection ("Punishment," pp. 42ff.) that the rules need *only* be maintained publicly; privately, what happens is regulated by act-utilitarian considerations, thus *not* precluding victimisations. But cf. also Flew, "The Justification of Punishment," pp. 97 ff., who attempts a rebuttal of Mabbott in terms of the actual effect, and possible risks, of 'keeping it dark'.

54. A rule-utilitarian worry; act-utilitarianism need have no concern for precedent.

55. Cf. Flew, "Justification," p. 98.

56. Cf. Sidgwick, *Methods of Ethics*, p. 442 on "normal expectations"; cf. Ch. 1.c.

criminals, should not be deterred by witnessing the suffering of a man whom we knew to be completely innocent, or of the criminal who did not commit the crime, or of the man of diminished responsibility. We should not be deterred because we would not suppose that the crime which now tempts us bears any relation to the man who is now punished. On the contrary, in order that the deterrent effect be felt, it is necessary that the punishment at least appear to conform with our intuitions about what restricts liability to it—the commission of some act and responsibility for it.[57] What is more, we are likely to repudiate the legal system that violates these intuitions so that the victimisations not only fail to deter but also bring the whole legal and penal system into disrepute. Such victimisations are, therefore, a disutility.

However, even if the victimisation of the innocent does not deter us, is the same necessarily true of the exploitation of the guilty (B and C), even under conditions of great publicity? This depends, surely, upon the particular example. Although we shall be appalled by some victimisations, as the indirect utilitarian suggests, we may well be deterred by others, as he denies. The example of B may tell us to avoid acquiring a criminal record at all. The example of C may (usefully) make us shun situations where we might risk being coerced into committing a crime, in much the same way as we avoid situations where we risk becoming a victim. The suffering of both B and C usefully influences our behaviour; therefore the indirect utilitarian has failed to show that no case of victimisation can ever be called for by the calculus.

A further difficulty for the utilitarian lies in the objection that victimisations will deter as long as those who are to be deterred to not know that the victims are innocent.[58] Thus the only reason why the utilitarian should refrain from victimising is that he will be found out and the deterrent effect lost. Confronted with a victim whose punishment will usefully deter others, the utilitarian should go ahead, but be careful to 'keep it dark'.[59]

The two indirect counters to this line of attack are ineffective. The first is that keeping it dark is risky.[60] Yes, certainly the risk must be calculated, but this need not preclude its being taken. The second is that the victimisation will enfeeble the moral fibre of the victimiser.[61] This Kantian argument, however, will not do. Utility should not consider moral fibre *per se*, but only in its effects, beneficial or otherwise. There-

57. These, of course, are the criteria of desert, Ch. 3.a.
58. Cf. Mabbott, "Interpretations of Mill's Utilitarianism," in Foot, ed., *Theories of Ethics*, p. 141.
59. Mabbott's phrase, "Punishment," p. 44.
60. Cf. Flew, "Justification," pp. 97 ff.
61. Mabbott, "Interpretations of Mill," p. 142.

fore, only if moral fibre, as a factor in the calculus, produces a balance against the victimisation, will such considerations be critical. Certainly this will not always preclude the victimisation's taking place.

g. MILD UTILITARIANISM

The mild utilitarian admits that victimisation cannot be excluded on the grounds that it *must* be harmful overall.[62] But he concedes that there must be some limitation on the use of punishment so that victimisation will not take place.[63] The principle of utility, therefore, must be supplemented by the limiting principle of justice.[64] Thus any punishment is justified if it produces the greatest benefit of the greatest number, provided it does not violate the just distribution.[65]

Put like this, the theory seems unobjectionable. The limiting principle, *prima facie*, is a harmless and subsidiary proviso within the theory, to outlaw any unjust case of punishment. Justice, therefore, is a necessary condition of the punishment.[66] But is it not also a sufficient condition? Justice will, as required, limit cases of victimisation or excessive punishment. But it will also rule out insufficient punishment or failure to punish altogether. These cases, just as much as cases of excessive punishment, are unfair. This subsidiary principle ordains who is punished, that they are indeed punished, and also the severity or lightness of their punishment.

There is then no room for utility to exercise its influence, inasmuch as both the justification[67] and the distribution of the punishment are completely decided by considerations of justice. Furthermore, if justice is seen as a limiting factor, it must, in order for the limitation to be effective, be considered before utility. Consequently, utility will become a factor only when the requirements of justice in punishment have been met and thus only as a bonus accruing from the just punishment. If punishments such as these deter, they do so only because they are just, and only inasmuch as they are just. In short, a utilitarian theory of this mild type, whether to deter, to prevent, or to protect, is parasitic upon retribution.

62. Smart and Williams, *Utilitarianism*, pp. 30 ff.

63. Rawls, "Two Concepts," p. 150.

64. Or, as in Sidgwick and Bentham, by a principle of impartiality, *Methods of Ethics*, pp. 432 ff., 442.

65. Sidgwick, although an act-utilitarian, is caught up by the requirements of justice, p. 449; "the infliction of pain beyond the limits of just punishment" is presented as undesirable over and above its deleterious effects on the character of the victimiser.

66. Cf. Quinton, "On Punishment," p. 58.

67. Hence, as I have argued, Ch. 3.c, retributivism does *not* institution-beg.

Some modern writers[68] have proposed a more subtle way of integrating a limiting principle into the utilitarian theory. They argue that justice is a part of the definition of punishment, altogether separate from the matter of its justification. So to each of the proposed examples of victimisation, they would reply that if a punishment is thus grossly unfair, it does not qualify as a punishment at all. Thus they[69] employ the definitional stop[70] in resisting the victimisation objection.[71]

However, the same difficulties hold here. If justice limits the punishment, it must also determine it. It must be not only necessary but also sufficient for determining whom and to what extent to punish. But then if each punishment must be exactly just, can we add that we impose these just punishments for utilitarian reasons?[72]

First, this utilitarian function will be parasitic still upon the requirements of justice, which must be the prior (definitional) consideration. We may hope that these punishments will be useful, but we may only call this hope our justification in a restricted sense, inasmuch as utility will enter only contingently. Justice will not allow that the punishment be diminished or decreased in order to serve the purposes of utility.

Second, justice continues to enjoy a clear priority over utility, inasmuch as it will determine whether or not the punishment should take place at all. This suggests that the writers who propose this compromise feel some deontological pull, prior to utility. They do not admit it, however, and try rather to incorporate it in our definitions, which can then be apparently overlaid with further, utilitarian, appeals. Thus even the definitional stop fails to save mild utilitarianism from the charge of being covertly retributive, a deontological, no longer a teleological theory.

h. STRICT UTILITARIANISM

This offers a quite different approach to the problems of victimisation. The strict utilitarian insists that utility is the prior, indeed the only, consideration involved in determining whom we should punish, and how much.[73] If this is right, then useful victimisations must be allowed, since the only restriction on our public or private activity is that it must

68. Quinton, Rawls and Hart, cf. Ch. 1, n. 1.
69. E.g., Quinton, "On Punishment," p. 62.
70. Hart's stricture on the retributivists, "Prolegomenon," p. 6.
71. The defence is, as Rawls' article makes clear, rule-utilitarian, against the random cruelties allowed by act-utilitarianism. As such, it is open to the general objections to rule-utilitarianism; cf. above, a and n. 16.
72. As Rawls claims, "Two Concepts," pp. 150 ff.
73. Cf. J.S. Mill, *Utilitarianism*, ed. by M. Warnock (Glasgow: Fontana, 1962), p. 74.

maximise benefit and minimise harm. To our objections that victimisations are morally intolerable, the strict utilitarian may reply that there are no grounds for judging something morally unacceptable beyond the grounds offered by utility.[74] Should we argue, further, that we nevertheless have these moral feelings and inhibitions, he will tell us that our intuitions must be reformed and modified to fit with utilitarian principles.[75]

The major problem about his view is the effect it has on our understanding of what is a crime.[76] The strict utilitarian can allow no moral distinction between crimes and other harms,[77] including those inflicted by the judiciary. In this respect he faces the same difficulty as the *lex talionis* retributivist—how does the crime differ from the punishment?[78] According to strict utility, punishments, although directly harmful, are indirectly beneficial in that they prevent further harms (crimes).

Crimes, on the other hand, are unequivocally harmful.[79] Crimes are forbidden, therefore, while punishments are enjoined. But the only punishments that are justifiable on this basis are those which are actually effective. Correspondingly, the only crimes that can be subject to punishment, indeed, the only actions that can be thought of as crimes at all (as opposed to mere harms), are those which can be prevented. Whether they or their repetition can be prevented, however, seems to be a matter of particular decisions for the individual case; therefore this strict view is act-utilitarian.

This analysis of crimes as preventable harms seems both counter-intuitive and offensive to the expectations we have about the consequences of our social behaviour. Suppose, for example, that a particular unpredictable murder cannot be prevented by the offender's fear of punishment. This murder, on a strict utilitarian analysis, would be no crime, because it cannot be predicted or prevented either in this case or in others by the threat or the actuality of punishment. Or suppose that a man does some accidental harm (victim C) for which it becomes—suddenly and after the event—useful to punish. This man would complain, at least in circumstances that are at all familiar to us, that his punishment is unfair. Or consider the extreme deterrent position wherein all

74. Cf. Carritt quoted by Rawls, "Two Concepts," p. 151.

75. Cf. Flew, "Justification," p. 99. Strict utilitarians, unlike their 'keep it dark' fellows, seem to suppose that the community at large is composed of (aspiring) strict utilitarians.

76. Though cf. above, a.

77. "We do not call anything wrong, unless we mean to imply that a person ought to be punished in some way or other for doing it" (Urmson, "Interpretation," p. 132); but see Ch. 1.a on the oddity of this line.

78. Ch. 3.d.

79. This, of course, is dubious; some crimes, like any other *prima facie* harms, may turn out to be beneficial in the long run.

crimes are subject to the death penalty. We should, under such a statute, have no means of differentiating drunk and disorderly behaviour from sheepstealing or from murder.[80] In all of these examples, the instrumental approach of strict utilitarianism[81] rides roughshod over some values that we appear to hold independently of considerations of utility: our notions of what is criminal, of what constitutes a punishment, and of what are suitable grounds for ascribing responsibility and liability.

The objection to strict utilitarianism is therefore an emotional one. Utilitarianism in general contains a covert principle of distribution which uses deontological rather than teleological reasoning in its support. But the strict utilitarian must reject justice and argue that the distribution of benefit is irrelevant to the net utility. To this the reply is that we feel it to be unfair to ignore the principles of justice, in the same way as we are uneasy at the instrumental definitions of crime and responsibility. Why this is so, however, we cannot say, without recourse to the intuitions of the deontologist, which the strict utilitarian would say make no sense.

Consider, finally, the anxiety of all utilitarians to rebut the charge of victimisation. We object to the victimisation of the innocent and of the mildly guilty inasmuch as their desert, in the light of the past act, is thought to be limited. Correspondingly, we think they have a right not to be punished or victimised. Now, on the view I have suggested, our ideas of responsibility and the corresponding desert and rights do not derive from utilitarianism, but rather from more inchoate moral intuitions.[82] Nevertheless, the utilitarian, despite himself, tries to show how his theory does in fact conform to these intuitions. In undertaking this task, he lays himself open to the objection that he too shares in our preoccupation with justice.

Thus the confrontation between retribution and the utilitarian approach may be reduced to the dispute over justice. A utilitarian theory of punishment may be found to be deficient: either its efficacy is dubious, or its unlimited scope is offensive. If the theory is qualified by a principle of justice, that principle turns out to be prior, so that the

80. Von Hirsch, *Doing Justice,* p. 67, note, quotes the New Hampshire constitution—that such a system would, in fact, be a disutility, since criminals would commit serious harms as lightheartedly as petty offences. But for the sake of the present argument, imagine that the deterrence is in fact successful. I still question the strict utilitarian failure to distinguish petty from serious crimes.

81. E.g., Sidgwick's utilitarian interpretation of desert, *Methods of Ethics,* pp. 445 ff.

82. Cf. Urmson, "Interpretation," p. 130, who regards it as a "shattering objection" to act-utilitarianism that we do have duties conceived as other than indirectly useful or consequential. Cf. also Smart, "Extreme and Restricted Utilitarianism," who supposes that we do have moral "pro-attitudes," p. 174.

theory becomes deontological. If, however, justice is rejected on the grounds that it is incoherent, there may be residual moral feelings which have not been accounted for; therefore the utilitarian theory loses its persuasive force for those who believe that distribution is important. At the same time, the retributive theory is still open to attack on the grounds I have outlined. Thus the importance of justice may be affirmed or denied. It cannot, however, be ignored, since it remains a central factor in our moral reasoning.

CHAPTER
5

THE HUMANITARIAN APPROACH

Although still teleological, the humanitarian approach[1] stands in contrast to utilitarianism. The latter hopes to maximise the distribution of benefit and hence looks to the interests of the community at large. But a humanitarian theory of punishment concentrates its benevolence upon the individual criminal. The humanitarian argues that it is against the interests of the criminal to be criminal, either because it is intrinsically harmful to possess a criminal disposition, or because it is harmful *to the perpetrator* habitually to commit crimes. For his own sake, therefore, the disposition of the offender should be corrected. This can, and should, be achieved by means of punishment. Accordingly, sentences will be determined by what is necessary to achieve the reform of those upon whom they are passed. The humanitarian theory, therefore, is a theory of reform.

The reform of the criminal may also be urged for social reasons.[2] If the criminal no longer has the tendency to commit crimes, then his reform is in the interest of the community at large. Such a justification of punishment may appear as an additional benefit of a humanitarian theory, and it may look humanitarian in its methods, but it is utilitarian. As such, it is vulnerable to the objections against utilitarianism, rather than to those that may be marshalled against the humanitarian approach. A true humanitarian theory, by contrast, is individualistic and recommends reform in the interests of the criminal minority.[3]

1. I give the approach this title because, in general, the motives of these penologists are—or appear to be—humane. For a further discussion of humanitarian punishment, its justifications, and its difficulties, see Ch. 12.
2. Cf. Ch. 4.a.
3. Hereafter by "reform" will be meant "the humanitarian approach."

a. THE INTERESTS OF THE CRIMINAL

Crime does not pay, or so the reformist must maintain. Yet crime manifestly does pay. And the reformist is confronted with the task of explaining away this appearance.

First, he cannot argue that crime does not pay because it is subject to punishment, since, on the contrary, he wishes to say that punishment is necessary (and desirable) *because* crime does not pay. To invoke a subsidiary deterrent purpose of punishment in order to justify the reformative practice engenders hopeless circularity: 'Wrongdoing is harmful to you, its perpetrator, because it provokes a punishment. In order that you shall be protected from that harm, I am justified in subjecting you to punishment.'.[4]

Second, as long as the justification is to remain humanitarian, its proponent cannot appeal to the harm that follows for society at large from the criminal's activity. Eschewing utilitarian arguments, the reformist must exploit the self-interest of the criminal in order to explain how his punishment is justified.

The most promising line would be to claim that the disposition to commit crimes, rather than the actual criminal activity, is intrinsically harmful to its possessor. Thus, the reformist need no longer look for implausible explanations for why the apparent profitability of crime is but an illusion. Crime pays, perhaps, but criminality does not. There is something essentially corrosive about the criminal character; therefore its possessor would be well rid of it. Such a benefit would be conferred by his submission to reformative punishment.

In order for this thesis to work, it must be shown that there is a difference between the criminal disposition and its manifestation in criminal activity. The reformist must demonstrate that criminality is some aspect of character over and above the sum of its externals—the crimes themselves. This metaphysical approach might be exemplified in a criminological theory which claimed that a crime is simply the outward show of an inner, psychological disturbance.[5] The offender, by offending, is calling attention to his distress and is even asking for help. The penal authority obliges by reforming him. The difficulty attached to such a theory, of course, is that it appeals to notions such as the unconscious of the offender—notions which are themselves problematic.

The first step in the justification of reform, therefore, is to show that crime, criminality, or both do not pay. Clearly, for this purpose the humanitarian requires a good deal of proof, inasmuch as he is not appealing to the obvious. What is more, if he fails in this enterprise, his theory

4. Cf. Ch. 1.a.
5. Cf. Wootton, *Crime and the Criminal Law.*

is ruled out by his own principles of benevolence. For if the interests of the criminal are to be served not by reform but by continued offending, then the humanitarian actively harms his subject. The humanitarian's first task, therefore, is to convince both the criminal and the observers that he is genuinely humane.

b. LIABILITY AND RESPONSIBILITY

If crime does not pay, then liability to reform may reasonably be determined by the offender's having responsibly committed a crime. For, it will be supposed, committing a crime is the first step towards recidivism; therefore a man's commission of a crime is a symptom of his need to be reformed.

This account of criminal liability fits well with our intuitions about punishment: that it is *for a crime*. And the stipulation that the criminal be responsible rules out unacceptable punishments for accidental or unintentional acts. Apart from the difficulties attached to demonstrating that crime does not pay, however, such a thesis conceals two major difficulties about liability.

First, it supposes that there is a necessary correlation between being responsible for a crime and recidivism. Granted, the one-time offender is a step nearer to recidivism than his blameless fellow. Yet a one-time offence is not a certain indicator of the offender's future activity. To sentence a man on this basis risks the punishment—or exploitation—of those who would not need reform but would refrain from further offending of their own accord.

Second, this theory ignores those potential recidivists who have not yet committed a crime. Now this may be a very good protection against victimisation, since we do not know, of all those innocent members of the community, who is going to become criminal. Yet it separates liability from the question of who needs reform, a separation which is both confused and inappropriate.

Third, this account unwarrantably assumes that having committed a single crime indicates not only that the perpetrator needs reform but also that he is susceptible to reform. For without the latter condition, the infliction of punishment upon him will be needless suffering.

More plausibly, however, if it is criminality that does not pay, then reform will concentrate upon the criminal's character, which is intrinsically harmful to him. Thus all those and only those who have a criminal character should be punished. But the gravity of his criminal disposition is not, surely, to be measured according to the opportunities to offend that the criminal has had. For one man may commit a crime without being habitually disposed to do so, while another may have had no opportunity to give full rein to his vicious temperament and may remain legally innocent. Moreover, there is no certainty that the seriousness of the crime is in direct proportion to the worthlessness of the character of its perpetrator. Yet the traditional account of liability declares punishments to be for crimes.

If reform adopts this criterion of liability, it will assimilate all those who have committed a particular crime and exclude from reform all those who have committed no crime at all. Subject to punishment will be such vastly different characters as the once-only passionate murder, the cold-blooded homicide who kills during an armed robbery, and the homicidal maniac. Exempt from punishment will be the legalistic fraud, the would-be murderer who lacks the courage to do the deed, and, to use a Platonic example, the tyrant.[6] These examples suggest that there is no guarantee that all those and only those who have committed what are presently described as crimes and have been caught should be subjected to reform; indeed, there are odds against it. Alternatively, reform presupposes a radical review of what actions are designated as crimes to include all those and only those which symptomatise the criminal disorder.[7]

If, on the other hand, the humanitarian rejects orthodox ideas of liability, he will argue that those and only those who have a vicious disposition should be liable to punishment. Thus his first task will be to revise radically his own and our notions of what constitutes criminal liability. But his second task, and the trickiest, will be to show that he can pick out of the community just those members who have this disposition and who will be susceptible to reform. Any "false positives"[8] will be victimisations, and false positives will arise not only when the disposition is mistakenly diagnosed, but also when the future malleability of the criminal is optimistically assessed. The irremediable recidivist should not, on this account, be punished.

When it comes to the question of liability, therefore, the humanitarian has a choice. He may stick to the orthodox account of liability and avoid offending whatever of our intuitions reside therein. In this case, he runs the risk of taking a simplistic view of the criminal disposition and its manifestations, and of punishing those who do not need it or missing those who do. What is more, he must then give some account of relative responsibilities and confront the complex issue of determinism.

6. He, by definition, has the power to get away with it, at least in the common view. Cf. *Gorgias*, 469c ff.

7. One problem here would be institution-begging: what has such a system to do with crimes and punishments? Another problem, suggested by Morris, "Persons and Punishment," is that on this analysis, all our acts would degenerate into events.

8. Cf. von Hirsch, *Doing Justice*, pp. 21 ff.

Or he may revise the account of liability, so that it depends on the identification of the criminal character. Here what crimes the offender is responsible for will be irrelevant. But relevant still will be the extent to which the criminal disposition was voluntarily incurred—the extent to which the criminal is responsible for his own criminality. Now the reformist not only risks false positives, but he may find that those whom he wants to convince of his theory adhere obstinately to the view that it is right that only those who have committed a crime should be punished.

c. RIGHTS

The discussion of utilitarianism suggested that some—innocents and the mildly guilty—have rights against victimisation or exploitation.[9] A theory of reform provokes anxiety about rights equally strongly, in two different areas. The hiatus between the conventional account of liability and the aims and effects of reform suggests that some who conventionally are liable should not be reformed, whereas some who are not liable should be subject to reform. But do both these groups have rights or deserts which are violated by such a reformative penology?

1. The irremediably vicious man may deserve to be punished.[10] Both we and he may object to his being treated differently or not being treated at all.[11]

2. We may all have a right to our own autonomy, to preserve our characters intact[12] against the good intentions and the invasions of the humanitarian, whether we are conventionally liable to punishment or not.

One line of defence for the humanitarian is to say that the criminal has abrogated his rights by committing the offence. Thereafter, he places himself in the hands of the judiciary, to do with what it will. And the judiciary compassionately responds by conferring on the criminal the benefit of reform. By this argument, the humanitarian closes the

9. Ch. 4.d.

10. This, as Morris' analysis, may be explained as a right—the right to be treated as a person, "Persons and Punishment."

11. Cf. Feinberg's characterisation of one version of reform as "chilling," "Crime, Clutchability and Individuated Treatment," in Feinberg, *Doing and Deserving*, p. 266.

12. "A tribunal, given the power not merely of exacting a specific penalty, but of controlling and remodelling the whole life of a man, might easily constitute a threat to the hard-won liberties of the subject. Indeed in certain circumstances it might make the administration of justice more ruthless than under existing systems and enable it to invade areas of life and conduct which now escape legal control" (Ginsberg, "The Nature of Responsibility," p. 91).

Cf. also J. Glover, *Causing Death and Saving Lives* (London: Penguin, 1977), Ch. 5. This is Morris' "fundamental human right to be treated as a person" ("Persons and Punishment," p. 475).

gap between conventional liability and subjection to reform, with the implausible effects already noted.

But certainly the criminal and probably many of his fellows do not take this view of his rights as losable by a single, telling act. On the contrary, discussions about punishment, both legal and philosophical, centre often upon the question of how far the criminal should remain inviolate from the activity of the law. Questions of mitigation and excuse, as well as disputes about victimisation, exploitation, and excessive punishment, presuppose that the criminal has some rights in the face of his punisher.[13]

Furthermore, there may be some conflict between this view and our moral intuitions. The criminal, if he is to be rendered completely subject to the judiciary, must be thought to abandon his rights altogether, whatever his offence. Thus the man who has committed the mildest of crimes, no less than the vicious recidivist, will forgo his rights by so doing. Consequently, all our rights and autonomies will be subordinate to the prior principle of reformative efficiency. Does not this view, however, make a nonsense of our intuitions about what a right is? A right is simply the principle that we retain some inviolability against the manipulations of others.[14] Even if this principle can be contradicted, it is difficult to imagine that the commission of a petty crime is sufficient to contravene such a primary freedom.[15]

d. PATERNALISM

The alternative defence for the humanitarian against the charge that he infringes rights is paternalistic.[16] Punishment will make the offender a good man, the humanitarian will argue. Being a good man is in the offender's interests. Therefore the punisher justifiably consults those interests when he punishes. "It is for his own good" is the catch phrase, and this is supposed to justify any means used upon the unfortunate criminal.

The *onus probandi* that such a penologist's activity is in fact in the criminal's interests rests upon the punisher. Furthermore, he who pun-

13. So Morris argues that the basic right is inalienable and cannot be waived.

14. Hart, "Are There any Natural Rights," in A. Quinton, ed., *Political Philosophy* (Oxford: O.U.P., 1967), p. 55; R. Dworkin, "Taking Rights Seriously," in Dworkin, *Taking Rights Seriously* (London: Duckworth, 1977).

15. It will be obvious that our intuitions appear to insist on some proportionality between crime and punishment, which is inappropriate to reformative expediency. The reformist must persuade us that these intuitions are mistaken.

16. "We [if we are humanitarians] do not seek to deprive the person of something acknowledged as a good, but seek rather to help and benefit the individual who is suffering by ministering to his illness in the hope that the person can be cured" (Morris, "Persons and Punishment," p. 483).

ishes must acknowledge that even a paternalistic attitude may be thought by some an insufficient justification for the unwarranted encroachment upon the autonomy of the individual (right 2).[17] The two principles—benevolence from the punisher, autonomy for the punishee—must be offset against each other.[18] And there is no certainty that benevolence will come out with priority. In modern liberal thinking at least, autonomy ranks very high.

A more complex defence of paternalism would claim that inasmuch as punishment is in the criminal's interests, he consents to it, so that none of his freedom is impaired. This kind of benevolence, therefore, is not really paternalistic at all, since it is voluntarily met by the criminal.

Again, the problem here is the burden of proof. The penologist must show that, contrary to our own experience, punishment[19] is something its victims go willingly toward.[20] Failing that, he must demonstrate that retrospectively the criminal will agree that his interests have been served, and, at least after the event, give his consent to his punishment.

e. THE NORMATIVE CRITICISM

To put it at its crudest, reform claims to make the bad man good. But can we be so secure in our ideas of what is bad and what is good as to justify interfering with the criminal's personality? We can certainly draw some conclusions about what is harmful. And the criminal may be classified as bad because he causes harm (which is, according to the humanitarian argument, against his own interests); thus he is liable to be reformed. If, however, reform is aimed at some evil in the character of the criminal (rather than merely his tendency to harm others), then it begs a great many important questions about the norms that are used to determine who is good and who is bad, or at what point the bad man finally becomes good. This is not, in the first instance, a question of moral psychology, of what causes the bad man to be bad. The normative problem lies in the difficulty of knowing and justifying why *we call him* bad.

There are, I suggest, two problems in the issue of moral values. The first is whether the values according to which we judge this man to be good and that man to be bad are a sound enough basis for taking drastic

17. This is the burden of Morris' argument—that paternalism treats persons as persons no longer.

18. Cf. Glover, *Causing Death*, p. 75.

19. Beware the institution-begger. The reformist would be much better off to deny talk of punishments altogether.

20. Contrast the definition of punishment, Ch. 1.c. It is largely because punishment is thought of as, *prima facie*, a harm, that it needs justification—although, as the present chapter shows, even if it is demonstrated to be actually a benefit, problems still arise.

and irreversible action, or whether moral values are not inevitably slippery. The second is whether, in imposing our values upon the criminal—which is what we do when we punish reformatively—we are justified, when his values may be the opposite of our own and, possibly, internally just as coherent.[21]

There are some responses at the disposal of the humanitarian.

1. He may argue that moral norms are determined by the majority; that majority is therefore justified in forcing conformity to those values upon others. This response runs dangerously close to utilitarianism. It would thus avoid humanitarian difficulties but be obliged to meet the objections to utility.

2. He may argue that what is criminal is laid down by the law: the criminal is he who has broken the law, and he must be reformed into being law-abiding. This response appears to remove the tricky normative content of the reformative thesis and replace it with legalistic terms. But it still must explain whence the law derives its prescriptions.

3. He may argue that what is wicked, or what is illegal, is harm done to others. But this theory is either utilitarian or the humanitarian must still explain how harming others is disadvantageous to the perpetrator.

4. He may argue that there is some common ground to our moral notions, which may be discovered by intuition. There is still some scope for relativism, but this focuses upon an intuitive core. From our own experience, this approach has something to recommend it;[22] But we have seen how intuitionism may readily be construed as obscurantism.[23]

5. He may argue that, despite all this relativistic talk, there are moral truths, according to which we (or someone) may determine whether a man is good or bad and when he has been reformed.[24] This defence may be impossible to demonstrate, but if it were proven it would render reform invulnerable to the normative criticism.

f. MORAL PSYCHOLOGY

Suppose that the humanitarian has solved these problems of justification and has shown that reform is the proper objective of punishment. His difficulty then is to show how reform can be carried out. To this

---

21. "The evil in this would be most apparent in those cases where the agent, whose action is determined to be a manifestation of some disease, does not regard his action in this way. He believes that what he has done is in fact 'right', but his conception of 'normality' is not the therapeutically accepted one" (Morris, "Persons and Punishment," p. 487).

22. So throughout Chs. 1 to 5 I employ intuitive notions to illuminate the advantages and difficulties attached to the notion of punishment.

23. Ch. 3.d.

24. The power of this defence will be made clear in Ch. 12.

end, his first task must be to demonstrate what constitutes criminality—whether by criminality is understood a tendency to commit crimes, or some further defect of character which manifests itself in the commission of crimes. He must show what causes criminality and what might be expected to remove it. But is the moral psychology of the criminal penetrable? It could be argued that we know too little to explain the causes and composition of the criminal character or the treatments appropriate to deal with it.[25] And if we know too little, optimistic measures of reform are indefensible.[26]

g. METHODS

Humanitarian punishment is the means to the reform of the criminal. The actual punishment, therefore, will be chosen and executed by reference to the needs of the subject. In this operation three types of method may be discerned—to be variously described and criticised—and derived from three different moral psychological accounts.

1. *Conditioning.* Here the penologist aims to establish, by more or less crude means, a response in the criminal which will inhibit him, in the future, from committing crimes. At one extreme, conditioning is aversion therapy: the prospect of recidivism makes the criminal, literally or figuratively, nauseous, so that he will not be tempted to repeat his criminal behaviour. At the other extreme, the punisher merely hopes to bring home to the criminal the folly of his behaviour by exacting extremely unpleasant punishment. The criminal, upon realising that it is stupid to be criminal, ceases to offend.

The distinguishing mark of penal conditioning is that it operates at a superficial level, employing the stimulus of fear.[27] Its aim is equally superficial: to repress behaviour.[28] If the criminal disposition is something over and above what is manifested in behaviour, then conditioning will only indirectly and contingently affect that disposition. And in all this the criminal is neither intellectually nor morally involved. Consequently his reformed behaviour is automatic, not chosen.

Now, since conditioning operates merely to inhibit the actual commission of crimes, it stands a good chance of success. For fear does indeed inhibit behaviour. And so long as punishments are effective, it matters

25. Morris' attack on therapy is, I think, implicitly predicated upon the idea that *we do not know for sure* that criminals are so because they are insane.

26. For a start, they either victimise or exploit.

27. Cf., e.g., Skinner's account of "aversive stimuli" in *About Behaviorism* (New York: Vintage Books, 1976), pp. 68 ff.

28. *Ibid.*

not how or why. Conditioning, therefore, least of all the versions of reform, begs questions of moral psychology.

However, this version of reform, more than any other, infringes the rights and freedom of the criminal. For he does not choose to be punished; on the contrary, he is punished against his will. Furthermore, in his life after punishment, he will be acting involuntarily, for he will refrain from crime as a matter now of habit, never of his own choice. Thus conditioning suppresses any rights the criminal may be thought to have to lead his life as he will.

2. *Therapy.* Here the criminal is thought of as sick, his disposition as an illness of which the crimes he commits are the symptoms. The appropriate action to be taken, therefore, is to treat his illness, with a view to curing it. For example, criminals may be thought to be mentally abnormal and in need of psychiatric treatment.[29]

The great virtue of this account of reform is that, if criminality were shown to be a disease, the criminal, himself convinced of this, might well submit willingly to treatment. His rights, therefore, would least risk infringement.[30] The great failing of therapeutic punishment, however, is that our understanding of moral psychology is too limited to allow us to say whether crime is a disease or not, let alone what medical measures are appropriate for its treatment.

3. *Education.* According to a different explanation, crimes are committed as a result of intellectual deficiency—maybe the criminal does not know right from wrong or does not understand the harm that he is doing. Punishment, therefore, should teach him what is right and what is wrong and should induce him, acting on his knowledge, to follow the right and eschew the wrong. Hence the purpose of punishment is to educate the criminal out of his disposition.

The primary difficulty raised by this explanation is the supposition that criminality is a matter of ignorance. How do we know that this view of moral psychology is the right one? A secondary difficulty here is that the reformist who proposes education invites the normative criticism: what is the provenance of these "rights and wrongs" that the criminal must learn?

This version of reform, however, is strong against the objection that

29. Cf. Feinberg, "What is So Special About Mental Illness?" in Feinberg, ed., *Doing and Deserving*, pp. 272 ff.

30. Against Morris, it is my opinion that conditioning is more outrageous a version of reform than therapy. However, cf. Quine's account of induction as conditioning—an intellectualist version of behaviourism—in *Ontological Relativity* (New York: Columbia University Press, 1969), p. 31.

the rights of the criminal are being infringed by the punishment. For education must work by informing the choice of the offender. It teaches him what is right and that doing right is in his interests, and it assumes that he will pursue his interests. The criminal, having emerged from the educative process, will act thereafter of his own free will, without inhibition or coercion from the judiciary.

However, he still may not have chosen to be enlightened in this way; hence his initial liability to punishment/education needs further explanation. The exponents of this view, like the therapists, could point out that both medical treatment and education (the commonplace analogues of these types of punishment) are self-evidently in the interests of the patient or the pupil. The initial compulsion, exercised by a paternalistic doctor or teacher, is justified, they would argue, by the patient's own interests, which he himself comes to recognise. This is a strong, but not immovable, argument. In its disfavour, consider how deplorably limited are the options of a hypothetical adult, who is forced to go to night-school in his own best interests but against his own enduring preferences. He would rather go to the movies, and who are we to say that he should not?

A humanitarian theory of punishment, in these three versions, confronts two major objections in varying degrees: either that it begs questions of the moral psychology of the criminal, or that it infringes his rights. Conditioning is vulnerable to the latter objection at its most severe; education and therapy can be called to task by the former. At the same time it is clear that the penologist's view of moral psychology, however unsure or incomplete, will determine the account he will give of reform. Thus, depending on whether he sees criminality as a matter of habit, of illness, or of ignorance, he will espouse conditioning, therapy, or education.

h. INSTITUTION-BEGGING

This analysis of the methods of reform makes it clear that the humanitarian begs the institution. He supposes that—whether conditioning, therapeutic, or educative—penal suffering is the efficient means of removing or treating criminality. Yet, particularly in the case of education, there is no necessity that any suffering need be involved, and no requirement that humanity need prescribe punishments at all.

This difficulty arises, I suggest, from a lacuna in the humanitarian's argument. Criminals are liable to punishment. The criminality of some is caused by, for example, disease or ignorance; therefore the humane way of dealing with these criminals is to remove the cause of their criminality (the disease or ignorance), and this may best be done by therapy or education. When such criminals are punished, therefore, they should be subjected to therapeutic or educational punishment.

The lacuna occurs between the assumption that criminals are liable to punishment and the declaration that their criminality should, for humanitarian reasons, be removed. For the notion of penal liability bears no necessary relation to humanitarian thinking, and indeed may often contravene humanitarian attitudes.[31] A humanitarian theory utilises punishments either because it must, unsatisfactorily, be tacked onto an already existing penal system, in an attempt to humanise that system; or as a result of the humanitarian's uncritical acceptance of the view that criminals are automatically or necessarily liable to punishment. What the humanitarian needs, by contrast, is to adopt a radical approach to the institutions that will effect the reform of the criminal and to refuse to take it for granted that punishment is the best means to humane ends. In this case, he runs the risk that we will resist this abolition of the institution of punishment.

i. HUMANITY, UTILITY AND JUSTICE

A humanitarian theory of punishment, therefore, adopts an individualistic and humane attitude towards the criminal. According to principles of benevolence, it considers the measures that are necessary to remove his criminality—whether this is thought of as simply the reform of his behaviour or as something more radical, the reform of his character. Such a theory, therefore, is characterised by its focus upon the individual criminal; his interests have priority.

In this concern with the individual criminal, of course, a humanitarian theory of punishment runs directly counter to the purposes of the utilitarian. Both theories are benevolent, and both are interested in punishment as a means to a beneficial end, but they consider quite different sections of the community. Classical utilitarianism directs its energies towards the majority, while humanitarian principles, perhaps supposing that criminals are initially disadvantaged, concentrates upon the minority. It is easy to see, therefore, that two such theories may conflict, each urging the priority of different interests.[32] Consequently, humanity and utility cannot be held *conjointly with equal priority* as the principles of

31. Consider, for example, a humanitarian view that all criminality is both involuntarily acquired and unwillingly exercised.

32. For example, the life-imprisonment of the persistent thief may deter others and *de facto* prevent his recidivism; but it may embitter him, rather than effecting that reform of his character which benevolence towards him would recommend.

punishment. And the utilitarian may well complain against humanitarian punishments just because they only benefit the minority.

It might then be supposed that the humanitarian had some affinity with the deontologist who urges just punishments. After all, it must be some feeling that criminals are unfairly treated—their dispositions are not their fault—that first prompts the humanitarian to focus upon the individual. Here again, however, the two theories are incompatible. I have urged that justice will exactly determine both the distribution and the measure of punishment,[33] so any reformative effect of a deserved punishment will be incidental. Conversely, reform must first look to what will be efficient to achieve its ends and must disregard the fitting of efficiency to justice. So, although reform might be a subsidiary benefit of retribution, the retributivist cannot hope always to reform, nor the reformist to provide just punishments in every case.

In conclusion, therefore, the three main types of penal theory may be distinguished according to their objectives: whether they aim to benefit the majority or the individual, or to meet the requirements of justice.

They may also be distinguished according as they see the criminal as a means (utility) or as an end (justice,[34] humanity). Considerations of justice suggest that the criminal has rights, an autonomy, whereas considerations of humanity and utility would sacrifice those rights to a benefit, for himself or for others. Some theories (justice and mild utilitarianism) regard the responsibility of the agent as a paramount condition for his liability to punishment; other theories (strict utility and reform) either disregard or fudge the question of responsibility.

Each of these theories, though possibly accounting for a side-effect of another, is strongest when held alone. Attempts to join retribution with utility, utility with humanity, or humanity with retribution are doomed to failure so long as the principles are held with equal priority. At the same time each theory, singly held, is vulnerable to a series of objections, some of which appear to tell conclusively against the theory in question. Three questions, therefore, remain. If theorising about punishment is so fraught with difficulty, why, if not from ignorance of these difficulties, do it at all? Or is there any difficulty attached to denying penal institutions?[35] And can any theory of punishment be put forward which is proof against the objections outlined here?

33. Ch. 3.a and b.

34. Hence Kant's advocation of the *lex talionis*—retributivism treats men as ends in themselves. Cf. *Groundwork of the Metaphysic of Morals* (New York: Harper, 1964), p. 95.

35. These two questions raise the problem of institution-begging, to which justice, alone of the penologies discussed, is invulnerable.

Part II argues that the institution of punishment has deep cultural roots, taking as an example the evolution of punishment in ancient Greece. Thus, although penologists may always suppose the institution to be necessary, they do so not thoughtlessly but under considerable historical pressure. Alternatively, they have difficulty in denying the institution altogether. Part III presents one penology, that of Plato, to illustrate how a complex theory of punishment might be defended against the objections, and, at the same time, to show the price that must be paid for penological coherence. In the end, the example of Plato shows how the inherited institution exerts its own pressures in the face of system and analytical theory.

PART
II

THE CLASSICAL TRADITION

CHAPTER

6

HOMERIC VALUES

To develop a theory of punishment, three conditions must hold: first, there must be penal institutions; second, the institutions must be rationalised, explained or justified; and third, the rationalisations must be subjected to critical scrutiny. In classical Greece, true penology appeared late, associated as it is with general philosophical analysis. The antecedents of Plato's theory of punishment are to be discerned, however, in the moral tradition of early and classical literature—poetry, drama, history, oratory and science. The present chapter, and the two that follow, will outline the conditions of penology as they evolved during this period.

a. INTERPRETATION[1]

Yet this procedure begs several questions. First, a critic might deny the propriety of the use of literary evidence in a study of a philosophical problem. The objection is twofold—both against the treatment of literature as philosophy and against the assumption of continuity in the transition from non-philosophical to explicitly philosophical sources. To this the answer lies partly in the nature of Greek culture. Until the sophistic age there existed no moral philosophy as such. Yet the Greeks were capable of considering and solving moral problems, such as the questions surrounding the practice of punishment. Thus while we should distinguish between this unphilosophical approach and the sys-

---

1. Sections a, b, and d are reprinted, revised, from *Philosophy and Literature* (1978).

tematic analyses of the philosopher, the problems with which they deal remain the same.

Second, although I shall begin by discussing the *Iliad*,[2] the society Homer depicts is fictional: it is a common contention that we therefore have no grounds for attributing consistency or historical reality to any of the institutions described in the poems. Thus the proposition is that, not content with inventing a story to tell, Homer imagined all the trappings of the fiction as well; that the conventions and the sentiments bear no relation to conventions or values of his own or any other time. The same argument might be applied to other literary works which make no claim to historicity. But its plausibility depends upon an inflated notion of fiction in which nothing of the story approaches the familiar experiences of its hearers. It is, of course, more reasonable to suppose that fiction generally derives its impact from familiarity,[3] and that Homer's popularity was founded on his appeal to the audience's imagination in the context of their own lives. Thus while the story itself is fiction, it is associated with fact in its detail—the commonplaces of social life and human reaction among which the heroes move. Our task is to look to the commonplaces, for here will be found the social practices and the assumptions which Homer's audience would take for granted.

And third, we may generally suppose that the context of a particular source is determined chiefly by its antecedents. If, however, we are to treat the Homeric poems as the earliest Greek literary sources available to us, there is a major difficulty in this establishment of context: the absence of antecedent. The discussion of Homeric society has been severely hampered by the lack of contemporary referents and by the consequent temptation to import our own values as yardsticks for the measuring of the idiosyncrasies of Homeric thought. To a large extent this is a useful enterprise. It is possible, for instance, to point out the differences between Homeric military structure and our own, or between the kingship system and the political structures of later Greek societies. But

---

2. Which is to assume that the *Iliad* is at the beginning, followed, later, by the *Odyssey*, then by Hesiod, etc. (but cf. West, *Hesiod: Theogony* [Oxford: O.U.P., 1966], pp. 40 ff.). I shall argue below that the *Odyssey* presents a different, and evolving, moral picture from the *Iliad*. But this could be explained by the wartime context of the *Iliad*, contrasted with the peace of the *Odyssey*. Thus Tyrtaeus (e.g., Fr. 10), writing of war, and Pindar (e.g., *Ol.* 6, 9–11, *Nem.* 4.6, *Isth.* 2.28), writing of athletic competitions, revert to the values of the *Iliad*. The explanation of the difference between the *Iliad* and the *Odyssey* lies, I believe, partly in their chronological ordering and partly in their contextual contrast—hence the moral notions that see their beginnings in the *Odyssey* are developed further in later, noncompetitive, literature.

3. Science fiction works the other way round—the stories are familiar, the details outlandish.

as soon as the discussion turns to values, the issue becomes complicated: to compare two values, in our own society and in the Homeric poems, tends to presuppose some common ground where there need be none, to assume that the way we might translate a word reflects significantly upon its original use.

This third difficulty gives rise to a dilemma of a type common in the history of ideas: how do we know that a transaction is a punishment unless we already know that it is a punishment? Or if we are uncertain whether punishment occurs (and if we have no common language to help in the identification), where should we look for it?

The first question may be answered with the benefit of hindsight. The practice of punishment should be sought, if not expected, in situations in which either the later Greeks or we ourselves would impose it. We punish 'crimes', but it is unreasonable to claim to recognize any act as a crime if the moral context is unknown. Moreover, it could adequately be argued that 'crime' presupposes punishment and that one of the identifying marks of a crime is that it is subject to punishment; therefore, again, it would be prejudicial to the inquiry to label any set of actions as crimes. When we believe that a series of actions is offensive, however, the focus of our objection seems to lie in the fact that such acts injure,[4] and their injury quotient may, to an extent, be independently evaluated.[5]

Accordingly, I discuss incidents which might be described, in an attempt at neutrality, by the word 'injury', and which, in a later society, might provoke a punishment. I have tried to show how the Homeric heroes reacted to being injured and how they described both the injury and the reaction.

I have argued for a definition of punishment as "suffering deliberately inflicted, by a penal authority, upon a criminal for his crime, insofar as he is responsible for that crime."[6] The reactions of the heroes of the *Iliad* to an injury do not qualify as punishments, as we shall see. In later centuries, however, the concept of punishment does become current. This development may be seen in the light of the criteria of punishment I have suggested:[7] that there should be a crime, that the criminal should be held responsible for it, and that his treatment should be penal.

4. Cf. Ch. 1.a.
5. In certain cases, of course, the assessment of the injury may vary according to who is the assessor. This does not detract from the supposition that the objective content of crime lies in its injurious nature.
6. Ch. 1.
7. Ch. 1.a,b,c.

b. ACHILLES AND AGAMEMNON

Recent debate has focused upon the values of Homeric society.[8] The findings of Dodds and Adkins have been contested and discussed,[9] with the result that rigid schematization of these values is no longer acceptable. Nevertheless certain characteristic priorities of the society can be identified which vitally affect the nature of any subsidiary manifestation of the values held by its members. Adkins tells us it is

a society whose highest commendation is bestowed upon men who must successfully exhibit the qualities of a warrior, but must also be men of wealth and social position, men, too, who must display their valour both in war and in peace to protect their dependents: a function in which they must succeed, for the most powerful words in the language are used to denigrate those who fail. . . .[10]

The two evaluative terms that represent this situation are the words *aretē* and *timē*. *Aretē*, excellence, carries with it a corresponding estimate by others which is the vital determinant of status: this is described as *timē*.[11] *Aretē* and *timē*, therefore, are interdependent and of supreme importance.

It is generally assumed that both these attributes, when possessed in full measure, give to the hero a freedom from all sanctions apart from the strong force of public opinion, which is the determinant of *timē*. In other words, as long as the hero continues to possess *aretē* and *timē*, thus obeying the ultimate sanction, no constraints will operate over his behavior:

To be *agathos* [i.e., to possess *aretē*] . . . is to be in all circumstances free and independent of the constraint of another, for to be so constrained is viewed as intrinsically insulting to one's manhood and, indeed, to one's very humanity.[12]

8. By "Homeric society," "Homeric man," etc. I mean, throughout this chapter, "Homeric society as shown in the *Iliad*," etc.

9. E.R. Dodds, *The Greeks and the Irrational* (Berkeley: U.C. Press, 1966); A.W.H. Adkins, *Merit and Responsibility* (Oxford, Clarendon Press, 1965); A.A. Long, "Morals and Values in Homer," *J.H.S.* (1970):121–139; V.A. Rodgers, "Some Thoughts on *Dikē*," *C.Q.* (1971):289–301; H. Lloyd-Jones, *The Justice of Zeus* (Berkeley: U.C. Press, 1973); G. Vlastos, *Plato's Universe* (Seattle: U. of Washington Press, 1975); M.W. Dickie, "*Dikē* as a Moral Term in Homer and Hesiod," *C. Ph.* (1978):91–102.

10. Adkins, *Merit and Responsibility*, pp. 34–35.

11. To translate *timē* would prejudice my subsequent argument; I therefore transliterate throughout. At this juncture, it may be borne in mind that Liddell, Scott, and Jones (LSJ) give three sub-headings for the word: 'honour, dignity', 'worth, value', and 'compensation, satisfaction, penalty'. I shall argue that the three senses are originally one. Words etymologically related to *timē* are *tiō*, 'value, honour'; *tinō*, 'pay a penalty' (I shall argue for "pay *timē* to"); *atimos*, 'dishonoured, lacking in *timē*', and *poinē*, 'penalty'. For a discussion of these words, see Adkins's valuable "Honour and Punishment in the Homeric Poems," *B.I.C.S.* (1960):23–32.

12. A.W. Gouldner, *Enter Plato: Classical Greece and the Origins of Social Theory* (New York: Basic Books, 1965), p. 12.

But this picture, however adequate as a description of one man's *aretē* and its concomitant *timē*, is singularly deficient as an account of the structure of the society as a whole. Not only does the *timē* of the gods exercise an influence over the protagonists of the *Iliad*, but the *timē* of their fellows inhibits their actions to an important extent. For it should not be forgotten that each man has *timē*; the interplay of the characters represents a tension and a resolution of varying degrees of *timē* derived from various sources. Conflicts may arise when two men claim equal *timē*, as we shall see. The resolution of such conflicts depends on the reality of the value they invoke, and this reality relies upon the close connection of *aretē* and *timē*. The latter is the mark of the agent's ability to maintain the former; it is an actuality that preserves itself and whose loss can only be ascribed to an inability to retain it, which in itself justifies the loss.

In contemporary society the elementary and minimal reaction of the victim of an injury is to demand recompense for what he has suffered. Injuries are seen to fall roughly into two categories, material and emotional (a word which covers a multitude of non-material sins). Recompense may be classified correspondingly. In general we make the attempt to correlate material loss with material recompense and emotional loss with emotional recompense. It is true that the assessment of an injury may become blurred, and thereby an apparently material loss may have a primarily emotional significance. As long as the assessment is subject to variation, so is the response. Nevertheless, the original correlation is in general upheld.

In Homeric society, however, the situation is more complex. At *Iliad* 1.40 Chryses prays to Apollo that the Greeks should pay for his tears (*teiseian*). Chryses has suffered the loss of his daughter to Agamemnon. Under such circumstances we should expect the priest to demand material satisfaction in the form of the return of his daughter, since Chryseis is still alive. Indeed, he does appear to be asking for some kind of recompense. However, for some unspecified reason the Greeks must not pay for (*tinesthai*) his daughter, but for his grief.

Arguments may be advanced to show that Chryses, in the face of Agamemnon's superiority, proved unable to recover his daughter, and that this request to the god is second best. Certainly Agamemnon is more powerful than Chryses and has been seen to be so, for, after all, he was powerful enough to take Chryseis in the first place. But he can hardly be more powerful than a god. Why, then, should Chryses not ask Apollo to help him recover his daughter, instead of advancing the apparently weaker plea for recompense for his grief? The conclusion must be that for some reason compensation for his grief is more important than the return of his daughter.

The converse also occurs. At 9.632 ff. we are told of the procedure following a murder. A relation of the victim received the payment.[13] The murderer is then allowed to remain in society, and the victim's family, on receiving the payment, is satisfied. The material exchange, therefore, has cancelled out the injury.

In these two instances what actually happens is the opposite of what we should expect. Chryseis is still alive; therefore she could be returned to her father. Chryses' apparent concern, however, is with the tears he has shed. In the second transaction the victim is dead and his relations, who now replace him in the role of victim, are admitted to have suffered, presumably emotionally. They are satisfied, however, financially. There is not, therefore, an immediate correspondence between these events and the prescriptions of the *lex talionis*, which deals with an injury by exactly imitating it in recompense, having a flexible standard— namely, the simulation of the offence—for equating material with material and emotional with emotional loss and recompense.

The rape of Chryseis by Agamemnon sparks off the plot of the *Iliad*. Chryses goes to Agamemnon to ask that his daughter be restored, is harshly rejected, and turns to Apollo for assistance. The Greek army is visited by a plague at the instigation of the god, so the Greeks then demand that Agamemnon return Chryseis to her father. Agamemnon submits,[14] on the condition that he may have Achilles' prize, Briseis, for he in turn is concerned that he shall suffer no loss:

Lest I alone of the Argives should be without a prize (*agerastos*), since that is not fitting. (1.116–19)

Achilles refuses, and they quarrel. The upshot is that Agamemnon declares that he will take Briseis by force. Achilles insists upon keeping her:

I do not think to pile up wealth and riches for you here, while being myself without *timē* (*atimos*). (1.171)

Consider the similarity between the claims of the two heroes. Agamemnon argues that for him to be the only Greek without a prize would not be fitting. The force of this must be that he, being the most powerful of the chiefs, deserves a prize above all. Achilles, in the same vein, is asserting his own claim to a prize. The implication of what he says is that he should not win prizes for Agamemnon, while he himself goes

13. *Poinēn edexato*: the verb *edexato* here suggests that the victim physically receives the recompense, and therefore that the transaction involves material exchange.

14. It will subsequently appear (e.g., at 19.86 ff.) that Agamemnon's action should not be regarded as a matter of choice, but of necessity—he is compelled by the superior force of the god. Cf. below, c.

without. It appears, therefore, that the quarrel is initially about Briseis herself. Agamemnon, however, feels impelled to explain why being *agerastos* is undesirable, which he does by saying that it is not fitting.

Simply being *agerastos*, without a prize, is clearly not a sufficient explanation of his demand to be given Briseis, which leads one to suppose that the prize itself is not in fact the primary issue. This suspicion is confirmed by Achilles' use of *atimos*. If he loses Briseis, his rightful prize for the part he has played so far in the war, he will be *atimos*; he will suffer a loss of *timē*. And this, we infer, is self-evidently undesirable. Agamemnon, in contrast, has consistently been awarded greater prizes than Achilles. He thereby gains wealth as well as a mark of esteem, and wealth is an indication of *timē*.

In the transfer of Briseis, therefore, Achilles loses *timē*, and Agamemnon continues to gain it, or, more accurately, to regain such *timē* as he must have lost in the return of Chryseis. *Prima facie*, *timē* is equated here with material possessions. It would appear that with the return of Briseis the *status quo* between Achilles and Agamemnon would be restored.

Achilles' argument is that he has deserved the reward for fighting well: prowess in battle and the reward for success in the field go hand in hand. Without the reward the prowess goes unrecognized, and recognition is all-important. When Achilles is deprived of his prize, he loses the mark of his success; thus he might as well not have fought at all.

He declares, therefore, that he will retire from the fighting. Agamemnon and the other Greeks will soon realize how much they must suffer for treating him in this way:

And you will chastise your heart within you, in anger that you paid no *timē* (*ouden eteisas*) to the best of the Achaeans. (1.243)

Herein lies the ultimate sanction of the Homeric hero. His *timē* is based in fact,[15] in the harsh reality of the Homeric battle scene, and he has *timē* because he excels in the field. Achilles excels above all others, or so he argues, and this guarantees that his compatriots will suffer from his withdrawal.

Nestor then attempts to mend the rift between the two heroes. His grounds for asking Agamemnon to leave Briseis with Achilles are always practical: the quarrel is harming the Greek cause, and therefore Agamemnon should return the girl, *agathos per eōn* (although he is *agathos*, a phrase which indicates that there is no inherent sanction to prevent him from doing what he likes).[16] Agamemnon should yield in order to

15. Cf. L. Gernet, *Droit et société dans la Grèce ancienne* (Paris: Sirey, 1955), pp. 13 ff.

16. The interpretation of the phrase has been contested by Long. I do not believe that he makes a strong enough case against Adkins, *Merit and Responsibility*, p. 37, to warrant adopting the strained reading he suggests.

prevent the defeat which, without the support of Achilles, is imminent. No word of moral condemnation of his action has been spoken. He is *agathos*, and, since he rules more men, he is the superior of the two (1.281). He seems therefore to be entitled to enhance his own *timē* by robbing Achilles, as long as Achilles does not have an equally powerful card to play.

So Achilles should not insult Agamemnon and should, on the contrary, recognize and admit Agamemnon's superiority, since by his action he is jeopardizing the Greek position at Troy. But this final sentiment reveals the ambiguity of Nestor's argument and the strength of Achilles' position: Agamemnon's superiority, his *aretē*, may be measured in terms of his ability to win the war; if, however, Achilles' retreat adversely affects the army, Agamemnon is shown to be in turn dependent indeed on Achilles' ability to do what he claims.

In the event, therefore, Achilles must be justified in claiming equal status, since he is so crucial to the attack on Troy and since Nestor needs to interfere.[17] Nestor implicitly acknowledges the claims of both heroes; his counter-claim is based upon prudence alone. Agamemnon is doing what his values compel him to do in a crisis situation: asserting his superiority over others and in the process profiting himself. Achilles also acts according to the values of the time—he must not accept losing *timē*, because *timē* is of supreme importance. The only reason that Nestor interferes at all is that the quarrel affects others besides the protagonists, including himself.

In this position, however, neither party can give in. A man's life is governed by his *timē*; therefore Achilles must regain what he has lost. Similarly, Agamemnon must not lose what he gained; loss is equivalent to failure. There is a deadlock.

Briseis herself is only a mark of what Achilles has suffered. His real injury is the loss of *timē*. This to some extent consists in the fact that Agamemnon was able to take anything at all from him. Everyone can see that he is less *agathos* than Agamemnon, whereas his constant contention is that he is independent of Agamemnon, and just as *agathos*, if not more so (1.150 ff.). Agamemnon is in a similar difficulty when he must admit to needing Achilles' help in the sack of Troy.

Achilles now declares his intentions: he wants the Greeks to be driven back to fight by their ships, so that they will recognize Agamemnon for

17. Here I disagree with M.I. Finley: "His [Agamemnon's] status also prevented the aggrieved Achilles from expressing defiance other than in the passive form of a mighty sulk, though in valour Achilles was the admitted superior" (*The World of Odysseus* [London: Chatto & Windus, 1964], p. 82). It seems, on the contrary, that the "mighty sulk" is simply the most effective way for Achilles to exercise his powerful sanction.

what he is, a fool "who paid no *timē* (*ouden eteisen*) to the best of the Achaeans" (1.407 ff.).

The exact position of the protagonists and their supporters is revealed in Thetis' prayer to Zeus (1.505 ff.). Agamemnon *ētimesen* (took *timē* from) Achilles. Zeus must get back *timē* for Achilles, by giving the Trojans the upper hand until the Greeks *tinesthai* Achilles and give him *timē*.[18] This may be simplified as follows: Agamemnon must lose *timē* and Achilles consequently gain it in recompense for what he has suffered. Clearly the loss and the gain are two aspects of the same transaction: Agamemnon's loss of *timē* with defeat (Achilles' priority) will be identical to Achilles' gain of *timē* with the defeat of the Greeks when he is not participating in the battle (Thetis' priority). The fact that Zeus' help is to be employed in bringing this about is immaterial. It is not thought to reflect on Achilles' *timē*, nor does it detract from his opinion of himself; results are what matters. It should further be observed that Zeus is involved not as an authority but as a god whose superior power will be effective. The same is true of Chryses' invocation of Apollo.

This exchange reveals two important characteristics of *timē*. First, it appears to operate as a finite commodity, such that one man's gain constitutes another's loss. Second, each hero appears to be demanding *timē* from the other, thus affirming its universal importance. Agamemnon is inhibited by Achilles because he needs help, which need may be explained in terms of Achilles' *aretē* and hence his *timē*. However, because of Agamemnon's *aretē* and *timē* (which might be translated into his ability to retain his prize in the teeth of Achilles' opposition), Achilles must exercise an indirect sanction, rather than recover Briseis by force. This means that the limits of each man's activity are imposed by the other, even though the men might be equal in status. Not only are they not free of the demands of their own *timē*, but the Homeric heroes are also restricted by the complex of *timai* of their equals and superiors.

In Book 9 the Greeks are driven back to their ships. Agamemnon rightly ascribes his defeat to Zeus, saying that the god has decided that Agamemnon shall return to Argos dishonoured (*dusklea*). But Nestor explains (9.96 ff.) that his disgrace is a consequence of his treatment of Achilles. Agamemnon yields and promises to give vast wealth to Achilles. Nevertheless he still asserts his superiority. The price Achilles must pay for his recompense is that he must acknowledge Agamemnon's *aretē*:

And let him give way to me, inasmuch as I am more royal and inasmuch as I claim to be his senior by birth. (9.160–61)

18. Cf. Adkins, "Honour and Punishment," for a discussion of this passage.

Ajax and Odysseus are sent to Achilles to offer the bargain. Odysseus then explains that, by giving in to Agamemnon's request, Achilles will put himself in a position to defeat Hector, which will win him additional *timē* among the Achaeans:

They will give you *timē* (*teisousi*) as to a god, for you could win very great glory in their eyes. (9.302)

The terms of the bargain can be schematised as follows:

1. Achilles gains *timē* from Agamemnon's compensatory gifts.

2. Agamemnon loses *timē* by giving Achilles the gifts (the same thing happens to Alcinous, *Od.*, 13.14) and by admitting that he was partially wrong.

3. Achilles will then be able to win additional *timē* by defeating Hector. (This, however, is incidental to the transaction.)

4. But it is a part of the bargain that Agamemnon gains *timē* when Achilles recognizes his superior *aretē*.

Achilles' gain, therefore, according to the bargain, is the *timē* of the gifts from Agamemnon (his possible victory over Hector is irrelevant). He will not be compensated for Agamemnon's assertion of his own *aretē* when he took Briseis, even though Briseis is returned, for the bargain requires that Achilles acknowledge this superiority. Each party to the bargain, therefore, will gain *timē*, and Achilles will thus be the overall loser, because he is still suffering from loss of *timē* from the original injury.

There is no question here of Achilles demanding an extra penalty from Agamemnon in addition to recompense; his demand is simply to be restored to the status he occupied before Agamemnon's injury to him. I would therefore take issue with Finley, who claims that

It was when Achilles refused this proper, and under all normal circumstances satisfactory, gift of amends, that the real tragedy of the *Iliad* began. "Sing, goddess, of the wrath of Peleus' son Achilles." The hero's mistake was not made at the beginning; it came at the refusal of the penal gift, for that placed him temporarily beyond the heroic pale, that marked him as a man of unacceptable excesses.[19]

Achilles counters the proposal with the assertion that in battle he has

19. *World of Odysseus*, p. 130. T.J. Saunders, in a paper delivered recently to the Cambridge Philological Society, argued that what the victim demanded was first of all recompense, but secondly an extra payment above and beyond the requirements of restitution. Herein, Saunders claims, lies the basis of subsequent penal practice and theory. It is my opinion that seeing an 'extra' payment in these transactions is based on a mistaken reading of the nature of the injury itself. Granted, if the injury had merely been the removal of Briseis, Achilles' subsequent demands would appear excessive. I have shown, however, that the injury consists principally in the affront to his *timē*, and until that is restored there can be no question of any 'extra'—and Agamemnon is steadfast in his refusal to admit Achilles' claimed equality.

more *aretē* than Agamemnon, though Agamemnon is depriving him of recognition of this. The proof of this is that Hector is defeating the Greeks now, whereas he never dared approach the ships when Achilles was fighting (9.351 ff.). We then come to the crux of the matter. Achilles refuses the gifts; he refuses any gifts that Agamemnon might offer. Agamemnon will never win him over, he says, until he *gives Achilles back* all the grief that he has suffered (9.386–7). This grief, as we have seen, is not contained in the loss of Briseis and is not assuaged by her return. Achilles suffered when Agamemnon first refused to recognize Achilles' *aretē* and then deprived Achilles of *timē* by taking Briseis. Achilles demands payment in kind.

The earlier demands of Chryses spring immediately to mind. Chryses' attitude towards his loss is one of concern for his own emotions rather than for his daughter; the insult he has suffered assumes priority. This is explained thus:

Because the son of Atreus took *timē* from (*ētimasen*) Chryses the priest. (1.11)

Chryses has lost *timē* in the affair; his first thought is to rectify the loss. This is confirmed and explained by his prayer at 1.40, in which he demands repayment for the tears he shed.

It is considered as a commonplace that Chryses' loss of *timē* is the most important aspect of his exchange with Agamemnon. Furthermore, in each case the reaction of the man who has lost *timē* is to make every effort within his power to recover it from the injurer. In effect, all relations between men appear to be reducible to their *timai*, whose loss fundamentally affects their lives, to the extent that they exert themselves to the utmost to return to the *status quo*.

A similar situation seems to obtain in man's relations with the gods. For the gods too, within the anthropomorphic outlook, have their own *timai* (e.g., 9.498). This being so, we should hardly be surprised to find that the same expressions used by gods as by men—*timē* and its cognates *timaō, atimos, tiō, tinō*—are used in contexts where gods and men are associated together. This is the real force of Zeus' giving *timē* to Achilles (1.505), for Zeus is Achilles' superior and may protect him in this way. The same effect may be seen in Phoenix' account of the Litai, who exact a recompense for mortal disrespect towards Zeus (9.505 ff.). Similarly, Scamander's anger against Achilles may be seen to stem from the same source, the preservation of self-esteem (21.315). And it is concern for the divine *timē* that provokes Poseidon's wrath in Book 7 (7.446 ff.). Moreover, the system whereby the gods bestow *timē* upon the least favored of men[20] involves the divine prestige in any transgression. There is a significant use of *apotinō* in connection with oathbreakers:

20. Beggars and guests; cf. Adkins, *Merit and Responsibility*, p. 25. To be someone's

Even if the Olympian has not fulfilled (the consequences of men's oaths) straight away, he does so in the end, and the oathbreakers have paid dearly, both themselves and their wives and children. (4.160)

It is not necessary to read into such contexts any idea of the gods as moral underwriters, when the situation may be explained by reference to the commonplaces of social values at the time. We may suppose, therefore, that, as was the case in later literature,[21] an offence against a god constituted an affront to his *timē*, to which his reaction would be to assert himself over the mortal involved. Similarly, relations between one god and another seem to operate according to a hierarchy of *timai*; thus Thetis may remark,

so that I may know well how I am the god with the least *timē* (*atimotatē*) of all. (1.515–6)

Or Poseidon may claim equal status with Zeus and Hades (15.185 ff.). Effectively, therefore, when it comes to the according of *timē*, the gods are on the same scale as mortals, but superior to them, both in the amount of *timē* they possess and in their ability to preserve it, although the ability to preserve one's *timē* is in fact an aspect of it. Among themselves, the gods seem to struggle in precisely the same way as Achilles and Agamemnon.

From the accounts of the effects of injury, it is made clear that although *timē* can be lost in active failure, it can also be lost in passive suffering; thus the major characteristic of being injured is loss of *timē*, which explains both Chryses' and Achilles' emphasis on the emotional aspect of their loss. In addition, the injurer gains a corresponding amount of *timē* by having been in a position to assert his superiority over his victim. The victim, therefore, in order to recover from the injury, exerts such pressure as he can command to restore the *status quo* by demanding from the injurer an equivalent loss of *timē*; in the granting of his demand, he gains in the same way as the injurer did in the first half of the transaction.

Built into the protagonists' *timē*, however, is a measure of their ability to preserve it; the victim will only recover his loss, therefore, if he has the *aretē* to do so. Thus it is that Chryses is helpless in the face of Agamemnon's superiority; Chryseis would have remained in Agamemnon's hands had not her father turned to a more powerful agent still—a god. It is only when the god intervenes that Agamemnon gives in. Achilles

---

patron, of course, is one way to enhance your *timē*, for you are seen to be strong enough to protect your clients. Thus Achilles' grief at the death of Patroclus is at least partially explained by his sense of failure as a patron, 18.98 ff. Cf. Adkins, "Friendship and Self-sufficiency in Homer and Aristotle," *C.Q.* (1963):30–45; Gernet, *Droit et société*, p. 10.

21. Cf., for example, Athena's sense of affront in Sophocles' *Ajax*.

demonstrates the practicality of these exchanges, for he, asserting equality with Agamemnon in the form of mutual dependence,[22] is proved right by the event. His sanction depends entirely upon the reality of his claim to be equal in *timē* and *aretē*, and he is vindicated by the failure of the Greek army in his absence.

The prudential nature of Nestor's attempt at reconciliation underlines this point: Achilles is in a strong position only because his sanction works. There is no indication that moral pressure (as we understand the term moral) can be applied to either hero to make him give in. If, however, Achilles' sanction failed, nothing would happen at all; Agamemnon would lead the army to victory without him. Nestor would have no need to complain, and Achilles himself would merely remain sulking in his tent. Yet there is no suggestion that Achilles would, on the success of his sanction, oust Agamemnon from his position altogether. As Nestor points out, Agamemnon commands more men, which is an attribute of *aretē*. The *status quo* would simply be restored.

It transpires, therefore, that injury and reaction, together with the ability both to injure and to retaliate, may be resolved into the single notion of *timē*. One effect of this will be to make commensurable the emotional and the material in loss and recovery. For if any loss, of whatever form, could be measured in terms of *timē*, the reaction to restore the *status quo* need only restore the requisite amount of *timē*, irrespective of the form this process takes. This state of affairs is rendered possible by the flexibility of *timē*, which can be expressed in any form of *aretē*—excellence of any kind or wealth of any kind. In short, *timē* may be determined by any Homeric asset.

Furthermore, the exchanges of *timē* that take place in the *Iliad* (either in an injury and its consequences or in any recognition of another man's status, whether according to his physical prowess or according to his wealth) occur without the moral overtones that typify modern crime/punishment transactions. Thus Agamemnon is not blamed for asserting himself over Achilles or over Chryses. He is simply asked to remember the consequences to the Greek army, and therefore to himself, of his action.

There is no moral sanction as we know it; the sanctions are based on expediency[23] and in the last analysis depend on the concern of every

22. Agamemnon depends upon Achilles to sack Troy, although Achilles is not powerful enough to overcome Agamemnon's position as the leading chieftain.

23. Dickie, "*Dikē*," argues that even if the imprudence of an act is urged on the grounds of its unpleasant consequences (e.g., punishment), this does not preclude the act's being decried for moral reasons. This, of course, is true. He also argues that such prudential arguments do not show that the society in which they appear is run on considerations of expediency alone. This, too, is true. So a society that appeals to the consequential 'because'

hero to maintain and hopefully to increase his *timē*. This concern in itself forces him to give in to the demands of others, and Agamemnon is therefore susceptible to pressure from Nestor because his *timē* is representative of his ability to protect the troops, an ability which he betrays if he makes no attempt to heal the breach between Achilles and himself. In addition, the *timē* of an opponent, whether actual or potential, to an extent dictates the actions of the protagonist, for when he tries to encroach on the *timē* of another, he can only get away with it insofar as he is genuinely superior to the other. By contrast, "the man without *timē* . . . may be harmed with impunity."[24]

Timē is the measure of a real attribute; thus the *timē* of each man must act as a check on all others, for his strength is commensurate with his status. *Timē* is, therefore, a far more concrete idea than is conveyed by our translation 'status', for it encompasses not only the position of its owner, but his actual ability to maintain that position by whatever means are available. It is a precise measure of a man's desert, inasmuch as he deserves and must deserve what he has, after the struggle of injury and reaction has subsided. But a man's 'desert' in the *Iliad* does not reflect what he should have but does not—in other words our moral condition of 'ought'—but only what he should and does have. In short, his desert describes but never prescribes.

Turning to the complex transaction of injury and reaction to it, it becomes clear that the neutral and prudential notion of *timē* affects the approach of Homeric man to injury. The absence of moral criticism of the agent,[25] along with the presence of a currency, *timē*, to measure gain and loss, seems to mean that it is the action, not the agent, which is of primary interest. Thus Nestor displays no concern for Agamemnon's character, but an anxiety to avoid the consequences of his action. Although it may be fully realized that Agamemnon's self-importance pushes him into this impossible situation, the failure to apportion blame indicates that Nestor and presumably his fellows are interested in the effects of actions, not in the agents who do them.

The transactions accordingly attempt to remove these effects by canceling out the original injury and returning to the *status quo*. This will take place, however, only under certain circumstances. The reaction to injury is not statutory, by any means; as we have seen, it will take place

---

also must have some other account to be given why the imprudent act is not recommended. This is false. In a society in which what happens is what matters, unpleasant consequences are both necessary and sufficient reason for an act's being avoided. Although it is true that in general the reason for an action is to be distinguished from its consequences, in a society such as that of Homer, this distinction cannot be made.

24. Adkins, *Merit and Responsibility*, p. 25.

25. Cf. below, c, on Antilochus who cheats in the chariot-race, *Iliad* 23.

only when the victim is in a position to exact payment from his opponent. This can happen when the victim and the injurer are either equal
in status or, as will happen if a god is affronted by a failure to sacrifice,
when the victim is superior in power.

It cannot be sufficiently emphasized, therefore, that the process is not
one of equalization, but of restoration to the *status quo*. This is only an
issue of equal shares among equals; to unequals, such as the wretched
Thersites, must go unequal shares. These transactions preserve the hierarchical structure of the society depicted in the poem. In the case of
the quarrel between Agamemnon and Achilles, the conflict is prolonged
because Achilles is claiming that he should be restored to a position
equal to Agamemnon's own, which Agamemnon denies him.

All this evidence suggests that the traditional distinction between *timē*
as 'honour' and *timē* as 'punishment' should be revised. For the latter is
merely a restricted aspect of the former: 'honour' is the currency of
'punishment'. Thus to say that I will give you *timē* is merely to indicate
the medium of the transaction, a medium that is not restricted to enter-
prises which appear to some as punishment.

c. RESPONSIBILITY AND BLAME

If a man is responsible for an act, that act is thought to be his act and
neither a natural event nor the act of another. Modern views of responsibility, moreover, allow that for the acts of which a man is at least the
mechanism, he may be varyingly responsible, according as he acted
freely, intentionally and deliberately.[26]

Achilles and Agamemnon could distinguish between one man's act
and another's,[27] and between an act and an event.[28] But it has been contested whether they could distinguish varying levels of responsibility for
those acts which do belong to one man. Three arguments support this
view:

1. Homeric man so externalises his mental processes and so reduces

---

26. Cf. Austin, "Three Ways of Spilling Ink"; Feinberg, "Action and Responsibility."

27. Even between an act which should be attributed to one man but is done through
the instrumentality of another—we may recall Henry Lightfingers' dog, Ch. 1.b. Thus at
Il. 1.335 ff. Achilles recognises that it is Agamemnon, not Talthybius and Eurybatus, his
heralds, who takes Briseis from him.

28. Although this distinction might not be straightforward. Acts, of oneself or of another, are distinct from natural events, whether regular or otherwise, but natural events
are very often explained as the acts of a person—of Dawn, for example, or Zeus (cf., e.g.,
Il. 2.48; 2.5 ff.). This notion of the gods as causes of natural events will confuse their
emergence as penal authorities, as we shall see, Ch. 7.a. Also there are difficulties here
about a god causing a man to act; cf. below.

his awareness of himself[29] that he cannot arrive at a comprehensive view of intentionality.

2. He attributes many of his actions to the gods—"They drove me mad," asserts Agamemnon—and thus subscribes to a determinism that forbids subtle differentiations of what is done with intent.[30]

3. The society as a whole is a results-culture;[31] therefore intentions do not count.[32] Variations of responsibility are thus irrelevant and fail to evolve.

These three arguments should be treated with caution, partly because of their extreme generality. Nevertheless, there appears to be some substance in the view that responsibility was attributed upon fairly wide criteria, and that it was not subject to variation or excuse.

An excuse can diminish responsibility and hence affect culpability; a justification can diminish culpability. A man might argue that he was pushed and so was not responsible for an accident, or he might claim that he was right to do as he did and therefore not to blame.[33]

'Responsibility' signifies the relation between an agent and his acts,[34] such that his acts are treated as his own and not as mere accidents or as actions done by someone else. 'Culpability' signifies one relation between the agent and what happens to him (what he is liable to) as a result of his acts.[35] Thus culpability may be moral or legal. If moral, the culpable agent is subject to blame and his act is described as bad; if legal, the culpable agent is subject to punishment. 'Culpable' therefore means "liable to blame or punishment."[36]

---

29. The evidence for his externalised mental processes is good, and well presented by Dodds, *Greeks and the Irrational*, Ch. 1; B. Snell, *The Discovery of the Mind: The Greek Origins of European Thought* (Oxford: Blackwell, 1953), Ch. 1. The psychologising inference that he has a low awareness of himself, however, is questionable by its very nature and so, correspondingly, is the assessment of the Homeric view of intentionality. But it is the conclusion of this argument, not its premises, that should be attacked. Contra Vlastos, *Plato's Universe*; Lloyd-Jones, *Justice of Zeus*.

30. Cf. Adkins, *Merit and Responsibility*.

31. Gouldner's term, *Enter Plato*. This, effectively, is what I have argued above, b.

32. Or vice versa, intentions do not count (maybe for reason 1 or 2), and the society is thus a results culture. Intentionality may be the chicken or the egg.

33. Cf. Austin, "A Plea for Excuses," pp. 20 ff.

34. Here, and in Ch. 1.b, I suggest a notion of responsibility as distinct from culpability; both 'responsibility' and 'culpability' should be distinguished in turn from 'moral responsibility,' which apparently relates not only the agent to his acts but also his acts to the reactions against them. Thus 'moral responsibility' covers the agent's responsibility and his culpability and fudges the issue which I canvass in the present study, that a man may be responsible *without being culpable*. When I speak of 'responsibility', I do not mean 'moral responsibility' in this sense.

35. Cf. Ch. 1.b. Culpability is one type of liability.

36. The responsible agent could also act virtuously or legally. In this case he is not, of

Some responsibility is a necessary condition of culpability, but it need not be sufficient. In a context wherein the legal or moral conditions for culpability are missing, a man's acts may still be his. Suppose that the act is done in a context wherein there are no statutes requiring or prohibiting it. In this case, the relation between what a man does and what happens to him is either a matter of natural effect, where he causes the effect, rather than being liable to it; or of the unpredictable reaction of others, where that very unpredictability precludes our being able to say, before the event, "He is liable to that."

Or again suppose that determinism is true. We may still describe a man as the agent of acts, in order to distinguish the acts that he appears to initiate from those he does not, or from events in which he is mechanically involved. But we would be unlikely to blame him for his determined acts; therefore he is exculpated.

When Agamemnon gives in at last and offers reparation to Achilles, he explains why he acted as he did; the gods had driven him mad (9.17 ff.). Nevertheless, he offers compensation, and, ultimately, his offer is accepted on this basis.

To us, it comes as a surprise that Agamemnon, having offered so compelling an excuse for why he acted as he did, should still be liable to full jeopardy. In our moral system, the man who offers an excuse which is accepted gets off or at least escapes some of the penalty. Now Agamemnon's excuse seems quite a good one, for who could withstand the superior power of the gods? So it seems to us that he pays full reparation in spite of his plea, hence "nevertheless".

"Nevertheless" is the weasel here: the Greek text has no "nevertheless". "*Since* I was driven mad," says Agamemnon, "I will pay the price for my actions." His words are no excuse at all, nor are they a justification; they are an explanation.[37] And this is revealing.

That he pays the reparation indicates that Agamemnon is thought to be fully responsible to Achilles for what has happened. It is he who deprived Achilles of *timē*, and it is he and no one else (such as the gods who drove him mad) who must restore it. Thus what happened is Agamemnon's responsibility.

But if this is all there is to it, why the explanation? Vlastos has argued that this situation embodies a logical conflict which is to beset the development of Greek moral thought, but which is obscured by the modern tendency to view Homeric society as a 'results-culture'.[38] A plea of coer-

course, culpable—liable to punishment or blame. But, particularly if his act were supererogatory, he would be liable to praise or even reward—he would be laudable. Hence the converse of culpability is laudability.

37. Cf. Dodds, *Greeks and the Irrational*, pp. 3 ff.
38. *Plato's Universe*, p. 16.

cion should relieve Agamemnon of blame (why else make the plea?) *and hence from responsibility*. Yet his responsibility for what has happened is upheld *de facto*; he still has to give reparation. So the status of his plea is dubious.

Three reflections are provoked by Vlastos' dilemma.

1. His argument only works if Agamemnon is offering an excuse, whereas the words are explanatory, not defensive.

2. If it were an excuse, it would only be effective if it were accepted. But there is no sign of Achilles saying, "Oh well, in *that* case, I shall let you off ten tripods."

3. Consider the question of Agamemnon's culpability. He is indeed responsible. Vlastos supposes that if a man is responsible, then he is culpable. This is false. A man may indeed be responsible for making compensation without deserving blame for what has happened.[39] Hence Agamemnon's explanation reveals that although Homeric man attributes responsibility for acts, he does not blame those who are responsible;[40] there is no culpability. Agamemnon's explanation is treated as commonplace; it is not commented upon or thought to affect the case. The fact that it is an explanation rather than an excuse tells its own story. The society is a results-culture in which, although responsibility is upheld and compensation demanded accordingly, the causes and intentions behind responsibility are of academic interest only. There is no blame, so an excuse cannot help a man avoid it. But there is responsibility, measured strictly according to the effect of the act and irrespective of any excusing conditions. Agamemnon needs only to offer an explanation, for the curious, of why he made the mistake of depriving Achilles of *timē* when he could not get away with it.

Therefore, the example of Agamemnon suggests that we be wary of 'responsibility' and 'culpability' in the *Iliad*. Culpability is absent altogether—witness the fact that Agamemnon is not blamed for what happened. Responsibility for an act, on the other hand, is upheld, and it is measured strictly according to what happens. No account is taken either of the intentions of the agent or of the possibility that he may have been coerced and hence only partly responsible.

An episode in *Iliad* 23 offers ammunition to those who suppose that Homeric man does distinguish between actions according to what was intended, rather than according to their results.[41] In the chariot race

39. Insurance companies, guarantors and underwriters deliberately take on responsibility for damage for which they are not culpable.

40. As we have seen, there is no element of blame in the arguments between Nestor and Agamemnon.

41. E.g., by Vlastos, *Plato's Universe*, p. 98. I am grateful to an anonymous reader for

that forms a part of Patroclus' funeral games, Antilochus, who beats
Menelaus into second place by cheating, is about to walk off with second
prize when he is challenged. He should not have the prize, Menelaus
argues, because he won only by cheating. After some dispute, Antilochus gives in, and Menelaus takes the prize. Interpretations of this passage have supposed that it is the immorality of Antilochus' action to
which Menelaus objects,[42] and that it is the moral imperative not to act
in such a devious way that causes Antilochus to give in. The result,
therefore, depends not on what happened but on what was intended
and on what is fair.

If so, the prudential and descriptive interpretation of the *Iliad* that I
have suggested breaks down—particularly the idea that responsibility is
attributed for *what* happens, not for *how* or *why* it happens. This interpretation of Antilochus' concession, however, is not the only one available to us. The results of the race depend upon two factors: on the one
hand, upon who wins the race; on the other, upon who has the best
horses. The former is supposed to be an indicator of the latter, unless
natural events get in the way.[43] In Menelaus' case, however, his *aretē* is
flouted (23.571) by Antilochus' action, since Antilochus beat him by
cheating and positively in default of any excellence of his own (23.515).
Menelaus' claim is that he has in truth[44] the better horses and should
have the prize that goes with them.

The significant thing about the affair is that Antilochus gives in upon
Menelaus' inviting him to a trial by oath. Two factors, and two only,
dictate Antilochus' decision. First, Menelaus challenges that Antilochus'
claim that he has the better team is false, *de facto*; thus Antilochus cannot
get away with it. Second, by suggesting a trial by oath, Menelaus brings
on the big guns, for if Antilochus takes the oath and his team is then
seen to be the weaker—which it is—he has affronted the *timē* of a god
(cf. 23.595) and will certainly not get away with that. Antilochus' response is to give in and to acknowledge that he is the younger and the
weaker. Strength, not intentions, carries the day.

---

the University of California Press for provoking me into discussing this passage. Détienne
and Vernant discuss the race but explain the outcome in terms of the failure of Antilochus
to be cunning enough. They make insufficient allowance, in my view, for Menelaus' account of what should happen, M. Détienne and J.-P. Vernant, *Cunning Intelligence in Greek
Culture and Society* (Sussex: Harvester Press, 1978), Ch. 1.

42. Gernet, *Droit et société*, pp. 9 ff., sees Antilochus' action, implausibly, as one of
"générosité."

43. As they do in the case of Eumelus, who nevertheless receives a prize, as the best
man in the race.

44. Cf. 23.576, Antilochus' victory was *false*.

d. HOMER AND PUNISHMENT

How then does the Homeric practice relate to the definition of punishment? To begin with, it is evident that the Homeric incident takes place between individuals, a factor which reflects both on the nature of the authority involved and on the description of the original injury as a crime. Authority is involved in these affairs in the traditional acceptance of the way in which they happen. Thus when a reaction occurs it is apparently unexceptionable. But authority in the meaningful sense of the external and statutory agent of punishment is entirely lacking, even in exchanges with the gods, where the individual approach continues to prevail.[45] This removes a major defining mark of punishment, without which the activity must be reduced to the status of revenge.

Even the expedient of calling the activity revenge, however, may be found inadequate. Revenge penalises. But these are not penalties; they are payments made to a recipient. Liability to pay depends on the debtor—unlike culpability, which is liability to blame and is prescribed by the moral or legal climate. And blame, hence culpability, is missing here.

Moreover, the individual nature of the transaction creates a difficulty about the offensiveness of the injury or, more strongly, about its criminality. These injuries have consisted in damages done to the fundamental value of the victim, but they do not contravene any rule. On the contrary, they may be seen to be recommended by the values of the time. Their direct offensiveness, therefore, is against the individual victim alone; they are only undesirable to a wider section of society when their consequences are unpleasant to others, as happens in the case of Achilles and Agamemnon. There are no crimes here, then, and no criminals.

There is, however, a more fundamental and revealing difficulty attached to the description of these Homeric transactions as 'punishments'. For not only is there no factor of prescription (no previously established code which may govern them), but they lack a statutory nature altogether. The reaction takes place if the victim has the power to react; otherwise the affair lapses. These exchanges therefore simply account for what actually happens, not for what ought to happen. A punishment, in contrast, may be actual or potential; it is determined by what is considered to be appropriate—according to various criteria—in reaction to a crime that has been committed.

It may be, therefore, that a punishment is prescribed but never exacted. In Homeric society, on the contrary, the reaction is only consid-

---

45. Even oath-breaking is committed *against* someone, namely the Erinyes; cf. *Il.* 19.265.

ered to be appropriate if it takes place. This contrast may be encapsulated in the opposition between what does actually happen and what ought to happen, Homeric society having no time for the 'ought'.

This in turn influences the moral status of the protagonists. For it would be incorrect to say of the *Iliad*, "The archaic view of *adikia* is just this, that one who is guilty will always pay the penalty."[46] On the contrary, even were 'guilt' the appropriate word, it would be determined only by whether the penalty is paid or not. The man who is forced to pay recompense for an injury is guilty in the sense that he is unable to take an advantage and to keep it, whereas that man who gets away with an injury is automatically justified in so doing. But even this restriction of guilt is not sufficient to preserve it, because again the moral overtones are quite inappropriate to the practical atmosphere that pervades the *Iliad*.[47]

46. C.H. Kahn, "Anaximander's Fragment: The Universe Governed by Law," in A. Mourelatos, ed., *The Pre-Socratics* (New York: Doubleday, 1974), p. 105.

47. In "The Tears of Chryses: Retaliation in the *Iliad*," *Philosophy and Literature* (1978):3–22, I go on to relate this analysis of Homer to some fragments of Anaximander and Heracleitus. Here I shall adopt a different tactic, continuing to the *Odyssey*, archaic poetry, and the varied literature of the classical period.

CHAPTER

7

THE DEVELOPMENT
OF JUSTICE

a. PUNISHMENTS

In the *Iliad* there are no punishments. But in the centuries after Homer, the moral climate alters and there are crimes,[1] there are criminals,[2] and there are punishments.

Among men, the institution of punishments and judicial proceedings in general is commonplace. The poets of the archaic period take legal and penal institutions for granted. Thus, for example, Hesiod (*W.D.* 221 ff.) complains about the crooked judicial decisions (*dikai*) of the princes. His argument is not that the princes have no right to pass judgements, but that they should pass good (straight) judgements. His objection is therefore moral (to the quality of human justice), not procedural (against its illegitimacy).[3] A seventh-century law, Draco's law of homicide,[4] shows that legal authorities could also punish, for it clearly stipu-

1. Cf. below, c.
2. Cf. below, d.
3. Cf. below, c. Havelock's argument, *The Greek Concept of Justice* (Cambridge: Harvard U.P., 1978), Ch. 11, that justice is only procedural in Hesiod tends to conflate the distinction I make here between a legitimate institution (procedural justice) and a legitimate institution administered with propriety (moral). Havelock's use of "procedural" is misleading, cf. my review, *J. Hist. Phil.* (forthcoming). I shall argue below, c, that the use of *dikaios* in *W.D.* 270 ff. cannot be merely procedural, as Havelock might be interpreted as claiming. Nevertheless, Havelock's book has a great deal to offer. Its thoughtful approach to what "just" means, and how it operates logically, legally and morally, stands in sharp contrast to Lloyd-Jones' *Justice of Zeus*, who fails to observe, among other things, that "just" is ambiguous. Cf. Ch. 3.b, Ch. 13. The focal meaning is justice in distribution, the just state of affairs. The virtue and the punishment are both described as "justice" inasmuch as they promote or preserve the just state.
4. The evidence here is derived from a late fifth-century inscription; cf. R.S. Stroud,

lates the crime, the conditions of responsibility under which it must be committed, and the authorities designated to punish for it. The appropriate sentence is supplied.

Hesiod's admonitions to his princes, however, foreshadow the problem of human penal systems. Men are authorised to make judgements, to pass sentence or to commute sentence.[5] They are so authorised by statute, not merely by virtue of superior force,[6] and the statutes themselves are created by those who are authorised to do so.[7] Therefore those who are subject to the laws acknowledge and expect that they will be enforced. This is the recognition of legal and penal authorities. But both legislators and executors are men, and as such they are fallible, as a story from Herodotus shows (V.71–2).

Cylon, having failed in an attempt to seize the Acropolis, found himself as a suppliant at the feet of Athena's statue there. The authorities,[8] however, persuaded him to come out from sanctuary and to submit himself to justice, with the proviso that he would not be put to death. Cylon emerged and was put to death, apparently by the Alcmaeonidae.[9] Thereafter, the murdering Alcmaeonidae were called "the accursed," and banished.

Clearly these Alcmaeonidae were authorised to pass or to commute sentence. But factors other than legal ones also should have affected their behaviour. They should have been governed by restrictions both moral (not to break their word—to have done so made their action murder, *phonos*) and religious (Cylon was a suppliant to the goddess, which should have rendered him secure against them). But, being men and Alcmaeonids, these considerations did not enter, and, as it turned out, the family's political activity was therefore inhibited for long after.[10]

Dracon's Law of Homicide (Berkeley: U.C. Press, 1968), who dates the law at 621/620, after Cylon's attempted coup and before Solon's legislation.

5. The suspect evidence of the *Ath.Pol.* describes the power of the Areopagus to convict and punish before Draco (3.6), under Draco (4.4–5), and under Solon (8.4).

6. Contrast the Athenians' repudiation of Cleomenes, who tried to force constitutional reform on Athens in the late sixth century, with their voluntary election of Solon as a legislator early in the same century (Hdt. 5.71–72, I.29).

7. Such as Solon.

8. The *prutanies tōn naukrarōn*, "fiscal and administrative authorities" (LSJ) instituted by Solon, on the evidence of *Ath.Pol.* 8.3. The rest of the story implies that these men had not only civil but criminal administrative powers; cf. Thucydides 1.127.8. Herodotus says "They managed (*enemon*) Athens at that time." Thucydides says the nine archons (his equivalent of the *prutanies*) "held chief political power in Athens at that time."

9. The story does not make it clear whether the Alcmaeonids *were* the *prutanies* or whether they violated an assurance given, independently, by those entitled to do so. The evidence of Thucydides, 1.127.11, suggests the former.

10. Which is the point of Herodotus' story.

The laws of men are executed by men. Human justice is often seen to be done; the criminal is caught and punished. But, just as often, it fails. Men are fallible, ignorant and corruptible, and the laws and punishments that they administer are as inadequate as they. And this is the problem besetting the early poets:[11] the failure of mortal judges to do their job properly.[12]

In a society where theism is widespread, however, there is an alternative to human punishment: punishment at the hands of the gods. Divine punishment may be imperceptible[13] and even vulnerable to the sceptic,[14] but it has the supreme advantage that it may be said, by the believer, to be inevitable. Consequently, although the literature of the period incorporates the notion of human punishment, the poets concentrate upon the activity of the Olympian hierarchy.

Anthropomorphism, however, causes some difficulties of interpretation here, for the gods may be involved in a transaction in one, or more, of three different ways:

1. They may be conceived as the causes of natural events. To explain what apparently lacked cause, the gods were invoked as the mechanism of natural events[15]—hence, for example, the personification of the sunrise in Homer (*passim*; cf. e.g., *Il.* 1.475 ff.), or the attribution of dreams to Zeus (*Il.* 2.1 ff.). Following from this, an argument that a particular act is imprudent because unpleasant consequences naturally follow might attribute the necessity of the unpleasant effect to the fact that the gods were its cause. For example, the demise of the fifth race (Hesiod, *W.D.* 174 ff.) occurs as a natural consequence of its members' contempt of *dikē*. But it occurs through the mechanism of Zeus, who made them that way (180).

2. The gods may be the protagonists in an injury, either as offenders or as victims. For example, at *W.D.* 42 ff. Prometheus' philanthropic activities are a direct and individual affront to Zeus, and the retaliation upon Prometheus and upon mankind is carried out with the joyous egoism of the Homeric heroes.[16]

11. Cf. Hesiod, *W.D.* 202 ff.; Theognis, 373 ff.; Solon, fr. 4.
12. The wrong man may be punished; or the culprit may get away scot free; or the punishment may fail, either by excess or deficiency, to fit the crime—for whatever purposes the 'fit' is intended.
13. A divine punishment could be slowly mounting unhappiness, rather than a sudden catastrophe.
14. Who would argue that a catastrophe has natural causes and need not be attributed to the supernatural.
15. Anaximander uses the imagery of human life in this way to explain natural causation; DK12B1. Cf. my "The Tears of Chryses," pp. 17 ff.
16. Cf. also Hesiod's *Theogony*, throughout; e.g., 164–166.

3. The gods are seen, in the archaic period, as the authorities to exact punishments.

The distinction between 1 and 2 may only be derived from an argument that the gods are not the causes of all misfortune. And such an argument is possible. For example, Zeus, presented vividly in this context as a person, not a mechanism, complains that men say that all their evils come from the gods; but this is untrue, since all their evils come from their own stupidity (*Od.* 1.32 ff.). Similarly Theognis (833–6) observes that the chaos of human affairs comes about as a consequence of human vice, not at the whim of the gods.[17]

The distinction between 2 and 3, which concerns us most here, may be made upon the basis of three criteria.[18] First, gods who are personally involved will be partial in the affair, whereas penal authorities should be impartial. Second, authorities are appointed on the basis of their superiority or excellence in some respect. Third, those subject to an authority must recognise it to be such and, for this to be a matter of authority rather than merely *force majeure*, this recognition should precede the exercise of the authority. In human affairs, the expectations of the subject are enshrined in statutes and penal institutions; in man's relations with his gods, his expectations will take the form of a prediction that divine punishment will happen, coupled with an acceptance that this is so.

The offence of *hubris* was originally the unwarranted (*de facto*) incursion into someone else's sphere of influence.[19] So *hubris* could be committed against another mortal or against a god. Increasingly, however, *hubris* is conceived as an offence against no one in particular, human or divine.[20] Nonetheless, Zeus watches those who commit it and, as Hesiod attests, makes the *hubristēs* suffer (*W.D.* 238 ff.). Equally, Theognis' prayer to Zeus (377 ff.) demands Zeus' involvement in human affairs irrespective of the consequences (such as increased *timē*) to the god himself, on the simple grounds that he dislikes unfairness. Thus both god and man will be disposed towards the same evaluation of what is fair. Beyond that the god stands outside the action.

Impartiality alone, however, is insufficient to qualify someone as an authority. Mere power is similarly insufficient. For the weaker may be subject to the stronger—as men may be subject to gods—simply as victims, not because the stronger have any authority over and above their

17. Cf. also Pindar, *Ol.* 1.55 ff. where the unfortunate consequences of Tantalus' offence are *compounded by* his punishment at Zeus' hands. Contrast, however, Theognis, 149 ff.

18. Cf. Ch. 1.c.

19. Cf. *Il.* 1.202 ff.; but cf. below, c.

20. Cf., e.g., at *W.D.* 238–239; Solon 4.8; Theognis 379, etc.

strength.[21] But, in the archaic period, the individualistic picture typical of the *Iliad*, in which strength is the only factor in the balance of power, alters, and we move towards a view of the gods as omniscient moral scrutineers. It becomes their specific task to watch over—and to punish—the improprieties of mankind. Zeus' omniscience is a constant theme,[22] which gives strength to the prudential arguments against opportunism.[23] If the gods are omniscient there is no hope of escaping notice in our surreptitious criminality.

Suppose, however, that the gods are omniscient but immoral. Then they would have no interest in punishing crimes. But the poets make it clear that, on the contrary, Zeus concurs with the victims in wanting to punish wickedness and reward virtue. The gods do not subscribe to the heroic standard, at least for others, for inferior mortals. Instead, they advocate justice,[24] and they act, eventually,[25] against profiteering, corruption and victimisation.

Finally, everyone this time expects the gods to punish wrongdoing. This expectation is revealed in simple predictions—hence Hesiod's prudential advice to Perses to avoid violence and injustice (*W.D.* 213 ff.). Or it takes the form of a complaint—hence Theognis reproves Zeus for failing to punish some unjust men (373 ff.; 731 ff.). Or it forms part of the prudential argument—hence Solon's smug moralism: "I would like to be rich, but never unjustly, for always Justice comes down on you in the end" (13.7 ff.). In the classical period, even Lysias subscribes to this idea (VI. 20, 31).

The gods are governed by no statute. They are authorities because they are expected, even required, to act in a particular way and to punish what men think of as wrongdoing. Punishment from the gods may take several forms. It may be immediate, in this life;[26] it may be exacted

21. This, of course, is how the relations of the *Iliad* are determined.

22. E.g., *W.D.* 252, where the mechanics of omniscience are explained; Theognis 267–269; Solon 13.25 ff.

23. There are, for present purposes, three types of opportunist (a man who tries to get away with his crimes). The first is the powerful man, who is strong enough to act with impunity. But the gods are stronger still. The second is weak but sneaky—he tries to escape punishment surreptitiously. But the gods know all about him. The third has Gyges' ring—he is invisible and is unnoticed as he commits his crimes. But the gods see him. Zeus' omniscience, therefore, is the answer to the second and third opportunists. Cf. Ch. 8.b.

24. They advocate both procedural justice—straight judgements (cf. *W.D.* 248 ff.)—and the just state of affairs; hence Theognis' complaint, 373 ff., against apparent injustice. Havelock, *Greek Concept*, Chs. 11–14, argues that *dikē* in this period is purely legal; he misses, I think, the valuable evidence of the complaints against manifest unfairness. Cf. below, c.

25. Here lies the rub; cf. below, c.

26. Cf. *W.D.* 213 ff.; Solon 13.25 ff.; Lysias, VI.20.

upon the soul after death;[27] it may be exacted from the soul during reincarnation;[28] or the punishment may be exacted from the associates or descendants of the wrongdoer.[29]

Each of these methods of divine punishment has its advantages and its drawbacks. That it is a punishment from the gods may be a good and even satisfying[30] explanation of misfortune coming suddenly in this life upon a wrongdoer. And this 'divine punishment' is clearly of that individual for that crime.[31] But often the wicked live out their lives without catastrophe.[32] Then post-mortem punishment comes into play. Punishment after death—whether during separation from the body or during reincarnation—is not an interpretation of misfortune that actually occurs, but it is misfortune that is predicted to occur, after this life is over. It is still the punishment of that individual for that crime. But that the punishment will occur at all is an article of faith, not an empirical fact that merely needs interpretation.

Accordingly, to meet the objections of the sceptic, it may be argued instead that the descendants or the associates of the happy criminal are punished. Here again, what actually happens need simply be interpreted; this is no pious prediction of what will happen. As such, this account of divine punishment has empirical support. However, there is here no direct connection between the individual criminal and his punishment. In the early period, this may be unexceptionable, when family or other dependence groups were so closely knit[33] that the projected punishment of one might have a (deterrent) effect on the behaviour of another. But if the importance of group were to decrease and that of the individual correspondingly to increase, then trouble looms for this type of divine punishment, as we shall see.

The great advantage of divine punishment is that it will—if it is accepted at all—be recognised to be both infallible and inevitable. Its great disadvantage lies in its vulnerability to the sceptic. For human punish-

27. Cf., e.g., Pindar, *Ol.* 2.56 ff.

28. Cf., e.g., Empedocles, DK31B115. The reincarnation itself may be the punishment; see Plato's interpretation of this, *Rep.* X.

29. Cf., e.g., Solon, 13.31; Theognis 735 ff., Hes., *W.D.* 240, Antiphon, II.1.3. This happens in human punishment, too; cf. Lysias, XII.36.

30. Cf. Ch. 3.

31. That is, no complexities of interpretation are required to determine who is the criminal in this case.

32. Cf. Theognis 373 ff. This is the problem confronted by Plato, when he deals with Polus' happy tyrant; *Grg.* 470 ff. The more pessimistic approach to the same problem, of course, is Solon's dictum, "Call no man happy until he is dead," Hdt. 1.29 ff.

33. Cf. Ch. 6.b, the system of *timē* welds together a group by their mutual dependence. Cf. Adkins, "Friendship and Self-sufficiency"; Finley, *The World of Odysseus*, Ch. 4.

ment, the converse is the case. Such punishment is seen to happen—when, and if, it does. So human penal institutions complement the belief in divine punishments: both men and gods are accepted as penal authorities.

b. MORAL DEVELOPMENTS

The institution of punishment is a commonplace of legal or religious history. But the philosophy of punishment is concerned with problems of morality. Thus to discover the tradition in which Plato composed his theory of punishment, we should look not so much to institutional history as to moral development, to the moral imperatives and prohibitions that governed his predecessors. In this way, it may be possible to determine what kind of approach we should expect from any penologist when moral philosophy finally gets off the ground in the fifth and fourth centuries.

Punishment is entangled in a complex of moral values. In particular, it raises two moral questions: "Who should be punished?" (distribution) and "why should we punish?" (justification).[34] But the Homeric background of Greek culture denied these two questions any currency. On the one hand, although responsibility for acts was allowed for, the descriptive value system of the *Iliad* gave no room to culpability. For in Homer explanations do not excuse and do not relieve the responsible agent from liability *to pay*. But the assessment of liability *to punishment* must take into account excuses and defences which, while they may not affect the damage done, do affect the agent's responsibility for the damage, or his culpability as a consequence of it. The fact that excuses and justifications affect culpability distinguishes punishment from commerce. So it remains to be seen how the notion of culpability evolved during the centuries after Homer.

On the other hand, the question of justification has wider moral import. For this invokes the general values of the time; it begs questions of what is right and what is wrong, what is justifiable and what is not, both from the point of view of the offender and from the point of view of his judge.

At this juncture, therefore, we need to know what was the moral climate within which punishment became instituted. To discover this, we should look at reflective comment—the thoughtful, and sometimes critical, remarks on morality made by poets, dramatists, historians, orators, and even philosophers. It is in these thoughtful contexts that there may be found the true antecedents of Plato's justifications of punishment.

34. Cf. Ch. 1.d.

c. JUSTICE

Conspicuous by its absence from the *Iliad* is any suggestion that inferiors could be victimised, that any harsh treatment of inferiors is subject to criticism. Thersites, for example (2.212 ff.), is belaboured by Odysseus but appears to suffer thereafter from no sense of grievance; nor does anyone else feel sympathy for him. The confrontations of the *Iliad* occur between equals or near-equals, and the complaint of the victim, "That is not fair," is never heard.

Justice (the just state of affairs) in the *Iliad* consists in the facts of the matter as they appear after all the striving is done, and once power has found its own *timē*. Thus Agamemnon is accused of *hubris* (going too far) (1.203) and of doing injustice (19.180) simply because he cannot succeed in his attempt upon Achilles. However, under prescriptive conditions, distributive justice will reside in what ought to be the case at any point both before, during and after the event. "This is just" will not be a contention of the strong (as is Achilles' accusation against Agamemnon, 1.203), but an appeal of the weak, in an attempt to ward off victimisation.

The victim is, by definition, powerless to retaliate. If he is deprived of goods, he cannot take them back by force. So he claims that the deprivation was theft, and he hopes, by this persuasive moral imperative, to induce the thief to restore what was lost. Callicles will suggest that it is the weak who evolve the moral imperative, as their only defence against the strong, hoping to arrive at general agreement about what is not to be done (*Gorgias* 483).[35] As the development of Greek moral terminology shows, Callicles was right.

Telemachus and the suitors

In the *Odyssey*, whether because this is a later work than the *Iliad*, or because the context is a peaceful one, or merely owing to the exigencies of the story, the victim occupies a prominent place. Telemachus' insistent claim against the suitors is that they have gone too far (they are *hubristai*, *huperphialoi*),[36] and he is constantly regretful that he is powerless to do anything to retaliate (e.g., 3.205–9). Telemachus is a perfect example of the weak victim, and, on the standards of the *Iliad*, he would have no recourse at all. Here, however, he makes the moral claim against the suitors that they are guilty of *hubris*, independent of the fact that he can do nothing against them.

35. Cf. Ch. 8.b on the immoralists.
36. E.g., 1.368; 2.266; 4.321, etc. The common factor in all these contexts is the idea that the suitors have gone *too far*, hence the prefix *huper*.

In the event, the values of the *Iliad* carry the day: Odysseus recovers the lost *timē* of his house by a violent retaliation, with the help of a goddess. Nevertheless, the *Odyssey* marks the first move in the direction of a deontology wherein it is of independent importance that a state of affairs be just.[37]

Hesiod, *Works and Days*, 174–285

This important but obscure passage of Hesiod is, as Havelock has observed, a poem to justice.[38] It opens with a story about the problems of being a victim. The hawk preys on the nightingale (203–12) and admonishes him, with the confidence of the strong, to endure what is happening to him, for there is no alternative.[39] Then abruptly—and significantly[40]—Hesiod starts to talk about justice, *dikē*. His line of argument is complex, and its interpretation is considerably vexed.[41] He urges his brother, Perses, to avoid *hubris* and to observe *dikē*, and he attempts to put the same advice across to his political masters, the princes who give crooked judgements.

Now there is no doubt that one sense of *dikē* in the passage is legal, that it means "judgement."[42] The princes are apparently corrupt and biased judges, whom Hesiod, by a variety of prudential arguments, is trying to straighten out. But the climax of the argument comes at 270–72, where he comments bitterly:

I would have neither myself nor my son be *just*, since the inferior man gets the *portion appropriate to justice*, the *unjust* man gets the greater *portion*.

The force of these lines is derived from the punning use of *dikē* and

37. Which is not to suggest, of course, that to arrive at such a deontology is the protagonists' intention.

38. *Greek Concept*, p. 194.

39. Compare the interpretations of Rodgers, "Some Thoughts on *Dikē*," and Dickie, "*Dikē*."

40. Cf. below.

41. Cf., e.g., Gernet, *Droit et société*, pp. 61 ff.; Havelock, *Greek Concept*; Gagarin, "*Dikē* in the *Works and Days*," *C. Ph.* (1973): 81–94; Rodgers, "Some Thoughts on *Dikē*"; and Dickie, "*Dikē*." Closest to the truth about the tangled concept of *dikē* is M. Ostwald, in my view: *Dikē* "seems originally to designate claims or rights which define the place a person occupies within a community, often with the connotation that this place is actually or potentially assigned by the verdict of a judge" ("Ancient Greek Ideas of Law," in *Dictionary of the History of Ideas* [New York: Charles Scribner's Sons, 1973], p. 675). For a man to be *dikaios*, therefore, will be, on the one hand, for him to behave in such a way as to merit those claims and, on the other, for his claims to be met. The former meaning is the most common; but the latter should not be ignored (cf., e.g., in the classical period, Antiphon, III.3.7, Lysias, XX, 9–10, not to mention Plato, *Rep.* IV).

42. E.g., at 250. Cf. Havelock, *Greek Concept*.

its cognates.[43] But it does not serve to make the point against the corrupt judges that Hesiod has been urging earlier. This passage, on the contrary, may be understood only in terms of distribution[44]—in terms of the just state of affairs. It is not fair, Hesiod complains, that the just man should have less than the unjust—and this complaint is moral.[45] He offsets two ways in which a man may be just: he may receive the reward appropriate to justice,[46] or he may behave in a just fashion.[47] Being just, therefore, is not merely a matter of what you get, but also a matter of what you do and how you do it. It is the latter, justice as virtue, that Hesiod is trying to recommend in the face of the powerful egoistic appeal (having the reward for justice greater, we may suppose, than that appropriate to injustice) founded in Homeric values.

The story of the hawk and the nightingale gives point to these two aspects of justice. Hesiod, like the nightingale, has no defence against the hawklike princes. Despite all their virtues—a sweet voice, a virtuous character—the victims cannot rely on getting what they deserve. But Hesiod claims they *should* have this security and that there *should* be a just distribution, a state of affairs where what you get matches how you behave—where there is justice. The poem to justice is an attempt, by the victim, to persuade the aggressor to participate in these standards.

Hesiod's poem illustrates the conflict between the values of the aggressor and the values of his victim. Thereafter, into the classical period, the claims of the strong and of the underdog continue to compete.[48] The crimes of the strong are committed very often against the stronger still—hence the tragic crime of *hubris* in the face of the gods committed by Agamemnon or Ajax.[49] At the same time, the other-regarding virtues begin to make their appearance, so that successful actions, where the

43. Underlined here. The close juxtaposition of *dikaios* (twice), *dikē*, and *adikōteros* in three lines must be deliberate, intended, in my view, to call our attention to the ambiguity of these words.

44. For one thing, the idea of a *greater dikē* (272) makes no sense if *dikē* means "a judicial decision," but very good sense if it refers to a general distribution.

45. I would not deny, however, that the basis of the distribution may be legal; cf. Ostwald, quoted in n. 41.

46. That is, the reward appropriate to just behaviour. Hesiod does not mean that the man who is *dikaios* in this sense gets his just deserts, for it is the failure of just apportionment to which he is objecting.

47. The specifics of just behaviour are not filled out, but earlier lines of the passage suggest that justice, as opposed to *hubris*, means not going too far. Cf., e.g., 213.

48. Cf. Lysias XXIV.18.

49. Agamemnon's walking on the purple carpet is *hubris*, and he knows it (Aesch. *Ag.* 921 ff.). Ajax, too, provokes the enmity of the gods and is punished for his arrogance (Soph. *Aj.* 127 ff.; 766 ff.).

agent gets away with it, are nevertheless criminal, because such successes are proscribed by the values of the victim.[50]

By this time, several factors have influenced the development of moral values:

1. Moral evaluations are universal, applying equally to the strong and to the weak. For the victim can only convince the aggressor if everyone, including the aggressor, subscribes to the victim's values.

2. As an alternative to moral persuasions, the underdogs point out that however strong their aggressor, the gods are stronger still. This argument began with Chryses,[51] and it continues in the archaic period with a series of generalisations: we who creep upon the earth are all insecure, weak and unimportant, by comparison with the omnipotence of the immortals.[52] These two arguments become reconciled into the idea that the gods, powerful as they are, scrutinise and punish human immorality.[53] The gods, then, may be strong, but they are not dissociated from human morality.[54]

3. If men are weak, they may become strong by joining together in a group.[55] Hence the pyramidal structure of the group in the *Iliad*[56] becomes replaced by a *polis* wherein mutual dependence is more clearly

---

50. In archaic poetry, cf. Theognis 145 ff., 197 ff., etc., Solon 4, 13; in the classical period examples abound in the confrontations of tragedy—Sophocles' *Philoctetes*, for example. Cf. also Herodotus 7.164 on the unself-interested behaviour of Cadmus, tyrant of Cos, or 6.85 ff. on the evil intentions of Glaucus.

51. *Iliad* 1.35 ff. Cf. also Telemachus, at *Od.* 1.378 ff.

52. Cf., e.g., *Od.* 18.130; Theognis 157–158; and the account of the races of men in Hesiod's *W.D.*, whose genesis and destruction are completely controlled by Zeus.

53. E.g., Solon, 13.25 ff., Hesiod, *W.D.* 248 ff., discussed above.

54. I have tried to avoid, here, the controversy raised by Adkins, *Merit and Responsibility*, pp. 62 ff., and taken up by Lloyd-Jones, *The Justice of Zeus*, Ch. 1., that the gods of Homer are *non-moral*. By this I understand Adkins to mean that the anthropomorphism of Homer extends human behavioural values into the sphere of the divine; thus the gods operate a *de facto timē* system as well. Lloyd-Jones repudiates this (despite the fact that he recognises the *timē* system).

It will already be clear that, in my view, the evidence is in Adkins' favour; cf. Ch. 6.b. But here I do not wish to maintain that later there is a system of morality attributed to the gods which imitates the new, victim's morality of mortals. My point is merely that as far as gods' relations *with mortals* are concerned, the gods support and subscribe to the morality of the victim. This might plausibly be thought to have evolved from the system of divine patronage in Homer. Cf., e.g., *Od.* 3.218, etc.

55. This functional account of the evolution of justice is supported in antiquity by Plato, *Republic* 369b ff.; and in modern philosophical writings by Rawls, *A Theory of Justice*. Cf. also Ch. 8.b on Callicles.

56. Governed by the patron, who may be king or parent. Cf., e.g., *Il.* 12.310 ff., where the Lycians are represented by their kings, Glaucus and Sarpedon, and the kings recognise that to retain their *timē* amongst the Lycians they must excel in battle. Or consider Telemachus' total subordinacy to the suitors, lacking the support of his father.

recognised.[57] This has the effect of allowing the autonomy of a Hesiod, who is not, apparently, restricted in his freedom of speech, as was Thersites.[58] In the *Iliad*, the group was knit together by patronage, by friendship,[59] and by the indirect but equally powerful ties governing the treatment of guests, beggars, and suppliants.[60] In later times, the client develops some power of his own. Thus, for example, Herodotus tells us that it was by public request that Solon was appointed legislator at Athens at the end of the sixth century (I.29), and Solon himself (Fr.5) advocates modified equality between the classes and a modified autonomy of the weak.

4. The necessities of mutual dependence lead to the recognition of individuals having some rights against each other.[61] This might be expressed as modified equality, or as modified inequality, or as justice.[62] In the work of the philosophers, the relation between elements is one of equality, as the alternative to random change. "Cosmic equality was conceived as the guaranty of cosmic justice: the order of nature is maintained because it is an order of equals."[63] In the political sphere, this situation might be represented by the albeit limited franchise of democracies.[64] In poetry, it expresses itself in a complaint against manifest unfairness.

5. The dependencies of community life differ from those of the *Iliad*. In particular, the groups of the *Iliad* prospered or suffered according as their leader succeeded or failed; the lower echelons had neither independence nor identity. The leader represented the group, which rose or fell with him. But in the community life of the democracies, the same situation does not hold. Here, the fortunes of the individual are identi-

57. Cf., e.g., Tyrtaeus 12.13 ff.; or Solon, Frs. 4,36,37.

58. *Il.* 2.211 ff.

59. Cf. Adkins, "Friendship and Self-sufficiency."

60. Cf. Havelock, *Greek Concept*, esp. pp. 155 ff.

61. The notion of Greeks having "rights" is a controversial one. I mean to make no strong claim here, but merely to assert that sometimes victims felt that they had moral grounds for complaint against their aggressor, which had not been so before.

62. Cf. Vlastos, "Solonian Justice," *C. Ph.* (1946):65–83, and "Equality and Justice in Early Greek Cosmologies," in D. Furley and R.E. Allen, eds., *Studies in Presocratic Philosophy* (London: Routledge, Kegan Paul, 1970). The point here is merely that the Greeks did not, apparently, think of all franchised members of the state as absolutely equal. See, for example, the limitations imposed on the various classes in respect of which political offices they might hold; cf. Aristotle's evidence on the constitution of Solon, *Pol.* 1273b27 ff. Nevertheless, justice of some kind may prevail between unequals no less than between equals.

63. Vlastos, "Equality and Justice," p. 57. I am dubious, however, about the notion of *retribution* in early cosmology; in my view, the system is *restitutive*. Cf. "The Tears of Chryses," pp. 17 ff.

64. Cf. Lys. II.17 ff.

fied with those of the community; indeed, when it comes to foreign policy, these extend to protection from invasion and to imperial expansion.[65] But he also has his own individual fortunes within the group. It is the sufferings and joys of the individual that poetry and tragedy illustrate.[66]

As a result, the major principle in moral thinking at this time was the principle of justice. This is not merely a cooperative principle, not merely a matter of what you *do*. It is—perhaps most importantly of all—a distributive principle, a matter of what you *have*. At the centre lies the idea that everyone should have his just deserts; this is the just state of affairs. Derivative from this is the virtue of justice—that behaviour which promotes and observes the just state of affairs. Derivative also is the just punishment, of which more will be said below.

Hence we have the pious hope, expressed constantly in Greek literature, that what happens to you should match what you do, that we should all get our just deserts. And this, since the context is increasingly political rather than familial, and since the emphasis is on behaviour rather than mere allegiance, is now a matter of what the individual does, what he deserves, and what he gets.

Concern for justice is seen most clearly where justice has failed; complaints are the best evidence. We have seen that even in the archaic period Hesiod bitterly abjures right conduct because it fails of its reward. But, he implies, it is unjust that the just man should not be rewarded, the unjust not punished. Theognis, too, complains that just and unjust alike receive a similar portion (*moira*)[67] at the hands of the gods (373 ff.) and suggests that this is intolerable injustice. Indeed, very often what we do and what others do is not rewarded or punished as justice demands that it should be. This is manifestly unfair.

Manifest unfairness then gives rise to resentment and, more generally, to the indignation that is a hallmark of the sense of justice.[68] The dilemmas of classical tragedy exploit this emotion. For the pity and fear that is aroused in the audience at the sight of the hero suffering comes directly from the feeling that here is neither just punishment nor outrage, but rather the more insidious disaster of the moderately virtuous man undergoing immoderate suffering.[69]

Aeschylus' *Prometheus Vinctus*, for example, presents the conflict of

65. Cf. also the archaic picture of the identification of the city with its king presented in the *Oedipus Tyrannus*.

66. Strongest evidence of this is to be found in complaints by the individual at being treated as merely a member of the group. E.g., Theognis 731 ff; *Antigone* 856 ff.

67. Significantly *moira* is a distributive word; cf. L.R. Palmer, "The Indo-European Origins of Greek Justice," *Trans. Philol. Soc.* (1950):162.

68. Cf. Rawls, *A Theory of Justice*, Ch. 8, especially pp. 467–472.

69. Cf. Aristotle, *Poetics*, 1435a7 ff.

philanthropy with violent tyranny.[70] Both parties, Prometheus and Zeus, are inflexible and intolerant, yet both parties have a point of view which may be justified. The tragic outcome of the play is that neither party wins; neither justification is seen to prevail. The irresistible force meeting the immoveable object generates disaster, a disaster which affects us because from no point of view is it fair. Sophocles' *Antigone* culminates in catastrophe in the same way. Antigone's death is seen as a necessity, but its justice is denied (891 ff.). Our emotions are involved in the drama for that very reason: we are swayed because of our sympathy for Antigone, and our sympathy stems from indignation on her behalf.

Herodotus echoes the themes of tragedy, often explaining human misfortune by reference to divine jealousy (e.g., 1.34). It is the gods' concern to get their own just deserts that makes them repress the most fortunate of men. Consequently Herodotus makes a strong case that men should observe and promote the just state of affairs (6.85 ff.; 7.51 ff.). This prevails when each man has and keeps what he deserves (2.151 ff.). Violations, whether in man's relations with man (1.2 ff.) or in his relations with the gods (3.40 ff.), invite retaliation, which is thereby justified (6.137 ff.).[71]

All the literature of the archaic and classical periods betrays a preoccupation with justice. The lesson of tragedy is that not only did the poets subscribe to this standard of morality themselves; they expected their audiences to do so too. For it is by provoking pity and fear at manifest unfairness, and so through appeal to the sense of justice, that tragedy derives its impact. We may conclude that, from the descriptive values presented in the *Iliad*, Hellenic culture came, by the classical period, to be dominated by a morality of justice.

d. EXCUSES AND CULPABILITY

Justice is a matter of getting what you deserve. But if the values of the *Iliad* were to prevail, what you deserve would be determined simply

---

70. It is all too easy to read the play as an illustration of man's unequal struggle against the power of the gods, as do A. Podlecki, *The Political Background of Aeschylean Tragedy* (Ann Arbor: U. of Michigan Press, 1966), p. 103; and Lloyd-Jones, *The Justice of Zeus*, p. 95. Prometheus is unjustly punished for an action which is no crime at all, and we feel pity and fear at the struggle of the weak but virtuous against the vicious but strong.

But this is to miss the central point of the conflict. Each side has both strength and weakness, both morally and practically. Prometheus may claim justification for his crime before a sympathetic human audience, and he may even the balance of power by threatening to withhold the secret of the god's future dangers. Yet Zeus also is justified, since Prometheus has deliberately flouted his authority and disobeyed his decision to destroy the human race utterly—and this is indeed a crime (cf. 259).

71. Cf. Havelock, *Greek Concept*, Ch. 17 on the justice of Herodotus.

by what you do: the act is yours, and your desert is read off from it. The weak man, however, is interested not only in results, but also in intentions, for, after all, he himself has little power over what happens and great power over what he intends. This interest in intentions is revealed in a new currency of excuses: arguments that responsibility for an act should for some reason or other be diminished.

Someone who is accused of an offence may offer an excuse. He may also offer a justification. In this case, he argues not that the act was not his but that the act was not offensive, that he does not deserve to be punished. The two pleas—one of diminished responsibility, the other of diminished culpability—appear to differ in emphasis only, but the difference runs deeper than that. On the one hand, excuses consider the analysis of action and questions of intention and deliberation (and thence of responsibility). On the other hand, justifications consider the moral evaluation of the act—its rightness or wrongness. And a justification drives a wedge between a man's responsibility and his culpability.

Both responsibility and culpability provoke controversy. That is, whether an excuse is acceptable is, particularly when excuses are newly developing, a matter of reflection and moral dispute. Similarly, justifications are not in the first place legal, but moral, issues. They will occur first—and most revealingly—in the context of moral reflections; only after they gain currency will they be enshrined in law. Within a moral system where justice is the prevailing value, both responsibility and culpability are vital factors in assessing desert or in repudiating its assessment.

In the centuries after the *Iliad*, excuses begin to acquire some status. The distinction between a man's acts as his own and his fortunes as coming from the gods is readily available; thus the threat of determinism recedes. At the same time, the protagonists of epics and stories begin to accept excuses of coercion and of the gods' interference in individual acts; thus responsibility may be diminished.

Odyssey Book 22

Odysseus' retaliation against the suitors, as well as his summary execution of the renegade slavegirls, would be typical of the *Iliad*. He behaves exactly as we should expect, since his *timē* has been diminished by others (21.332; 19.428). In keeping with this, he rejects out of hand the attempted excuse of Eurymachus—that he was influenced by Antinous—on the grounds that only by killing the suitors will Odysseus recover a satisfactory amount of *timē*. The excuse, in fact, is ignored altogether.

By contrast, his treatment of Leodes, Phemius and Medon takes their excuses into account. Leodes argues that he was only the priest of the suitors and was not involved with their crimes. Phemius makes the excuse that serves both for himself and for Medon, that he was coerced into helping the suitors. Leodes' excuse is rejected, Phemius' and Medon's accepted. For Leodes denies responsibility altogether, which is manifestly untrue, whereas Phemius admits that he helped the suitors but claims *force majeure*. Phemius' argument was apparently not available to Agamemnon; Phemius can argue what Agamemnon could not: that coercion diminishes his responsibility.

Herodotus 9.93

Evenius fell asleep taking his turn at shepherding for the Apollonians, with the result that the sheep were slaughtered by wolves. Evenius was therefore punished by having his eyes put out. It transpired that the gods disapproved of Evenius' punishment on the grounds that he was punished for an act which they themselves caused, for they set the wolves to devour the sheep. So the Apollonians were punished in turn for their injustice until they made such amends as Evenius thought fit.

This passage contrasts sharply with Homer's account of the case of Agamemnon in the *Iliad*. In this story from Herodotus the responsibility for the act is lifted on the grounds that, in this particular instance, the gods interfered. The claim is not that determinism is true, but that sometimes divine causation restricts responsibility. Responsibility should be ascribed, it is suggested, only when the agent exercised some control over what happened.

Herodotus' story illustrates one effect of subtler notions of responsibility. In the *Iliad*, a man was completely responsible for what he did. But what happened to him as a result was a matter of the power of his victim or the strength of a group to prevent him from getting away with it. In the fifth century, however, it appears that limited responsibility engendered limited culpability, for the consequence of the excuse urged on Evenius' behalf was that his punishment was considered to have been unjust.

The society of the *Iliad* is one wherein neither moral nor legal conditions of culpability hold, although acts still belong to agents. With neither legal nor moral prescription, what happens to an agent as a result of his act is not a punishment, but rather the unsystematised reaction of others to what he did. After the *Iliad*, however, the picture begins to change, and a relation of culpability begins to develop. The injury that one hero could do to another becomes a crime done by one man to another; thus the victim, lacking the strength to retaliate, imposes a moral prescription against his victimisation and hopes to prevent it that way. Acts, therefore, may be right or wrong, and their agents may be praised or blamed, rewarded or punished. Thus it is Telemachus' contention that the suitors are acting wrongly; he blames them and wishes that their punishment may come in the end.[72]

The hope is that only those who are responsible are liable to punishment; indeed, Theognis complains against occasions where the child is punished for the crimes for which the parent is responsible (731 ff.). But the relation between responsibility and culpability causes difficulties.

Aeschylus: *Oresteia*

The thoughtful approach of this trilogy to the problems of crime and punishment is to be seen particularly in Aeschylus' account of responsibility. The final play exploits the question of whether culpability should be increased or diminished in a strict correlation with the level of responsibility or whether culpability may also be affected by moral considerations.

Three main variations of responsibility may be discerned: the agent may be seen wholly as the instrument of a higher force; he may be thought to act solely on his own initiative; or he may be seen both as an instrument and as sole responsible agent. The problem is that these ascriptions may be severally attributed to the same act; and the culpability of the agent should thereby be affected.[73]

Agamemnon, for example, is given full credit for the fall of Troy by the Herald. But in the same speech, he is said to have achieved his victory by the spade of Zeus, and the first Chorus of the *Agamemnon* confirms that the Atreidae were sent against Troy as Zeus' agents, *husteropoinos Erinus* (58–9). Similarly, Clytemnestra believes herself to be independent—at first. Later she comes to realise that she is but a pawn in the hands of higher powers and that her action was therefore caused by the ancient avenger of the house (*palaios alastōr*). Upon recognising this, she tries to argue that she did not murder Agamemnon. But the Chorus turn upon her and demand to know how she could be thought not to have done it[74] (*anaitios*, *Ag.* 1505). Clytemnestra did it, so she is

---

72. *Od.* 3.205. Cf. also Hesiod's attack on the princes, *W.D.* 248 ff., and Solon's criticisms of injustice, Frs. 4, 13. Three separate strands of argument should be recognised in these passages: (a) the claim that the agent did the act (responsibility); (b) the assertion that the act was wrong (culpability at the moral level—praising and blaming); (c) the hope that punishment, usually divine, will catch up with him in the end (culpability at the legal level).

73. We should bear in mind that culpability is a matter of what happens to the agent as a result of his action; the severity of his punishment may be debatable before the event, but the punishment is determinate once it takes place. So the level of culpability cannot be left vague.

74. *Anaitios* may be understood, on the interpretation I offer, in terms of *causation*. Cf. Ch. 9. n. 30. For someone to be *aitios* means that they caused the action in question, they did it, they are responsible for it. Clytemnestra is arguing that she (alone) did not do it and

responsible. Whatever the power of her co-agent, she does not escape liability for punishment or blame as a consequence of her act.

This situation, wherein any action may be ascribed to several agents at once without contradiction, seems to us to resemble determinism. However, Greek theism is apparently able to accommodate a situation in which an agent is caused to do something by the gods, yet his action is still significantly his own—his own to the extent that he may be held liable to the consequences. We tend to view responsibility as something to be divided among co-agents, and we regard culpability as a constant companion of responsibility.[75]

If my account of the *Iliad* is correct, however, the Greeks did not see responsibility and culpability as mutually entailed. Consequently, in later literature, even partial responsibility for an act could render the agent totally culpable. It is only on some such account as this that the apparent contradictions of the *Oresteia* may be resolved. Orestes is culpable, even though Apollo made him kill his mother, and indeed Orestes could be said to have been coerced. Orestes, therefore, simply from his share in the responsibility for matricide, derives complete culpability for the act and is liable to punishment for it, unless he can convince the jury that his action was not a crime at all. In the end, his attempt at justification results in acquittal: he is not culpable at all.

The attempts of the protagonists in tragedy to argue justification[76] indicate that they feel their fate to be undeserved. To this complaint the general response is that suffering is natural to mankind. Moreover, many of the plays suggest that the suffering is deserved inasmuch as the agents were responsible for the acts which initiated the disasters. This is true irrespective of the force that appeared to operate upon the agents at the time: the dilemma of Agamemnon at Aulis, for example, is not considered to relieve him of responsibility simply because it was unavoidable. It is also true despite the justification or mitigation urged by the protagonists: Antigone, for example, claims that she is obeying the powerful demands of the gods of the dead, but this does not absolve her. Oedipus, more strongly still, could advance his ignorance as mitigation, but he does not escape the consequences of his crime. For although necessity is harsh, it is not random, since it obeys the sequence of responsibility and consequence.

However justified the agent, as long as he was responsible (this, pre-

---

thus that she should not be liable to punishment. The Chorus argue that she is liable to punishment at 1426 ff. and 1560 ff.; and liable to blame also, at 1625 ff., 1645, 1669.

75. Hence our notion of 'moral responsibility', which conflates responsibility with culpability. Cf. Ch. 6, n. 34.

76. The most striking examples of this occur in the *Oresteia*: Clytemnestra, *Ag.* 1397, 1406, 1525; Orestes, *Choe.* 144; 1028 ff.; the Erinyes, *Eum.* 490 ff.

sumably, would exclude mere accident), he suffers.[77] The unfairness resides in the assumption that responsibility is the only factor in assessing desert. For the protests of those who suffer indicate that in their view desert should be assessed according to intention and should take account of both responsibility and motivation. Realism dictates, however, that consequences follow irrespective of the rightness of the motive behind the act. In just the same way, it dictates that no man is happy until he is dead.[78]

The confused relation between responsibility and the evolving notion of culpability serves to make two points. First, it establishes a formal distinction, frequently blurred, between the two concepts. A man may be responsible without being culpable—and not only in the manner of insurance companies and underwriters, for a more striking possibility is now open. A man may under some or even all circumstances be thought of as criminal inasmuch as he is responsible for crimes. But yet he may be exculpated. Second, the very confusion that exists, by the fifth century, between responsibility and culpability, will itself prohibit justice.

There are now, at the very least, two different criteria for assessing culpability. One, derivative from the system of the *Iliad*, correlates total culpability directly with any level of responsibility. But the other denies so strict a relation and takes into consideration questions of excuse, of justification, and of mitigation. Whichever criterion is adopted—and one must be, to arrive at a sentence—it will outrage the other. So punishments will, ironically, promote that which they are instituted to destroy: injustice.

e. RESTITUTION AND RETRIBUTION

In such a moral climate, what justifications do men offer for the institution of punishment?

If there were punishments in the *Iliad*, they would be restitutive in purpose. For, as we have seen,[79] the objective of the Homeric heroes was always to ensure that they recovered from an aggressor the loss they had suffered. Hence, when punishments were later instituted, we might expect a similar account of their purpose to be given. And so it is.

Telemachus is too weak to recover from the suitors what they, in their

---

77. This view is actively criticised in the *Oresteia*, as I shall suggest in Ch. 8.a.

78. Recall Herodotus' celebrated story of the confrontation between the blissful tyrant, Croesus, and the sage, Solon. Croesus' subsequent misfortune is attributed to the gods, a punishment for his failure to acknowledge Solon's dictum, "Call no one happy until he is dead" (Hdt. I.34.1).

79. Ch. 6.b.

hubris, have taken from him. However, like Chryses before him, he can appeal to more than his own resources: he prays to the gods to get repayment for him.[80] Theognis, another underdog, adopts the same tactic. "May Zeus," he prays,

grant me repayment (*tisis*) to the friends who befriend me,[81] and to the enemies who have got the better of me. Thus should I seem to be a god amongst men, if the fate of death were to come upon me once I have achieved restoration (*apoteisamenon*).[82] (337–40)

The physical philosophers use the balance of restorative transactions to explain the rhythmical exchanges of natural events.[83] Anaximander: The elements interact "according to necessity; for they [the things that are, *ta onta*] give *dikē* and payment (*tisis*) to each other for their injury (*adikia*) according to the ordinance of time" (DK 12B1).[84] In a grimmer and later context, Medea murders her children in an attempt to recover from her enemies what she has lost at Jason's betrayal. For he has deprived her of support and made her laughable (Eur. *Med.*, 712, 797), and thus he has made her *atimos* (696). Medea's retaliation[85] aims to recover what she has lost, and to that end she invokes Zeus and the goddess Justice to support her in what she does (764 ff.).

Restitution, therefore, retains its force in the centuries after Homer. However, at the same time the focus of attention widens, and the purpose of punishment alters accordingly. In the *Iliad*, the injured hero was concerned at the facts of what he had suffered; thus the damage done was all important. So in general, restitution concentrates upon rectifying the offence at the expense of considering the agent, his motives, his intentions, and the evaluation of his act.

Restitution is commercial.[86] As such, it requires not only that the damage can be assessed but also that the victim is able to receive the recompense. In Homer, the continuity of the family[87] or the group[88] ensures that there is always a recipient for the recompense. But later,

80. E.g., at *Od.* 1.378 ff.

81. Adkins, "Friendship and Self-sufficiency," argues that the friendship relation is one of the mutual conferral of benefits, rather than primarily of mutual affection. This fits well with the commercial view of friendship expressed here.

82. The participle here echoes the *timē* vocabulary of the *Iliad*. The idea of "achieving restoration" embraces both giving (*timē*) to friends and getting (*timē*) from enemies.

83. Cf. my "Tears of Chryses," pp. 17 ff.

84. Cf. also, e.g., Heracleitus, DK22B80; Empedocles, DK31B17.27 ff.

85. Apparently designed not for revenge but for the restoration of her lost *timē*—hence it is still, grotesquely, the commerce of restitution; cf., e.g., 807 ff.

86. Cf. Ch. 2.

87. Cf., e.g., *Il.* 9.632 ff.; or the story of Chryses.

88. Cf., e.g., the interdependence of Achilles and his Myrmidons, *Il.* 18.79 ff.

the victim may be defunct and leave no substitute.[89] Or the victim may be abstract[90]—'the state' rather than 'this family'. In either case, talk of payment to the victim becomes awkward. Increasingly, as the individual, whether victim or offender, gains in autonomy[91] and importance,[92] cases of homicide or treason will be inappropriate as targets for restoration. Consequently payments will begin to be replaced by penalties.

The problems of the victim seem therefore to recede. But I have argued that the very prominence of the victim in the centuries following the heroic age engendered thoughtfulness about moral values, and about intentions, responsibility and culpability.[93] The weak had no recourse to individual retaliation, so they moved towards persuasive definitions of what ought not to be done, in an attempt to preserve themselves from victimisation. Thus certain actions were characterised as offensive in general, certain attitudes as malevolent in general, or certain types of man as wicked.[94] So a universal moral structure will, it is hoped, govern the victim, his aggressor, and everyone else. Condemnation will attach not only to my particular bully but also to anyone else's. Ironically, this has the effect of highlighting the character of the offender and dimming my personal grievance. Restitution will be devalued.

The individual victim nonetheless resents the wrong that is done to him, and he looks for retaliation to relieve that resentment. But he cannot retaliate, because he is too weak. Accordingly, by his eloquence and his persistence he forces a move away from the standard of what happens and towards a standard of what ought to happen. In doing so, he

89. At least as the recipient of compensation. Cf., e.g., Antiphon, I.3, 22, 25, etc., where the murdered man may be avenged by his kin, but he is not thought to recover the damage he has suffered thereby. The vengeance is not given by the original aggressor *to his victim*, as restitution would require. Cf. also Lysias, X.28; XII.100. But n.b. the possibility, expressed in Aeschylus' *Eumenides*, that the individual, although dead, might continue as a ghost.

90. Cf., e.g., Antiphon, I.3; VI.9.

91. Hesiod, for example, able to criticise the princes with apparent impunity, by contrast with Thersites, *Il.* 2.211 ff. The autonomy of the individual will increase as his intentions become recognised as important. Cf. above, d.

92. The importance of the individual, albeit entangled in his membership of various groups, familial or political, is acknowledged by the tragedies, where it is the personality of the protagonists that occupies the attention. Prominence is necessarily given to the intellectual performance of the individual by the philosophers, notably Heracleitus and Parmenides, forerunners of the elenctic method of Socrates. DK22B1,2,50, etc., DK28B2 etc. For these philosophers rely on their audiences being able to think—and only individuals do that.

93. Above, c, d.

94. Cf., e.g., Theognis 145 ff.; Solon, 13.7 ff.

initiates a sweeping change, as his individual resentment becomes generalised into indignation.[95]

Resentment on your own behalf is parallel to indignation on the behalf of others. The emotion that is triggered by your own individual suffering is transmuted as you witness, detached, the suffering of those who are unconnected to you, and your sympathy for them manifests itself in indignation. Even when I no longer have sand kicked in my face, I still pity others who suffer the bully. And I am indignant at the outrage of my now universal moral principles—at the football foul, at the plagiarism, no less than at the robbery or the iniquitous law. My cry is "That's not fair." And I find myself with a notion of justice.

If manifest unfairness is a problem, then its answer is retributive punishment. If distributive justice has become upset, it may be restored by retribution.[96] From early in the archaic period, the poets warn that justice comes in the end, that the outrage of the just state of affairs is always restored by the just punishment.[97] And in the *Oresteia*, where a formal debate is staged between different justificatory claims,[98] the argument is all about justice and retribution. Each party to the debate wants to claim that his own position is just and the position of his opponent an outrage to justice. However, the central principle, the philosophical core of the last play of the trilogy, is the *lex talionis*. "Let the doer suffer"—each character in the *Eumenides* asserts that his justice fulfills that principle.[99] Two things go unquestioned: first, that justice is desirable; second, that the retributive principle is an expression of that justice.

The sophist Critias, writing late in the fifth century, describes the founding of human and divine punishment, making clear its retributive function (DK 88B25). He contrasts civilisation with the wild state of primitive man, who had neither rewards for virtue nor punishments for vice. Men instituted a penal code in order that justice (distribution) might be sovereign, and *hubris* enslaved. To that end they punished

---

95. The distinction I use here between resentment—a personal, even egoistic, emotion—and indignation—an impersonal emotion, moral distress at the sufferings or the ill-gotten gains of others—was suggested to me by Strawson, "Freedom and Resentment," pp. 84 ff. The dichotomy may seem an artificial one, inasmuch as we may feel indignation on our own behalf (although never, I think, resentment on another's). I shall use the terms hereafter according to this crude dichotomy, for ease of argument.

96. Cf. Ch. 3.b.

97. Hesiod, *W.D.* 238; Theognis, 200 ff.; Solon, 13.7 ff.

98. Cf. above, d; and Ch. 8.a.

99. The Erinyes invoke the principle on Orestes on the grounds that there is no justification of matricide, *Eum.* 415 ff. Orestes concedes the principle but argues that in his case it does not apply because he was justified, *Eum.* 609 ff. cf. also *Ag.* 1564; *Choe.* 144 etc.

whoever transgressed, and punishment was now no longer a payment, but a penalty.

Retribution, therefore, is the instrument of distribution, and it expresses the allegiance of the society to the principles of justice. The expressive function of punishment is conceived by the fourth-century orator Lysias as the manifestation of society's anger against the transgressor. In a speech against Eratosthenes, who was one of the Thirty, Lysias records the importance of manifesting indignation. To condemn Eratosthenes is to show anger at what he and the rest of the Thirty did, and to acquit him is to acquiesce in, even to approve, such activity (XII.90 ff.).[100] On the other hand, from the point of view of him who is punished, retributive punishment shows him that his actions were wrong,[101] as the Chorus fondly hopes that Prometheus will have recognised ("Do you not see that you did wrong?"[*P.V.* 259]).

Punishment and reward, therefore, were expected to be retributive, coming to each man as he deserved and directed at the perpetuation and assertion of justice. Thus one punishment is justified because it is just, and the other resisted because it is unjust. But sometimes human penal expedients break down. On the one hand, mistakes—punishments of the innocent—often cannot be rectified, particularly if the punishment is capital. This argument is offered frequently on behalf of a defendant,[102] and exploited by Diodotus in the Mytilenean debate.[103] On the other hand, despite human laws, the wicked often get away with evil. "The Greeks were not so unrealistic as to hide from themselves the fact that the wicked flourished like a green bay tree."[104] Confronted by the prospect of punishment for overt wrongdoing, the criminal went underground and became a covert opportunist.[105] Then, comments Critias cynically,[106] someone invented the gods. For whereas men are fallible, gods are not, and they make sure that the just punishment comes along in the end.[107]

100. Cf. also XXVIII.3; but XXVII.16 suggests that mere condemnation is not enough; the punishment must actually be carried out. Contrast Feinberg's optimism for expressive punishment, discussed in Ch. 3.e.

101. Cf. Ch. 3.b. No deterrent function is necessarily involved in the recognition of wrongdoing, although this might be the first step towards deterrence. Cf. below, f.

102. E.g., Antiphon III.4.9; V.88; *Gorgias*, DK82B11a.36.

103. Thuc. III.45.1. Cf. below, g.

104. Dodds, *The Greeks and the Irrational*, p. 33.

105. Cf. above, n. 23; Ch. 8.b: the opportunist, covert or overt, is he who does wrong when and only when he can get away with it.

106. In the conclusion of the passage discussed above, DK88B25.

107. But n.b. Theognis' complaint that the gods are omniscient and omnipotent, and still the wicked flourish (373 ff.).

Thus human punishment, although effective against the overt criminal, is helpless against the covert opportunist, and this itself creates rather than solves manifest unfairness, for someone is able to get away with crime. But divine punishment, as a solution to the fallibility of human punishment, has its own problems.

I have argued that there were three major types of divine punishment: during this life, after death or during reincarnation, and collective punishment, whether of the family or of some other group such as the city.[108] The early poets complained that punishment from the gods in this life simply does not take place, and that this is unfair. "I am amazed at you, Zeus," whines Theognis, "that you, with all your power, treat both just and unjust alike, and fail to punish those who commit *hubris*" (373 ff.). Later, in his *Antigone*, Sophocles exploits the converse idea, that someone, albeit a respecter of the gods, even a martyr, should suffer for that respect as Antigone does.[109] In short, the problem is that opportunists get away with it, not only by evading mortal litigation, but also by continuing to thrive in apparent defiance of the authority of the gods; meanwhile the innocent suffer.

The most effective, if least demonstrable, argument against manifest unfairness, that retribution—whether reward or punishment—is carried out after death, is rare. The most common rebuttal of Theognis' complaint that Zeus is simply inefficient as a penal agent lies in the suggestion that punishment is not of the individual but of the group. This conveniently explains the apparently unfair suffering of one individual: he is the victim of inherited guilt.[110] Aeschylus, however, is clear that the idea that the individual's deserts are determined by his membership of the group is itself a violation of justice.[111] Accordingly, in the *Eumenides* he returns to the expedients of human justice, fortified by the support of the gods, to rectify manifest unfairness.[112]

Both human retribution, therefore, and its divine counterpart, may fail, either through mere inadequacy or through the violation of justice—violation of the idea that we should each create our own deserts and not have them foisted upon us by our grandparents. And when

108. Above, a.
109. Here the fact that her family is being punished by the gods is adduced as an explanation, but not a justification, of what happens to Antigone, 856 ff.
110. Cf. Aeschylus, *Oresteia*, Sophocles, *Antigone*. Equally, that a man is being punished for some crime committed earlier in his life may be an explanation of present misfortune; e.g., Antiphon, III.3.8.
111. Hence his sympathetic presentation of Orestes, who argues that he should be released from liability although he is a member of the house of Atreus, on the grounds that he was justified in killing his mother. Cf. Theognis, 731 ff.
112. Cf. Ch. 8.a.

retribution fails to do its job, it actively creates unfairness:[113] the remedy may be worse than the disease.

A different tactic is suggested by the tragedians, particularly by Sophocles. This is the principle of 'endure.' The plots of the tragedies make it clear that life is neither fair, kind, nor ordered. They suggest, further, that the only suitable response to this is to put up with it. The protagonists of the *Antigone* inveigh against the suffering they must undergo. Creon, confronted at last with utter disaster, is reduced to despair. The Chorus, however, reprove him (1337–8), as they reproach Antigone for railing against her punishment (853). Antigone, they argue, is responsible for her fate, for she was bold in her affront to *dikē*. Creon recognises the responsibility to lie with him but despairs in the face of his own suffering. The Chorus remind him, however, that no man escapes his allotted suffering. This must be accepted, rather than repudiated. Despair, therefore, is not the solution. On the contrary, we must come to terms with the harshness of reality and the helplessness of man. One aspect of this harsh reality is the inevitability of suffering.

Acceptance is the only attitude that we can, with rationality, take up in the face of the problems of manifest unfairness. Human retribution is weak, divine retribution inscrutable; and between the twain we must simply learn to endure. Unfortunately, this stoical line affects an important subsidiary of the retributive principle—the prudential argument that wrongdoing is against the interests of him who does it.

f. THE IMPRUDENCE OF WRONGDOING

The moral values of the classical period were instituted, I have argued, as a defence against victimisation, and they issue in a retributive account of punishment. But to reinforce right action, beyond the moral imperative, they exploit the deterrent effect of punishment that is parasitic upon retribution. This type of deterrence is not utilitarian; it is merely an exploitation of the unpleasant effects of becoming subject to a retributive punishment.[114] If justice governs the rewards and punishments for behaviour, then it may also be invoked to influence that behaviour.

Thus a teleological argument, constructed upon an appeal to consequences, may rely ultimately upon a deontological principle, the principle of justice. The argument runs as follows: "You should not do this because it is wrong; if you do it you will be punished as you deserve;

113. Cf. Ch. 3.a.
114. Cf. Ch. 3.c. This type of deterrence, for example, does not appeal to the benefit for many.

and so you should not do it for the additional reason that it is against your interests."

This prudential argument may be purely consequential. Hesiod, for example, warns Perses against injustice solely on the grounds that he will inevitably encounter retribution. But it may rely further on the expressive function of punishment. Tragedy teaches that the act was wrong—or at least mistaken—and only afterwards urges against its repetition.[115] The principle of 'learning by suffering',[116] so dangerously liable to an inflated interpretation as some kind of moral education, is surely nothing more than the awareness in the offender that retribution hopes to induce: that what he did was wrong. At the same time, he who suffers learns that suffering is endemic to being human.

If retribution fails, therefore, so will this prudential argument. Not only the observations of poets and historians but particularly the events of tragedy erode this protection of the moral structure. If a human sanction over moral behaviour is seen not to work, opportunism will flourish, accompanied by scepticism directed towards divine retribution.[117] Thucydides, describing the anarchy that followed the plague at Athens, suggests how men, unrestrained from human laws and made cynical by disaster about divine ones, lapse into lawlessness (II.53). Retribution needs to be secure to be effective as a prudential argument; very often it is not. Indeed, unfairness grips the virtuous and the vicious alike, and not only is the vicious man likely to avoid punishment, but also the virtuous—Antigone or Io—will miss their reward.

Initially, the response of the tragedians to this proposition seems to be that the moral imperative survives despite manifest unfairness. Just behaviour is still right even if the just state of affairs breaks down, and the vicious opportunist is still in the wrong. Neither Aeschylus nor Sophocles suggests that our moral principles should or even could be eroded along with the erosion of the just state of affairs.[118] On the contrary, they imply that there is an overriding rationality, albeit inaccessible to the feeble human mind, which protects the moral imperative.

The conclusions of Sophocles' plays[119] suggest that through the tragic

115. Cf. Aesch. *P.V.* 259.
116. Aesch. *Ag.* 176 ff. Cf. Dodds, "Morals and Politics in the *Oresteia*," *C. Ph.* (1973):81–94; Gagarin, *Aeschylean Drama* (Berkeley: U.C. Press, 1976), pp. 139 ff.
117. Exemplified by Critias, discussed above.
118. To recall the ambiguity of 'just,' it is quite possible for there to exist just men (men interested in promoting the just state of affairs) without there actually being a just state of affairs (without the just men being successful). From a logical point of view, however, justice the virtue cannot be understood before understanding its focus, the just state of affairs. Cf. Owen, "Logic and Metaphysics in Some Earlier Works of Aristotle."
119. E.g., *Ajax* 1332 ff.; *Antigone* 1347 ff.

experience the protagonists come a little closer to reaching this supreme rationality. The purposes of the gods are harsh and terrifying, but they can be understood, and what happens must be understood as coming from the gods (*Trach.*1264 ff.).

Euripides, however, tells a different story. His *Hippolytus* similarly presents irreconcilable conflict and its tragic consequences to guilty and innocent alike. Hippolytus, true to the tradition of inflexible heroes, obstinately denies the power of Aphrodite, goddess of love, maintaining instead his allegiance to the huntress goddess of chastity, Artemis. The play describes the action taken by Aphrodite in her anger at this disrespect: she causes Phaedra, Hippolytus' stepmother, to fall in love with him, and, from this beginning, disaster implicates Phaedra herself, Hippolytus, and his father Theseus.

The tragic impact of the play is heightened by the fact that both Phaedra and Theseus are innocents, involved in catastrophe despite themselves. But Euripides, unlike Sophocles, offers no relief, no idea that the gods, albeit terrible, are yet godlike and free from irrationality. In the *Hippolytus*, as in other plays of Euripides,[120] any higher rationality is positively denied. The effect of the appearance of the *deae ex machinae* at the beginning and end of the play is to reveal the wholesale caprice of divine intention, compounded by a malice which is all too human.

Aphrodite's anxiety for revenge does indeed square with the older approach to an affront to divine honour, but her careless implication of Phaedra and Theseus in the tragedy argues not for a higher rationality but for unreason. Similarly, the distant sympathy manifested by Artemis at the downfall of her adherent, compared with her fierce desire for revenge upon her rival, removes any confidence we might once have had in the government of morality by divine sanction. Thus the play suggests, as a whole, a moral cynicism which is alien to the older playwrights, as Euripides presents natural forces in our own image and contrives to convince us of their inscrutability to human understanding.

The effect of this is to weaken still further the weapons available to the moralist attempting to convince others of the necessity of right behaviour. Not only is there no guarantee of the expediency of virtue; there is apparently no room for anything but random sequence of cause and effect, of desert and receipt. We are at the mercy of irrational and, we may suppose, immoral gods.

g. TELEOLOGICAL ARGUMENTS

In the classical period, retributive arguments prevail. For the sense that we are equal in our helplessness, individuals whose sole hope of

---

120. The *Bacchae*, for example, or the *Medea*.

survival lies in acting as a group, leads to a sense of general sympathy, which, in turn, advocates distributive justice. Hence sprang the demand for retribution, the corrective of distributive injustices.

However, retribution fails. Be it human or divine, far from correcting manifest unfairness, it often creates it; and of this fact, the writers of this period were perfectly aware. It is all the more striking, therefore, that teleological accounts of punishment are rare at this time.[121] Individualism might give rise to either a humanitarian or even an egoistic[122] justification of punishment, although the sense of community might tend more towards utilitarianism. The two combined readily give rise to the utilitarian dictum, "each to count for one, none for more than one."[123]

The great advantage of all of these principles is that they will countenance deficiency. The egoist and the utilitarian will be content to maximise benefit,[124] and they will not feel that any falling short of the perfect benefit is in fact an active disutility, unlike their deontological counterpart, who must argue that any punishment that is not just is unjust and thence forbidden.[125]

Teleological arguments are rare but they do occur. Sophocles' *Antigone*, if thought of as the confrontation of principles rather than personalities, contains a comparison of the two imperatives to action. Antigone believes that she should act as the articles of her religion command.[126] She puts the commands of the gods above the laws of man (450 ff.), believing that it is right to do so (72) and despite the fact that she courts disaster by her action (as Ismene warns her from the outset, 98–9). Tragedy overtakes her despite her allegiance to the laws of the gods, a fact which even she finds hard to accept (921 ff.). Nevertheless, she maintains her stand in the face of Creon's quite different arguments. Antigone is the tragic heroine of this play: she is represented as unfortunate both in her ancestry and in her present dilemma, as tragic in her fate, and as obstinate in her allegiance to her principles. But she is never

121. I except the teleological argument of the previous section, which relies on a deontological penology.

122. I have suggested in Ch. 4, n. 3 that a completely egoistic account of punishment is inconceivable. It would, for example, require a very odd notion of the generalised, universally applicable, statute. In some contexts, however, a principle of punishment is advocated by those who are self-regarding rather than benevolent. But the contexts themselves are eccentric. Cf. below on the Mytilenean debate—a matter of foreign policy.

123. Cf. Sidgwick, *Methods of Ethics*, pp. 411 ff.

124. Although there are, of course, problems of calculation and choice here; cf. Ch. 4.b.

125. Ch. 3.a.

126. This might be thought of as the equivalent of intuitionism.

characterised as wrong; there is no suggestion that the moral imperative that she obeys is mistaken.

Creon, however, is a different case. His principle is utilitarian. He approves and disapproves (182 ff.); he makes laws and protects them by punishment (659 ff.) according to the single criterion of the general benefit—the interests of the city as a whole. This is the reason he punishes Antigone. But, like Antigone, he suffers as a consequence of his rigid adherence to one principle. He too is—or would be, if presented with greater sympathy—a tragic figure, whose world collapses as a result of the action of the play. But in his case, it is made clear that his very obstinacy in defence of his principle is the cause of what happens. Flexibility is advised by Haemon (707 ff.) and its lack bewailed by Creon as ignorance (1261 ff.); Creon fails to recognise the old retributive imperatives, as Teiresias points out, and he tries to operate on utilitarian lines. For this reason he himself will pay the just penalty, the death of his son for a death (1064 ff.).

This play, therefore, broaches the possibility of a utilitarian account of action in general, and of punishment in particular. But its outcome firmly suggests that utilitarianism is thoughtless (1262) because it ignores the more powerful moral imperatives of justice.[127] The same argument, of course, is levelled at modern utilitarians.[128] But in *Antigone*, the utilitarian is represented as having no counter. For here the intuitionist has power against the sceptic,[129] the power of the generally accepted religious belief that these imperatives are handed down from the gods.

Despite this early body blow, utilitarianism does survive in the fifth century and early in the fourth. The evidence of the orators is largely for retribution,[130] but some utilitarian arguments can be constructed from Lysias' speeches.[131]

When urging that a particular defendant be punished, Lysias sometimes suggests that retributive procedures will have the additional effect of deterring others[132] or protecting the state.[133] I have argued that a

---

127. The point about obeying the gods is that they are more powerful than mortals. The influence of Homeric values is still being felt, and indeed, it should not be supposed that a general abandonment of old values for new ever took place.

128. Cf. Ch. 4.d.

129. Contrast the problems of the modern intuitionist, Ch. 3.d.

130. E.g., Antiphon, I.3., etc.; IV.1.4; Lysias, I.49; XII. 99 ff.; etc.

131. Cf. also Andocides, I.68, 79–81.

132. N.b. this differs from the prudential argument parasitic on retribution, for it is the example of *one* that is to deter, and thus benefit, *many*.

133. XV.9; XXVII.7 ff.; XXX.23, etc. Cf. also, e.g., Antiphon II.10.

theory of punishment cannot, with consistency, be equally retributive and utilitarian[134] on the grounds that these principles are liable to give conflicting instructions for the particular case.[135] However, when Lysias urges considerations of both justice and expediency in a particular case, he is not committed to inconsistency or, worse, to the exact sentence being impossible to determine. All he is claiming is that this particular case will have the complex effect of both retribution and deterrence of others. This claim makes no promises for the joint effects of other punishments in other cases, and it makes no statement that justice and utility are principles in the justification of punishment which have equal priority when it comes to passing sentence.

However, there is more evidence in Lysias to show that he was indeed committed to a general utilitarian penology. From XIV.4 and 11 f. the following argument to justify punishment may be constructed. The duty of a jury is to execute the laws in such a way that the city will benefit in the future. When it comes to passing sentence, therefore, the jury should aim to punish the offender in such a way that others will become more restrained,[136] being frightened by his example. This will have the additional effect of making other states, both allies and enemies, respect[137] Athens all the more for this unswerving attitude to offenders. From this general argument, Lysias draws the conclusion that in this particular case Alcibiades should be punished.

All the marks of utilitarian reasoning are present in this argument.[138] The punishment is intended to influence the future, rather than reflect on the offence that is past. It is designed to confer a benefit on many, rather than to penalise one. It derives its impact from publicity.[139] And it will have both deterrent and protective functions—to deter others and to protect from those outside the state—although the prevention of recidivism is not mentioned.[140] But even here the marks of retributivism that characterise other of Lysias' speeches are not altogether absent. For he refers here (XIV.13) to the anger that we should display towards

134. Ch. 3.c; Ch. 4.d; Ch. 5.i.

135. And it is, of course, to provide for, and to justify, a series of particular cases, that we have theories of punishment.

136. *Sōphronesteroi*, or just, *dikaioi*, XXVII.6. It is significant here, I believe, that restraint and justice may be merely a matter of behaviour. We only have straightforward deterrence by fear here, no moral reform.

137. And hence fear?

138. Cf. Ch. 4.a.

139. XIV.12; the penalty should be exacted from the most conspicuous offenders.

140. Cf. Ch. 4.a. In those days of imprisonment for remand only, prevention of the offender from repeating his offence would only be achieved by the death penalty or by exile.

offenders,[141] and argues earlier that the penalty be exacted *for the crimes committed* (XIV.2). When this strongly utilitarian passage is considered alongside the other retributive passages, the dangers of conflict become increasingly clear.

What is more, by the time Lysias wrote the speech, these penological problems had already been aired in public. The debate over the fate of Mytilene, reported by Thucydides (III.37 ff.), is couched largely in terms of what is expedient. There are two speakers in the debate, Cleon and Diodotus. Cleon, an old adversary of Thucydides,[142] offers a muddled argument in favour of killing the entire male population of Mytilene, which had revolted against the Athenian Empire. Diodotus presents a clear, teleological argument as to why the Mytileneans should be spared, and disentangles the problems of the relative priority of justice and expediency.

Cleon argues that the Mytileneans should be punished as they deserve (*axiōs*, 39.6) for the great wrong that they have done to the Athenians. Such punishment, revealing as it would differential treatment for crimes of varying gravity, would deter others from emulating the Mytileneans. However, exacting the same punishment from those who are forced to revolt as from those who do so of their own accord would actually encourage others to revolt. The Athenians should carry out sentence on Mytilene. Either the Mytileneans were justified in revolting, or they were not. If they were not justified, then both justice and expediency dictate that they should be punished. But if they were justified, then failure to punish them would be to concede as much; therefore expediency alone dictates that they be punished. Accordingly, their punishment embodies both justice and expediency.[143] The hopeless tangle of this disjunctive argument may be encapsulated thus: on the one hand, it is just to punish them, therefore they should be punished, and this will also be expedient; on the other hand, it is expedient to punish them, whether it be just or not, therefore they should be punished.[144]

Cleon's use of 'expediency' may not be utilitarian. The context is an odd one, since it deals apparently with foreign policy, but foreign policy

141. Although an instrumental account of this expressive function of punishment might be available; cf. Ch. 4.a.

142. Cf. his characterisation as excessively violent, III.36.6; and other unflattering remarks—IV.21.3; IV.28.5; V.16.1. It may be for reasons of prejudice that Thucydides attributes to Cleon such a bad argument and then permits the second speaker to point out its faults. In that case, maybe the public debate was not quite as Thucydides presents it.

143. Both retribution (*axiōs kolazein*) and deterrence (*paradeigma katastēsai*), III.40.7.

144. The dangers of conflict reside in Cleon's apparent appeal to general principles to justify the action he proposes, which suggests that he actually subscribes to those general principles, both at once.

towards a subject (*de facto*) state. Two lines of teleological argument[145] are available. First, and most directly, this is an egoistic argument, to justify the behaviour of an individual city in terms of its own benefit.[146] Second, and more indirectly, it is the argument of one member of a community, the Athenian Empire, considering how best to hold that community together in safety and prosperity.[147] It makes little difference, however, whether the teleology be egoistic or utilitarian, for the two are comparable as teleological theories,[148] and both are liable to conflict with the quite different imperatives of justice.

Diodotus continues the debate. His argument is clean and accurate and invokes one general principle, that of prudence or expediency.[149] He maintains that capital punishment, which may be exacted for lesser offences than revolt, does not have a deterrent effect at all.[150] For when men are fixed on a course, rational considerations of what they should fear from taking such a course will never deter them.[151] But it is positively against the interests of the ruler to go through the business of reducing and then eradicating a state in revolt, for no benefit is to be derived from corpses and ruins. Consequently, the best thing is to prevent these revolts by better treatment of the allies in the first place. And the next best thing is to exact a lesser punishment than the death penalty: an indemnity which will allow the subject state to recover and to begin to bring in income to the imperial treasury. In this way, other states will be discouraged from revolting, and they will be prepared to surrender even if they do revolt. In general, punishments that are lesser rather than greater than the deserved should be exacted. The guilty should even be let off altogether, if necessary, if the objective of expediency is to be reached. Such a system of punishment, Diodotus declares

145. I.e., interpretations of *for whom* it is expedient.

146. Inasmuch as a city is a group, its internal principle of punishment will not be egoistic. When it proposes punishment as a matter of foreign policy, its action, if egoistic, is probably not a punishment at all—would there be a statute governing it? If benevolent, the state may be seen as an individual member of a group of states.

147. Cf. a parallel situation in the Melian debate, Thuc. V.99, where the Athenians argue in terms of the benefit of the whole empire, not merely themselves.

148. They both want to maximise benefit, rather than doing right. They differ only in the matter of the distribution of benefit, which, although a vital distinction in other contexts, is unimportant here, where the object is to contrast a teleological with a deontological approach to punishment.

149. "We are not concerned here," he says, 44.1, "with questions of justice, but merely with what is the prudent thing to do."

150. This line, of course, is familiar; cf. Ch. 4.b.

151. This amounts to an argument for the possibility of *akrasia*. Contrast Socrates' teleological penology, founded, in the first place, upon a denial of the possibility of *akrasia*; below, Chs. 9, 10, and 11.

in conclusion, may produce cases, like the present one, where justice
and expediency do not coincide (47.5). In such cases, considerations of
expediency must take priority.[152]

This, then, is a clear argument, run on teleological principles, to justify punishment. It carried the day for the Mytileneans, and talk of expediency continues to appear in such contexts as this.[153] But these teleological arguments tend to be egoistic rather than either utilitarian or
humanitarian. The principle of benevolence is not strong;[154] nor, despite the emphasis on individualism, is the humanitarian approach—
yet. Retributivism, despite its observed disadvantages, remains the central justification of punishment in the classical period.

152. Diodotus is, clearly, a strict teleologist; cf. Ch. 4.h.
153. E.g., the Melian debate, Thuc. V.87 ff.
154. Surprisingly enough, given the strength of general sympathy as evidenced in the
universal anxiety at manifest unfairness, particularly in tragedy. But n.b. the Anonymus
Iamblichi, virtue is a matter of conferring benefit on the most people; DK89.3.3.

CHAPTER

8

THEORETICAL REFLECTIONS

To rationalise and to justify punishment is the first step towards a penology. But the critical and analytic approach that will provoke theorising about punishment needs the spur of scepticism. The present chapter documents two sceptical approaches to the problems of punishment during the fifth century:[1] that represented in Aeschylus' *Oresteia*, and that of the immoralist[2] interlocutors of Socrates. The first was the constructive precursor of philosophical analysis. The second was destructive of contemporary morality, and therefore urgently requires an answer.

a. AESCHYLUS' *ORESTEIA*

The plots of Greek tragedies were, it is banal to point out, taken from traditional mythology. As a result, the audience was already familiar with the story being presented and had attention to spare for the arguments and the characterisation of the protagonists. These dramas were the ideal vehicle for the presentation of formalised debate, where not only might the playwright offer arguments on either side, but he might also pass judgement upon the arguments on his own behalf, by his char-

1. Thrasymachus and Callicles were, as Socrates' interlocutors, characters of the fifth century, although Plato wrote about them in the fourth. I adduce evidence below for the currency, at the end of the fifth century, of the views advanced by them.

2. Thrasymachus and Callicles are crudely so-called, to distinguish them from others of Socrates' interlocutors who adopt a more conventional position. But, as I shall argue below, only Thrasymachus is truly an immoralist, and then only by an unfortunate slide in his argument.

acterisation of their exponents.[3] Thus the characters of a play will represent ideas and sentiments whose interaction is being studied by the dramatist, and we need seek no further determinate answer from the play to the difficulties it illustrates. The object of the exercise may be not to solve but to pose a problem. The *Eumenides*, as we shall see, is a case in point.

The traditional response to injury appealed to principles of justice or fairness. The original aim to restore the *status quo* coordinated with the new prescriptive morality[4] to produce a declaration that there should be punishment for crimes, and that it should be retributive. So if a crime is committed, an equal and opposite reaction is required from the victim. But the reaction, being equal and opposite, is therefore also criminal[5] and thus demands a reaction as well, and so on *ad infinitum*. The regress will continue unless some element of the bare retributive principle is lifted. Either it must be accepted that not all injuries are crimes, that two actions, superficially similar ("an eye for an eye"), may differ in the fundamental respect that one is a crime and prohibited, the other a punishment and required, or else the retributive principle must be abandoned.

The classical tradition was already aware of the regressive problems of retribution. Odysseus, for example, makes provisions against civil war in Ithaca, in case the relations of the murdered suitors should come for revenge (*Od.*23.118 etc.). In the *Oresteia*, however, the dangers of regress are fully exploited. The plot involves a chain of crimes and revenges from Thyestes to Orestes, who, at last, seeks resolution, rather than submitting to the Erinyes. He does so by arguing justification, and indeed it is a strong theme of the *Oresteia* that acts, responsibility for

3. For example, Aegisthus is an unsympathetic character, which leads us to regard his arguments as specious.

4. 'New' is relative. Here all I mean is that the interests of the victim are not considered in what I regard as our earliest evidence, the *Iliad*. That the values of the strong (retaliation) and the values of the weak (that there are crimes) coincide in retributive attitudes serves only to emphasise that these different sets of values were not exclusive of one another at different periods. There are, however, problems in trying to reconcile them into a single system, as the example of Thrasymachus shows. See below, b. And here, of course, the retributive regress is set up by the conflict of non-moral—retaliate for injury—and moral—punish for crimes—approaches to the question of punishment.

5. There are two reasons for this. First, if crimes are so-called because they injure, then punishments, which injure, are also crimes. At least, they need justifying. Second, what actions are crimes is a general prescription, not specific to one case. If killing others is a crime, then the death is demanded for a death criminally. So it is because the reaction is *equal and opposite* that there is a regress. And that it should be equal and opposite (or at least that it should fit) is a requirement of both restitution and retribution. Cf. Chs. 2 and 3.

them, and reaction to them are infinitely complex.[6] But this means that by the end of the *Choephori*, the tangle of 'ought' and 'ought not' looks too complex to be resolved by anything less than the obliteration of the house of Atreus. The *Eumenides*, however, offers a different way out.

The final play of the trilogy may be construed as a dialogue between two opposing principles. The Erinyes claim the priority of a blunt *lex talionis*, whereby all criminal acts should be punished, and they are prepared to tolerate the regress. Orestes, however, wants to escape it, and he argues that some actions, although they injure, should not be thought of as criminal.

Orestes has been told to go to Athens, now that he has been purified,[7] in order that he may be tried and thus find release from the chain of murders. He arrives in Athens, pursued by the Erinyes, and seeks the protection of Athena. The Erinyes claim that he is their rightful prey, since he has committed matricide, a crime for which he must pay, according to the traditional morality which they represent.[8] Orestes points out that what he did was not only condemned but also required by the morality of the time.[9] Athena finds herself in a dilemma: she cannot ignore the claims of her suppliant, but, by sheltering him, she lays herself and her city open to the wrath of the slighted Erinyes. So she proposes that a jury court be set up to try the case. The Erinyes grudgingly submit, although reserving to themselves the right to punish the court for its decision should it go against them.[10]

The case is heard amid much argument. The Erinyes, on the one hand, appeal to the principle of the old gods that *dikē* consists in maintaining the crude *lex talionis* without equivocation or modification.[11] Orestes, on the other hand, argues that his action was justly done and thus should not be liable to punishment.[12] The dispute, therefore, revolves over where justice lies. The decision belongs to the jury, but the jury cannot reach a verdict. Athena steps in and adds her casting vote[13] in

6. Cf. Ch. 7.d.

7. It is worth noticing that the religious requirements of expiation are *de facto*; Orestes does not plead justification as a reason to avoid the religious rites to free him of pollution.

8. The Erinyes are represented as the 'old gods', Athena and Apollo as the 'new'; cf., e.g., 721–722, 778 ff.

9. Cf. Ch. 6.b, Ch. 7.c.

10. This is the implication of the chorus 490 ff., 719–720.

11. E.g., 427, 490 ff., 778 ff.

12. 443 ff., 609 ff., supported by Apollo, the new god, 213 ff., 614 ff.

13. There has been considerable debate on this topic; cf. the bibliography supplied by Gagarin, "The Vote of Athena," *A.J. Ph.* (1975):121–127. The issue is whether Athena has a casting vote or whether she, by casting her vote as the last member of the jury, creates the hung jury, which she then declares shall acquit. Gagarin, with an ingenious argument

favour of Orestes, for the spurious reason that she herself had no mother and so deems the crime of matricide of little account.[14] Orestes is acquitted and departs.

In this sequence of events, the jury, ostensibly central to the plot, affect the case not at all. The decision to acquit Orestes is taken by Athena, since she casts her vote in his favour. The outcome is therefore exactly the same as it would have been had Athena undertaken to make the decision alone in the first place. So why is the jury included at all?

It has been suggested that this is an aetiological account of the formation of jury courts at Athens, given in celebration of some legal reforms.[15] Why then does the jury not take pride of place by making the decision itself? Maybe the institution of the jury is meant to lift the onus of deciding the case from the individual goddess, to whom the defendant came as a suppliant.[16] But the jury does not decide the case; it is left to Athena to justify Orestes' acquittal. Altogether, it seems implausible

---

from the staging of the scene, supports the latter interpretation, many other scholars the former—notably, and with vitriol, C.O. Müller, *Dissertations on the Eumenides of Aeschylus* (London: 1853), pp. 149 ff., 215 ff.

My case rests on the fact that the jury is hung, however that comes about; so whichever interpretation is the correct one is irrelevant to the present argument. However, despite Gagarin's argument, considerations of rationality, not only stagecraft, must enter here. For Athena to abjure making the decision, then, with the human majority against Orestes, to cast her vote in his favour *and then* arbitrarily to declare a hung jury to acquit, seems inconsistent, or even bad drama. What is more, it risks the wrath of the Erinyes, which is what she is trying to avoid.

It should be remembered—and Gagarin plays this down too far—that however familiar the audience were with procedure in the Areopagus, the dramatic situation is one of the institution of that court; therefore we should expect some explanation of why hung juries acquit. Such an explanation is provided if and only if Athena has the casting vote. And, from the point of view of staging the scene, the dramatic impact of Athena adding her pebble to the urn after the votes had been counted and found equal (i.e., at 753) would be considerable. As for ancient interpretations of the vote of Athena, in addition to the evidence cited by Gagarin, Cicero (*pro Milone* 8) clearly takes the view I suggest.

14. But cf. Lloyd-Jones, trans., *The Eumenides of Aeschylus* (Englewood Cliffs: Prentice-Hall, 1970), p. 4.

15. This approach appears, with varying strength, in many commentators: e.g., Dodds, "Notes on the *Oresteia*," *C.Q.* (1953): 19; J. Jones, *On Aristotle and Greek Tragedy* (London: Chatto & Windus, 1962), p. 112; A.M.G. Little, *Myth and Society in Attic Drama* (New York: Columbia U.P., 1942), p. 33; or, as the converse idea that Aeschylus intends a criticism of contemporary institutions, cf. the appendix to Lloyd-Jones, *Eumenides*. But cf. Havelock, *Greek Concept*, p. 283, who offers, in general, a legalistic, though not aetiological, interpretation.

16. Cf. Lloyd-Jones, *Eumenides*, who suggests that Athena wants to avoid by her manoeuvres the hostility of the Erinyes being directed at herself. Certainly I agree that there is a strong element in the play of the move away from revenge, towards legally instituted punishments. Cf. Ch. 6.d, Ch. 7.a. This does not explain the hung jury, however.

that the author of the powerful first plays of the trilogy should allow the *Eumenides* to deteriorate into artifice.

On readings such as these, the hung jury and Athena's frivolous casting vote look like mistakes in Aeschylus' construction of a strong plot. But might they not be positive features of the dramatist's argument? Aeschylus' objective, on a superficial level, is to get Orestes off the hook and to terminate the regress. On a more profound level, however, he presents a thoughtful analysis of justice, fraught as it is with difficulties and incipient injustice. The outcome, on this level, is not important; the debate's the thing. Consequently, for Aeschylus to commit himself on one side or the other, by having the jury decide positively for new gods or for old, would be to bias the debate, to rob it of its analytical aspect, and to reduce himself to the level of a mere writer of plots. But to suspend judgement, to outline the opposing views, and to refuse to comment is the mark of true analysis.

Simply by being non-committal, Aeschylus goads his audience into reflection upon the answers to the vital questions that his trilogy expounds. First, the *Oresteia* casts doubt on a simplistic view of crimes and responsibility for them. Second, it presents an account of the regress engendered by a crude *lex talionis*, carried out without the sanctions of a court. Third, it tentatively suggests that by means of legal institutions, culpability may be assessed and justice administered in a sophisticated way and therefore without tragic outcome. Finally, the trilogy ends not with an aetiological anticlimax but with a philosophical *tour de force*, a dramatised analysis of different ideas and interpretations of retributive justice. And this is the necessary precursor of any philosophical approach to the problems of punishment.

b. CALLICLES AND THRASYMACHUS

Socrates, as he is presented in Plato's dialogues, had several opponents who have been loosely described as immoralists.[17] In fact, they are generally not immoralist at all, as we shall see, but they do pose a threat to the morality of the victim that preoccupies Plato. For they take up the challenge conceived in tragedy, suggesting that manifest unfairness is true. However, mere acceptance, they imply, is too flaccid an attitude, and they propose a more constructive treatment of the problem. As a consequence, they erode still further the prudential arguments for right action and, at the same time, they encourage opportunism which says, "Commit crimes if you can get away with it." Therefore, he who sup-

---

17. Cf. Adkins, *Merit and Responsibility*, p. 232 ff.

ports traditional morality[18] must find a counter that demonstrates the imprudence of opportunism and mitigates the problem of manifest unfairness.

To recapitulate, the problem of opportunism is a complex one. For present purposes, there are two kinds of opportunist: the overt opportunist, who is the strong man always able do what he likes and get away with it, and the covert opportunist, who appears to be just but covertly practises injustice only when he can get away with it.[19] In the archaic age, victims tried for protection against the overt opportunist by persuading him and everyone else that he should not have acted as he did. As a consequence, he went underground and practised his opportunism only when he would not get caught. For such a man, as Critias pointed out, divine punishment was invented.[20]

But Callicles, in the *Gorgias*, and Thrasymachus, in *Republic I*, represent the re-emergence of the overt opportunist, for they offer a morality of the strong, emerging from its eclipse in the centuries after Homer. The evidence of Thucydides shows that Callicles and Thrasymachus are not mere straw men, but representative of types of moral argument that were indeed current during this period.

Callicles (*Gorgias* 483 ff.) is a naturalist. He argues, to begin with, that conventional morality is indeed a morality of the weak, with laws drawn up by the victimised majority to protect their interests. But, he claims, the morality of nature is morality of the strong, wherefore it is right that the strong should have more than the weak.

So by convention it is said to be unjust and shameful to seek to have more than the many; and it is the many who call this acting unjustly. But I think that nature reveals that it is just that the better man should have more than the worse, the more powerful more than the weaker (483c6–d2).[21]

The argument rejecting conventional values might be thought to be a commonplace of moral scepticism. The subtlety of Callicles' approach lies in his attitude towards opportunism. For he is not merely allowing opportunism; he is justifying and even enjoining it. By the nature/convention antithesis he offers two moral standards, that of the strong and that of the weak. He argues that only on the morality of the weak is the

18. For whatever reasons, whether deontological or teleological, egoistic or benevolent.

19. The man with Gyges' ring is halfway between the two. In fact, he is a covert opportunist, but Gyges' ring makes him able to get away with it all the time, and in this respect he is like the overt opportunist.

20. Cf. Ch. 7.a.

21. Cf. the attitude of the Athenians at Sparta (Thuc. I.76.2) or in the Melian debate (Thuc. V. 105.2): "It is always true that the strong rule." But the Athenians slip over into amoralism; cf. below. Antiphon the sophist is a naturalist, too, DK87B44a.

activity of the strong opportunism at all; on the (superior and natural) morality of the strong, it is right action.

Hence, to the complaints of Theognis that it is not fair that the wicked get away with doing evil, Callicles would counter that it is precisely because they get away with it that the wicked are doing the right thing and are not naturally to be described as wicked.[22] Manifest unfairness, therefore, where it exists, is only unfair from the point of view of the inferior morality of the weak. The superior morality of the strong calls this justice.

This return to the *de facto* morality of Homer[23] puts the constructive moralist into a dilemma. On the one hand, the weak clamour for a solution to manifest unfairness; on the other, the naturalists dismiss manifest unfairness by permitting victimisation. This is the challenge that Socrates attempts to meet in the *Gorgias*—with only partial success.[24]

In the *Republic*, immoralism wears a different face. Thrasymachus, the most important interlocutor of the first book, does not have the cogency of Callicles, but he represents, perhaps, a more commonly held approach to the existence of opportunism.[25]

Thrasymachus has two principles according to which he outlines his theory of justice, and he takes two different (and increasingly vulnerable) positions with respect to them as the dialogue with Socrates continues. His first principle is contentious: justice is the interest of the stronger (338c); his second is a normal principle of what has been called cooperative morality:[26] justice is the good of another (343c). Thrasymachus' account of justice seeks to combine opportunism with altruism, and at times it is successful.

The first position that issues from these two principles might be described as amoralism. The weak act justly, and altruistically, by obeying the self-interested dictates of the strong. The strong act neither justly

22. The awesome dangers of this kind of position are exemplified in all "master race" arguments.

23. This is the answer to Santas' worry, *Socrates*, p. 258, about the provenance of Callicles' idea of justice.

24. Cf. Chs. 9 to 13.

25. A debate on Thrasymachus' actual argument has been conducted by G.B. Kerferd, "The Doctrine of Thrasymachus in Plato's *Republic*," *Durham University Journal* (1947): 19–27, and "Thrasymachus and Justice: A Reply," *Phronesis* (1964):12–17; G.F. Hourani "Thrasymachus' Definition of Justice in Plato's *Republic*," *Phronesis* (1962):110–120; and P.P. Nicholson, "Unravelling Thrasymachus' Arguments in the *Republic*," *Phronesis* (1974):210–232. There is a useful footnote by T. Irwin, *Plato's Moral Theory: The Early and Middle Dialogues* (Oxford: Clarendon, 1977), p. 289. In what follows, I agree on the whole with Irwin, although he does not allow for the shift at 343c ff.

26. Cf. Adkins, *Merit and Responsibility*; K.J. Dover, *Greek Popular Morality in the Time of Plato and Aristotle* (Oxford: Blackwell, 1974). This is a principle of altruism.

nor unjustly, since they are the beneficiaries, not the agents, of justice. Accordingly, their actions, described by the many as opportunist, are neither right nor wrong, but simply self-interested.[27] The condemnation of opportunism, therefore, is lifted by Thrasymachus' amoralist argument. Callicles actively recommended victimising others when you are strong enough to get away with doing so. Thrasymachus takes a neutral line, defusing the arguments of the victims against their aggressors. This approach, of course, not only threatens the entire moral structure so elaborately erected by the victims, but it denies the complaint of manifest unfairness and takes away the grounds for punishing successful aggressors.

Midway through the argument with Socrates, however, Thrasymachus appears to shift his position, with the unfortunate effect that his two principles become inconsistent.[28] For from 343c ff. he advocates a truly immoralist position whereby injustice, the activity of taking and having more than everyone else, is the prudent thing to do and therefore to be recommended, despite the condemnation that is attached to such opportunism by the weak. This line, therefore, disjoins what is recommended by morality from what is recommended by prudence, and advocates the latter. Such blatant immoralism is the target of the early moralising poets. It becomes Socrates' chief task to refute the notion that vice is happiness.

Thrasymachus and Callicles between them, therefore, present various positions on the opportunist scale: from actively recommending so-called opportunism, to neutralising its condemnation,[29] to disregarding

27. Hence before 343c, Thrasymachus does not speak of injustice at all. At that point, however, he changes tack and begins to advocate the prudence of overt opportunism, i.e., injustice. Cf. Irwin, *Plato's Moral Theory*, who tries to explain away the mention of injustice at 343c by arguing that this is the opportunist on his way to becoming strong, but incompletely so, hence classifiable as unjust according to the theory—he rebels against the interests of those who are currently strong. This analysis, ingenious though it is, does not seem to fit with the assumptions made during Thrasymachus' refutation (349b ff.) that the unjust man (he who has more) is, on the immoralist view, better off.

28. "Justice as the interest of the stronger, however, *is* inconsistent with justice as seeking another's interest, when looked at from the point of view of actions done by the stronger, since for him to seek another's interest will involve seeking not the interest of the stronger who is himself, but of the weaker who is his subject" (Kerferd, "Thrasymachus and Justice: A Reply," p. 15).

Of course, as long as the stronger's actions are classified as neither just nor unjust, this inconsistency does not arise.

29. We may well wonder whether amoralism works. After all, once value judgements have been instituted, as we saw in Ch. 7, can they be suspended? But that such a position was indeed held in Athens during the fifth century is suggested by Thucydides: e.g., V.89, justice is a matter between equals only; some are exempt from considerations of justice, notably the strong. Cf. also I.76.2–3; V.105.4.

the sanctions against it for reasons of prudence. Socrates concentrates his attention upon the immoralist represented by Thrasymachus in *Republic I*, but the more insidious threat to the morality of the underdog comes from Callicles. For not only does Callicles overturn the values advocated by the victim, perceiving that, founded in convention, they are safeguards against victimisation, but, by recommending opportunism, he threatens the retributive account that has preserved those values.

If opportunism is right, how can retribution be justified? The opportunist, and his effect upon the just state of affairs, had been a problem for earlier writers. But his existence now becomes critical, for he threatens not only to flout retribution but actively to recommend that it be held in contempt. Overt opportunism and satisfactory retribution cannot coexist. Early poets had hoped that retribution would stamp out opportunism, but Callicles and his like suggest the converse: that the imperatives backing retributivism are the pragmatism of the weak and are vulnerable to the strong, so that opportunism flourishes.

Thus the *Oresteia* paves the way to a philosophical approach to punishment by suggesting that the retributive principle is susceptible to analytical treatment. But the immoralists, whose existence Plato himself acknowledges, pose a more urgent question. To guard against victimisation, the victim had proposed a retributive system of punishment. To prevent opportunism, however, retribution must be stronger than those whom the victim would guard against, and the victim's values must be proof against the doubts of the naturalist.

Those values gave rise to the problem of manifest unfairness. Callicles, however, attempts a redefinition of manifest unfairness: that it simply is not unfair at all. As a consequence, Plato has two tasks on his hands: he must rebut immoralism and naturalism; he must provide some kind of answer, alternative to Callicles', to the problem of manifest unfairness. He might readily achieve both through the medium of a retributive theory of punishment. But he does not do so.

PART
III

PLATO

CHAPTER

9

PLATO'S
MORAL FOUNDATIONS

In the *Iliad*, reaction to an injury took the form of aggression by the victim, with the purpose of restoring the *status quo* upset by the injury. In the literature of the succeeding centuries, the *status quo*, which the Homeric heroes guarded so zealously, was increasingly viewed from a prescriptive standpoint. The hierarchical *status quo*, determined according to what actually was the case, therefore became transformed into a state of affairs determined by what ought to be the case. This was described as just.

The just state of affairs became the focus of man's political and moral activity, inasmuch as he was anxious to see fairness prevail both for himself and in the lives and fortunes of others. Consequently, he recommended the virtue of justice, which promotes the just state of affairs, and he relied upon the judicial activity (also described as justice) which restores the just state of affairs when it has been upset. Penal activity, therefore, tended to be on retributivist and deterrent lines. By this means, not only were criminals discouraged from infringing the rights and property of others, but manifest unfairness, the source of moral distress, was removed.

The tragedians, however, made the observation that the expedients of human and divine justice do not always ensure the prevalence of fairness. The prudential recommendation to right action was thereby weakened, since virtue does not meet its deserved reward. Equally, the tragedians undermined the fundamental satisfaction, provided by effective retributivism, that everyone encounters the deserts appropriate to their behaviour. Yet both the preservation of the prudential argument and the rebuttal of manifest unfairness are the immediate concern of the constructive moralist. Accordingly, we should expect Plato to provide a philosophic defence of the just state of affairs in a penology which combined retributive with deterrent measures.

However, it is not only the tradition that will exercise pressure upon Plato. His penology is an integral part of his general moral theory. The present chapter will demonstrate how his own ethical thinking is liable to affect his theory of punishment.

a. NO ONE FAILS WILLINGLY

Both the *Protagoras* and the *Gorgias* are concerned with the question of how to do what is prudent. Two extended arguments about the nature of choice allow Plato to conclude that all failure is due to mistake, whereas the only reliable road to success is knowledge or expertise.[1] No one, therefore, fails willingly,[2] and this is a dictum which encapsulates Plato's attitude towards him who fails.

Socrates proposes an intellectualist thesis:[3]

I. If a man knows what is good and what is bad,[4] nothing will induce him to

1. The only thesis required for the version of the Socratic paradox suggested here is that mistake is a necessary condition of failure. Moreover, Plato's approach to the reliability of the road to success suggests that knowledge is a sufficient condition of success. Plato treats these two propositions as equivalent. If success and failure are thought of as contradictory (i.e., any falling short of success is failure), and if knowledge and ignorance are also thought of as contradictory (as at *Prot.* 350), then indeed the propositions are equivalent. However, Plato does not always think of knowledge and ignorance this way: e.g., at *Rep.* 477, ignorance is the *contrary* of knowledge. This ambiguity about 'ignorance' will affect the logic of the intellectualist position, as we shall see.

2. Cf. G.X. Santas, *Socrates* (London: Routledge, Kegan Paul, 1979), Ch. 6.

3. Intellectualism is a characteristic of Plato's moral philosophy, for which I shall argue in some detail in both this chapter and the next. However, the term 'intellectualism' is itself unclear (cf. M.J. O'Brien, *The Socratic Paradoxes and the Greek Mind* [Chapel Hill: U. of N. Carolina Press, 1967], Ch. 1, etc.), and, as we shall see, the function of the intellect in Plato's moral psychology is open to interpretation. By using the term, I mean to make three points about Plato's account of action.

a. When he presents an intellectualist account, he is exploiting a view of action whereby *reason* (or skill or knowledge) is one, and sometimes the only, factor needed to explain why we act as we do—either with reason or without it—and to show how we should act.

b. A major aspect of his intellectualism is the view that knowledge and action are connected and hence that it is possible to know what you are doing, and to exploit your infallible knowledge (cf. *Rep.* 477e) in both your practical life and your moral life. Thus the fundamental factor is the idea of 'getting it right'.

c. A consequence of this association of knowledge with action is the idea that behaviour may be affected and altered by education. This, for the present study, is the importance of Plato's use of intellectualist ideas—knowing, reasoning, having a skill, getting it right—in his moral theory.

4. The context makes it clear that by 'good' Socrates means "good for the man in question," i.e., prudential, not moral.

do other than as reason bids [i.e., "Pursue the good"], *for knowledge is enough support for a man* (*Prt.* 352c).

Ranged against him is the opinion of the many,[5] who believe in the phenomenon of *akrasia*, that:

A. *A man may recognise the best, and be able to do it,[6] but yet he may refrain, and do something else, because he is overcome by pleasure, anger, fear or other emotions* (352d).[7]

Socrates believes that knowledge is noble and rules its possessor. The many hold that a man's better judgement may be overruled by the compulsions of pleasure or fear.

The demonstration[8] begins from 353c, with hedonistic[9] premises derived from 351d ff.:

1. *Pleasures, pains and all actions and passions are good or bad according as they maximise pleasure (in the long run) or minimise pain (in the long run).*[10]

2. *So we pursue pleasures as goods and avoid pains as evils.*

But, says Socrates, it is absurd to hold this in conjunction with A. If we reduce the values to a single currency, as *1* allows, we may translate *A*:

3. *A man knows evils for evils, and yet he pursues them, overcome by what is good.*

---

5. Since Protagoras refuses himself to defend the notion of *akrasia*.

6. This proviso allows for the eventuality of accident and requires, apparently, that the agent be free from external interference or coercion. I shall argue that these possibilities are taken up further in the *Gorgias* (509–10) and in the *Laws* (861 ff.); cf. Ch. 10.c and Ch. 11.d.

7. A modern discussion of the Socratic view of *akrasia* is in H. Frankfurt, "Freedom of the Will and the Concept of a Person," *J. Ph.* (1971):12.

8. Socrates' attack, as Santas points out, *Socrates*, Ch. 7, is directed not against the phenomenon of *akrasia* itself but against the explanation advanced by the many that we may be overcome by the various pressures of emotion. This leaves Socrates vulnerable to the criticism that he has failed to account for all of the overwhelming impulses (listed at 352b7), since his argument concentrates on the effects of pleasure on our behaviour. To this Socrates' answer might be that there is no other explanation of *akrasia* than being overcome by pleasure, in which case this is the only explanation he must refute.

But a stronger defence would be that whatever values we hold, they may be reduced into a single coin of what we pursue (a good) and what we avoid (an evil). One such reduction would be demonstrated in an earlier passage (351b), where Socrates' espousal of hedonism allowed all goods and evils to be explained in terms of pleasures and pains.

9. The absurd conclusion will follow for any system, hedonist or otherwise, which operates on a single currency of value. So Socrates' actual commitment to hedonism is irrelevant to the universality of the denial of *akrasia*. See C.C.W. Taylor, ed., *Plato: Protagoras* (Oxford: Clarendon, 1976), pp. 164 ff. for a discussion of Socratic hedonism. Hedonism does, however, have the additional advantage of defusing the irrational overtones of "being overcome by *pleasure*," inasmuch as, for the hedonist, pleasure is what is *rationally* pursued.

10. See Taylor, *Protagoras*, p. 179, for the qualification "in the long run."

This is claimed to be absurd. For the *akratic* man, *ex hypothesi*, does what he should not do, so it is clear that:

4. *What is good is not worthy of overcoming.*

'Worth' is then cashed in quantitative terms (355e): the situation is one in which the agent chooses evils in his pursuit of goods, but the choice he makes involves his taking more evil in return for less good, rather than less evil in return for more good. This, when other options are open to him, is absurd.

The absurdity is derived from two proposals. The first is that we pursue what is of most value. The second is that the agent in this case does in fact know, as the hypothesis declares, that he is taking greater evil in return for less good. However, the agent's reason, offered on his behalf by the many, was that he was overcome by pleasure. But 'pleasure' is now reduced to 'good', and the explanation disintegrates; for if we do pursue what is of most value, it is absurd to suppose that less good, recognised to be so, should induce us to seek greater evil.

The vital move, therefore, in the *reductio*, is to make all values commensurate. Either there is a balance of good, in which case we pursue it when we can, or there is a balance of evil, in which case we avoid it when we can. There can be no exceptions to this rule, since there is neither a way of explaining why we should deviate from this course of action nor an independent value in terms of which an explanation could be couched. The many originally supposed that such an explanation could be supplied by the irrationality of emotion, but Socrates, by translating this into a factor in the rational computation of what is best, explodes their account.[11]

Thus, since our behaviour is simply a matter of the proper choice of what to pursue and what to avoid, we need, Socrates declares, a science of measuring (*metrētikē technē*) pleasures and pains, goods and evils, in order to have a safe and happy life.[12] Failure to maximise pleasures and pains can *only* be attributed to ignorance.[13]

---

11. Although there is, I believe, an equivocation here between pleasure the motive and pleasure the object of that motive.

12. The stipulation that our life should be secure (356c8, *esōzen*) suggests not only that knowledge is sufficient for happiness but that it is necessary as well, since only knowledge gives security in right decisions (cf. *Meno*, 97c6). However, there are times, cf., e.g., *Prt.* 358b, when Plato assimilates knowledge and (unreliable) true belief.

13. That ignorance is both necessary and sufficient for failure is suggested by 357d, assuming (cf. the easy inversion at 350b) that knowledge and ignorance are contradictory.

But is Socrates justified in inverting "Success is to be attributed to knowledge" into "Failure is to be attributed to ignorance (and to ignorance alone)"? Plato has three possible standpoints, of increasing strength:

1. *Knowledge leads regularly to correct choice.*
2. *Knowledge always leads to correct choice.*

In the terms of the original dispute, therefore, knowledge is sovereign, and failure, vulgarly described as "being overcome by pleasure," should properly be ascribed to ignorance (357d). If a man fails, then it is because he is ignorant; and if he is ignorant, he is bound to fail. Failure, therefore, is always a matter of mistake.

A similar account of the nature of choice appears at *Grg.* 466e ff. The topic under dispute is Polus' reiteration of Gorgias' claim that the pow-

---

3. *Knowledge, and nothing else, leads to correct choice, and does so invariably.*

Taylor (*Protagoras*, p. 191) supposes that Plato has demonstrated *1*:

"At 357b1–4 Socrates gains (through Protagoras) the agreement of the common man that if anyone *regularly* makes correct choices of pleasures and pains he employs the appropriate sort of knowledge" [my emphasis].

And he goes on to point out that the weak thesis, *1*, gives Socrates no warrant for making the vital inversion that all failure must be attributed to ignorance. For even if regular correct choice were to be accounted for by knowledge, random or infrequent choice might have other explanations. Correspondingly, failure might have alternative sources. Therefore, if Socrates has only demonstrated *1*, he is guilty of fallacy.

Yet, whatever he has proved, he certainly does not want the weak claim. For, first, he does indeed make the inversion, proposing that success is explained by knowledge, failure by ignorance. Second, nowhere in the text does any equivalent of "regularly" appear; rather it seems to be imported by Taylor. At 357b Socrates has pointed out, by induction, that when it comes to the computation of greater and smaller (goods, pleasures or anything else) we need a measuring skill. We need that kind of skill just because these objects of pursuit are commensurable. So Socrates has not, as Taylor would have it, here committed himself to the weaker view.

The question still remains which of the two remaining options Socrates does in fact take. Option *2* is stronger than *1*, but still not strong enough to warrant the inversion. Only on the basis of *3* would it be possible to conclude that knowledge explains success (in every case) and ignorance explains failure (in every case).

First, if knowledge is the only factor involved (true belief may be assimilated to knowledge, cf. 358b), there can be no possibility of a mistake. If, therefore, knowledge ever indicates the correct choice, it must always indicate the correct choice. However, as the common man avers, other factors may inhibit the agent from pursuing that choice—notably, accident and emotion. The argument, by effectively reducing emotion to an element in the rational assessment of what is universally valued, rules it out as a factor conflicting with reason. Accident is largely ignored, apart from the provision that the chosen course must be available and not subject to external interference or inhibition.

Second, the argument assumes that we always pursue what we value. But Plato elicits the agreement of the company that what we value may be reduced to a single type, and thus either we pursue goods or avoid evils. Accordingly, not only will there be no conflict in the choosing faculty, but there will be no conflict about the object of choice. Since all goods are commensurable, our correct judgements will lead us directly to success. Conversely, since failure will lead us to lose what we value, failure can only be a matter of mistake (or coercion, again left out of consideration).

Thus by the device of establishing a common currency for what we conceive to be our interests, and by making the assumption that ignorance is the contradictory of knowledge, Plato is empowered to reach the strong intellectualist conclusion that knowledge is necessary and sufficient for success whereas ignorance is necessary and sufficient for failure.

erful are those with political influence, such as orators and tyrants. Socrates, however, claims that such men do not do what they want,[14] but only what seems best to them. This distinction, it transpires, turns on the intellectualist thesis; its purpose is to associate knowledge with power, and ignorance with weakness. The argument runs thus:

1. *Power is a good to its possessor.*
2. *What seems best to the foolish man cannot be a good (since he is foolish and therefore mistaken).*[15]
3. *The foolish man, therefore, will not achieve power, since power is genuinely a good.*
4. *Therefore, foolish men* [a group which includes the sophists] *will not be powerful.*
5. *On the contrary sophists, and foolish men in general, will, by doing what seems best, positively obtain what is bad.*

This sequence, then, claims that mistakes, albeit well-intentioned ones, lead necessarily to failure. This is the effect of the positive conclusion at 5. Accordingly, Socrates goes on to examine these good intentions, by focusing on the notion of "doing what seems best." To this end he offers an analysis of means and ends. We pursue good ends, in general; we also pursue evils, or neutrals, as a means to these good ends. Man's universal desire, therefore, is for what is good, and he desires specific goods in specific circumstances. But he desires what is evil or neutral only derivatively.[16] Then:

14. The qualification *hōs epos eipein* at 466e1 suggests that *boulontai*, the word qualified, is about to be redefined, as it is.

15. There is an illegitimate assimilation in the *Protagoras*, e.g., at 349, of knowledge (*epistēmē*) and wisdom (*sophia*), although 'knowledge' refers to what you know and 'wisdom' to your aptitude at knowing; cf. *Theaet.* 145d ff. Similarly, here 'foolish' is equated with 'ignorant', although 'foolish' means only 'bad at understanding', not necessarily ignorant. Conversely, the ignorant man, who does not in fact understand anything, need not be foolish. Plato assumes that ignorance is a 'faculty' for inevitably making positive mistakes.

It may be that a similar claim is made for *agnōsia* at *Rep.* 476 ff, where *agnōsia* is the contrary of knowledge. But in the *Gorgias* it appears that ignorance, however positive, is still thought of as the contradictory of knowledge: you either have *nous* or you have not. Cf. also the ignorant at 459 are those, simply, who do not know. Ignorance is the contrary of knowledge at *Symp.* 202a, but it is contradictory at *Theaet.* 188a, which suggests that at least for a large period of his life, Plato did not sort out the differences between contrary and contradictory terms, at least as far as his epistemology was concerned. But cf. Owen, "Plato on not-being," in Vlastos, ed., *Plato: I* (London: Macmillan, 1971).

16. But Dodds complains:

"Strictly speaking, there are no pure *adiaphora* in the sphere of action, since every moment of living has some value or un-value in itself, and no pure 'ends' since every event stands in a causal relationship to other events" (*Greeks and the Irrational*, p. 236).

Plato, of course, would reply that there is a single end, happiness, and that the "value or un-value" of each event was determined only according as it was conducive to happi-

6. *If a man does what seems best to him, and it turns out to be worse, he has still done what seems best to him* (ex hypothesi) (468d ff.).

7. *But everyone desires and pursues goods, yet he ended up with evils.*

8. *He has not, therefore, done what he wanted* [which was to obtain a good].

9. *Such a man, who fails, cannot have power, since he lacks goods, and power is a good.*

10. *Thus the man who only does what seems good does not do what he wants, and is powerless.*

Thus while all men desire the good, they do not always do (what is productive of) the good. This happens because of ignorance (from 2 and from 6, where the illusory nature of his judgement is emphasised), and ignorance entails powerlessness.

This conclusion is reached by two distinct yet related routes. First, the ignorant man necessarily makes wrong choices (2–5) and therefore ends up with those things we actively avoid, of which powerlessness is one. Second, his intellectual weakness is exhibited in his inability to make effective choices (6–10); thus, in this case, his ignorance is the same thing as his powerlessness. On both counts, therefore, ignorance is sufficient for failure.[17]

Taking the arguments of these two dialogues together, ignorance is both necessary and sufficient for failure.[18] "No one fails willingly": all failure is the result of ignorance about what is in our best interests. For, on the one hand, the ignorant man will necessarily make mistakes about his objectives, and since they are mistakes, they will turn out against his interests. On the other hand, if knowledge is the sure and only means to the achieving of what is good, then failure will be characteristic of the ignorant man, unable to make the right choices since he lacks the proper skill. Although he desires happiness, happiness will be beyond his grasp. His desire, however, renders his failure involuntary (cf. *Grg.* 509d) and

---

ness. Santas also ("Socrates at Work on Virtue and Knowledge in Plato's *Laches*," in Vlastos, ed., *The Philosophy of Socrates* [London: Macmillan, 1971], p. 181) criticises Plato for overstatement of the means/ends thesis although he displays a more charitable approach in *Socrates*, pp. 223 ff.

17. Step 9 could fit into both arguments: into the first if power is the object of desire, and into the second if power is the ability to achieve the objects of one's desires.

18. And assuming, still, that knowledge and ignorance are contradictories. The *Protagoras*, and at least the first part of the *Gorgias* (up to the encounter with Callicles) seem Socratic particularly in their espousal of a technical account of intellectualist virtue. Cf. *Grg.* 460; cf. below, d. It should be observed, however, that later passages in *Gorgias* shift towards the complex moral psychology of the *Republic*. Cf. Ch. 10.a. I have tried not to beg the Socratic question. But, if pushed, I should say that the shift towards Platonism begins in the (later passages of the) *Gorgias*.

therefore no cause for censure but simply for the recognition that he is deficient in that sovereign quality which leads to bliss.

Consider what attitude this account of prudential failure might lead Plato to adopt towards him who fails. Any action which turns out to be against a man's interests is done through ignorance, and all imprudent actions are in this sense mistakes. We tend not to criticise people for their mistakes, but rather to pity them. Some kinds of mistake are thought not to belong to their ostensible agent at all, but rather to have happened to him: a slip of the pen, a slip of the foot, and even a slip of the tongue. These uncontrollable mistakes are not only outside the range of the culpability of the agent, but also of his responsibility. They are attributed rather to the pen, the foot, or even the tongue,[19] and excused completely on that basis. The mistake of the persistent and ignorant failer, however, may be seen to arise from a fixed state of mind and to be symptomatic of the intellectual disorder that besets him. His mistakes are therefore indeed his. This unfortunate will thus still evade culpability, but he will be held responsible for what he does.

There are, therefore, three levels on which the agent may be related to his act. First, at the lowest level, his accidents are thought to *happen to him*, and thus not to be *his* at all. Consequently he will not be blamed for them but will rather be the object of sympathy, as both we and Plato would agree. Moreover, since these actions are not even his (they are more like events), he will not be held responsible for them either. (For insurance purposes, they should probably be considered God's liability, and so they are the insurance company's responsibility, not the criminal's.) At the second level, the man who "deliberately" fails, on Plato's view, will be held responsible; witness the fact that his activity makes him liable to treatment or punishment.

The two agents differ inasmuch as the first is not held responsible for what happens, whereas the second is. This reflects the fact that the relation between the first agent and the event is a contingent one, whereas the second is necessarily (dispositionally) related to his act. On the Platonic schema, however, the two agents are alike, for neither is held to be culpable for what happens/what he does. Consequently, Plato's account of the powerless failer drives a wedge between culpability and responsibility, for a man may be responsible for an act and yet not to blame.[20]

19. We may recall Hippolytus' famous remark: "My tongue swore, but my heart remains unsworn" (Eur. *Hipp.* 612). But cf. Austin on the effect of an excuse, "A Plea for Excuses," p. 21.

20. The difficulty here, as Ch. 12, f and g, will show, is that such a notion of liability or responsibility *divorced* from culpability leads to problems of institution-begging and of an odd idea of 'punishment'. Modern lawyers, by contrast, tie responsibility (in the sense I use it—your actions are *yours*) very tightly to culpability; cf. Gross, *A Theory of Criminal Justice*, Ch. 3.

It is only those who succeed who, according to the Socratic paradox, could possibly be blamed, for only they act voluntarily. They, therefore, are responsible at the third and highest level. But, as we shall see, they are far from being blamed.

b. NO ONE DOES WRONG WILLINGLY

What has failure to do with morality? Plato argues that all moral wrongs are harmful to their perpetrator. Consequently, whoever acts wrongly acts against his interests and so is under the influence of mistake. Thus Plato transforms the dictum "No one fails willingly" into a paradox: "No one does wrong willingly."

Crime pays, says Polus. At *Grg.* 473, Socrates' interlocutor takes up the common-sense position that some unjust men are happy. Socrates, however, maintains three propositions in the face of universal opinion:

S1. *Doing wrong is worse (for the agent) than suffering it.*

S2. *Wrongdoers are wretched.*

S3. *Wrongdoers who escape punishment are more wretched than those who do not.*

Although Polus will not admit *S1*, he is prepared to make a concession:

A. *Doing wrong is more shameful than suffering it.*

Yet he maintains that the shamefulness of doing wrong does not make it bad.

By 'bad' Polus clearly means 'bad for the agent'.[21] As for 'shameful', Polus is offering here the conventional view that wrongdoing is shameful, and he has no need to specify who feels the shame or why it is described as shameful. During the course of the argument, however, Socrates will force him to specify and hence to destroy his own position.

B. *We call things fine* (kalon) *according as they confer pleasure or benefit or both.*

C. *Thus we define the fine in terms of pleasure or good.*[22]

D. *We define the shameful in terms of pain or harm.*

E. *Therefore, of two fine things, that one is finer which exceeds the other in pleasure or benefit or both. Similarly, of two shameful things, that one is more shameful which exceeds the other in pain or harm or both.*

The principle established here looms large for the remainder of the dialogue.

21. We should beware throughout of Plato's tendency to present *agathon* or *kakon* without qualification or explanation of who is benefited or harmed—the agent or the patient. But see Appendix I.

22. There is a shift here from "benefit" to "good"; this is reasonable as long as Plato sticks to the prudential usage of "good." Cf. Dodds, *Plato: Gorgias* (Oxford: Clarendon, 1959), pp. 249–51.

F. Therefore, if A, *doing wrong must exceed suffering wrong in pain or in harm or in both* (475b).

G. But there is no pain involved in doing wrong.

H. Therefore doing wrong cannot exceed in pain or in both criteria.

I. Therefore, it must be more shameful in respect of its harmfulness.

J. Therefore S1.[23]

But if doing wrong is worse than suffering it, then wrongdoing cannot be in our interests. The pursuit of vice must therefore be undertaken through ignorance, since it only *seems* good to us, rather than being what we really want.[24] All wrongdoing is therefore involuntary; no one does wrong willingly.[25]

The paradox reappears in the discussion of vice at *Timaeus* 86b ff.[26] Here Socrates argues that, although we commonly suppose the bad man to be so voluntarily, in fact no one is voluntarily evil. Evil is a matter of physical weakness, or disease, compounded by a bad upbringing.[27] But disease, weakness, and upbringing are all beyond our control and, being undesirable, are in fact not desired.[28] Therefore, no one is evil, or sick, willingly. It follows, Socrates then claims, that the blame which is commonly apportioned to the evil man is inappropriate. To recapitulate then (87b), through disease, compounded by a bad political[29] and edu-

23. On the soundness or otherwise of this argument, see Appendix I, "The Refutation of Polus."

24. Cf. above, a, for these distinctions.

25. This conclusion is explicitly drawn in the confrontation with Callicles, 509e5–7. The reference to the discussion of choice, at 466 ff., I take it, is made explicit by the use of *boulomenos* at 509e6, and the claim that this has already been agreed. For the intervening arguments with Callicles, cf. Ch. 10.a and Ch. 11.a.

26. If the *Timaeus* is late, the reappearance of the paradox here fits well with its discussion in the *Laws*. However, there is then a long middle period where the absence of paradox needs explaining. My answer to this would be that the middle period accounts for the imprudence of vice by heavy dependence on a complex moral psychology, rather than on paradox, and by the use of the analogy with health (cf. c below). This analogy, however, if pushed too far, results in the *Timaeus* version of "vice is disease"; cf. Ch. 10.c. If, however, the *Timaeus* were dated early, to explain this connection with the Socratic dialogues, then the appearance of the paradox in splendid isolation in the *Laws* again needs explaining.

I incline to the view that a decadent body/soul analogy is shored up by paradox and the superficial appearance of strong intellectualism in Plato's late work—in the *Timaeus* and the *Laws*. I do so with hesitation, however, since the dating of the *Timaeus* before the *Parmenides* would seem to solve many of the difficulties of interpreting the latter work. Cf. Owen, "The Place of the *Timaeus* in Plato's Dialogues," in R.E. Allen, ed., *Studies in Plato's Metaphysics* (London: Routledge, Kegan Paul, 1965).

27. For an interpretation of the passage, cf. Ch. 10.c.

28. This echoes the *Gorgias'* account of choice.

29. The intellectualist slant is prominent here; note the reference to "words spoken in public," 87b1.

cational background, men become wicked most unwillingly. So we should attribute the cause[30] of their wickedness to their parents, if to anyone, and to those who bring them up,[31] who should encourage their charges to avoid evil and to seek what is good.

This passage urges exculpation on two grounds. The first is that sickness is always involuntarily incurred, without exception. A man does not deliberately court disease; rather, his constitution and his bad upbringing render him prone to infection.[32] Once he is infected, his cure is not his own responsibility but is in the charge of others.[33] He cannot, therefore, be accused of dereliction in the way he becomes diseased nor in the way he behaves thereafter. The second claim for the exculpation of the criminal looks Socratic, for it relies upon the notion that if a thing is undesirable, we do not (really) desire it. So if something turns out to be against our interests, even if we have aimed for it, our aim was mistaken and hence not genuine or deliberate.

Consequently, the wicked man is involuntarily so on two counts. First, wickedness is against his interests and is therefore not the genuine object of his desire. Second, the process whereby he becomes wicked is one wherein upbringing and education fail to rectify congenital weakness. Here both the cause and the remedy are outside the individual's control. Therefore, again, he is involuntarily wicked.

The *Laws* reiterates the Socratic account of choice. Mankind's common objective is that everything should happen according to the dictates of our souls, and that whatever we desire (*boulēsis*, 687c9) should come about. But if ignorance infects our desire, we may end up with the opposite of what we intended. Our ambition, therefore, should be not that everything should happen as we desire it (for this leads to failure when

30. *Aitiateon* is tricky. It could be translated "We must blame." However, blame is excluded altogether by the foregoing analysis. For even if the parents and upbringers are wicked to neglect their charges, this must be the product of their own vice, which is equally a matter of bad upbringing, etc., and thus also involuntary. But to translate "We should hold responsible" will confuse the legal issue, since these bad men, however involuntary, are still thought to be liable to punishment—for paternalistic reasons. Plato is surely, here, trying to establish *why* these bad men are bad, and the parents and upbringers are introduced by way of a 'because'. Cf. Vlastos, "Reasons and Causes in the *Phaedo*," in *Platonic Studies* (Princeton: Princeton U.P., 1973) and Feinberg, "Action and Responsibility." Cf. Ch. 7, n. 74.

31. Contrast Aristotle's approach: "It is odd that Aristotle never (to my knowledge) asks himself why the discipline of parents and teachers is not to be taken as an external cause of a man's dispositions" (D.J. Furley, "Aristotle on the Voluntary," in J. Barnes *et al.*, *Articles on Aristotle*, Vol. 2 [London: Duckworth, 1977], p. 53).

32. Plato seems not to envisage a man becoming diseased late in life.

33. Both in the public and the private sphere. Contrast the attitude of the *Gorgias* here, discussed in Ch. 11.a.

we are ignorant) but much rather that our desire should follow our reason (687e7).[34]

This idea, that informed choosing meets with success whereas failure
is a necessary consequence of ignorance, echoes the original Socratic
position. So, too, does the distinction between what we really desire, and
may achieve by following the dictates of reason, and what we only think
we desire. This notion is picked up in the renewed discussion of the
Socratic paradox in Book 5 (731c), where the Stranger explains that no
one willingly seeks the greatest evils. By implication, therefore, if we
pursue what is in fact damaging, then we do not really want it. Hence
our dishonourable treatment of our souls (by practising wrongdoing) is
involuntary. Our excessive self-love (731e) blinds us to the true nature
of ourselves, so that we make bad judgements about what is just, good
and noble. A man in this condition is convinced of his own knowledge-
ability and fails to leave to others what he himself is incompetent to do.
In this way he is bound to fail.

In Book 9 the Stranger introduces his theoretical account of punishment with a reconsideration of the legal implications of the Socratic paradox, "No one does wrong willingly." He comes up with a new distinction between voluntary and involuntary acts in the Socratic sense, and
acts committed deliberately or by accident (voluntary or involuntary in
the legal sense).[35] Throughout he retains the original proposal that a
man does not willingly seek the effects of injustice. In order to determine the value of a man's actions, therefore, we must look to his disposition, which will tell us of his intent (862b3).[36]

The effect of the Socratic paradox is to exculpate the criminal. For a
man's blameworthiness is to be judged by his intentions, and his intentions are in turn determined by his true objectives, according to Plato
(*Grg.* 466 ff., *Laws* 731 ff., 863 ff.).[37] But everyone's true objectives are
uniformly for goods, and goods include virtue,[38] whereas wrongdoing
is unequivocally an evil. Anyone who apparently pursues evil by acting
wrongly has his true desires perverted by some factor beyond his con-

34. T.J. Saunders, *Notes on the Laws of Plato, B.I.C.S.* Supplement 28 (1972):14, seems
to make unnecessarily heavy weather of the translation of this passage. I follow Burnet's
text.

35. Cf. Ch. 11.d.

36. Cf. below, d.

37. But cf. the copious modern literature on this topic, including Anscombe, *Intention*;
D. Davidson, "Actions, Reasons and Causes," in A.R. White, ed., *The Philosophy of Action*
(Oxford: O.U.P., 1968); Hart, "The Ascription of Responsibility and Rights"; Feinberg,
"Action and Responsibility," etc.

38. A stronger thesis, cf. c. below, is the *the good is virtue*; virtue is identical with happiness; all the virtuous, and only they, are happy.

trol[39] and should not be blamed (*Tim.* 87). On the contrary, he should be the object of pity (*Laws* 731).

At the same time, however, the criminal continues to be held responsible for his misfortune. For, in the first place, he is still spoken of as "the bad man" (e.g., *Tim.* 86e2) or "the unjust man" (*Grg.* 509e6). In the second place, although the causes of his actions are beyond his control, the actions themselves still belong to the criminal (*Grg.* 467, they seem good to him), for they stem from his settled disposition towards wrongdoing, whatever that may be.[40] As such, his criminal actions are distinguished from those accidents for which he is not responsible, accidents which "happen to him" (*Laws* 860d).

The distinction of the *Laws* between voluntary and involuntary on the one hand, and deliberate and accidental on the other, marches with the schema I suggest[41] to differentiate who is responsible from who is culpable. At the highest level, the man who acts voluntarily in the Socratic sense is responsible for what he does, and, were he not virtuous, he would also be culpable. Since he is virtuous, he is conversely laudable.

The intermediate class of agent is the deliberate wrongdoer who acts, in Socratic terms, involuntarily. Insofar as his action is deliberate and his, he is responsible; insofar as he acts involuntarily, he is not subject to blame. He is responsible from a legal point of view, but culpability is excluded by Socratism.

At the lowest level comes the man who is involved in accidents: his action is both accidental and involuntary (on my interpretation of the *Laws* analysis), and thus he is neither responsible for it (hence liable to treatment for something that expresses his fixed disposition) nor culpable.

But if the criminal is the object of compassion, he is also, then, the target for benevolent action. If pity issues in action, it issues in benevolent action. Such action, if it does take place, would surely aim to remove the criminal's misfortune at source, if only for reasons of economy. His criminal disposition,[42] therefore, should be removed, and he reformed in order that he will no longer make mistakes in his objectives. This treatment, however, must take into account the fact that he does act involuntarily; thus some attempts to remove his disposition—such as

39. This depends on Plato's moral psychology, but it seems, on the whole, that disorder, ignorance and disease are afflictions not deliberately courted. After all, if these afflictions pervert true desires, they, in turn, cannot truly be desired.

40. Cf. Ch. 10.a,b,c.

41. Cf. above, a.

42. Cf. below, d. This expression is deliberately ambiguous here between 'the habit of committing crimes' and 'the psychological state that causes a man to commit crimes'.

deterrent punishments—will turn out to be ineffective, since he cannot help what he does. The Socratic paradox, therefore, will both determine and restrict the benevolent action that should be taken, in his own interests, upon the individual criminal.

c. VIRTUE IS HAPPINESS

The Socratic analysis of the nature of choice suggests that vice has evil consequences, whereas virtue produces good. This, were it the only account of the relation between the moral and the prudential good, would result in a consequential approach to the prevention of wrongdoing. The Socratic account, however, is neither the only nor indeed the most powerful prudential argument that Plato has to offer. He frequently suggests that the real recommendation of virtue lies not in its consequences but in its intrinsic relation to happiness. That thesis will affect his theory of punishment.

In the *Gorgias*, Callicles proffers a naturalist thesis (483b)[43]: that suffering wrong is more shameful than doing it.[44] For natural law dictates that the stronger should use force and rule over the weak.[45] Consequently the stronger should have the greatest share of any distribution. But Socrates attacks this consequential analysis by suggesting that the stronger—those who have true control and power—practise self-restraint; strength and wisdom produce temperance and virtue. It is not, therefore, by his rewards that you will know the powerful man, but by his virtuous disposition. The powerful man is indeed happy, but his happiness consists in his virtue, not in his taking advantage of the distribution of goods. The intemperate man, however, suffers the permanent and intrinsic misfortune of a leaky soul, whose appetites are insatiable (493a ff.).

The *Republic*, like the *Gorgias*, is explicitly directed at demonstrating that virtue is in our interests. Thrasymachus puts forward the immoralist position that injustice, given free rein, is in the interests of its perpetrator (344c). This line is taken up by Glaucon and Adeimantus in Book 2, who ask Socrates to show that, on the contrary, virtue, or justice, is in fact in our interests (367e). To elucidate, Glaucon offers a classification of goods (357b ff.): we distinguish between things which are good in themselves (happiness and unadulterated pleasure), things which are good in themselves and in their consequences (intelligence, health), and things which are good only in their consequences (medicine, training).

43. Cf. Ch. 8.b.
44. Admitting the converse, it will be remembered, was Polus' downfall.
45. Cf. Ostwald, "Plato on Law and Nature," in H. North, ed., *Interpretations of Plato*, Mnemosyne Supplement (1977):41–63.

Socrates undertakes to show that justice is one of the higher goods, desirable both for itself and for its consequences.

To this end, he concentrates on the discussion of justice as an intrinsic good. The precise significance of this claim is hard to determine,[46] since arguments which are clearly intended to show the intrinsic value of justice often have recourse to a consequential analysis. It is clear, however, that Plato wants to make two claims: living justly is the same as living happily,[47] irrespective of the trappings of worldly reputation; whereas living wickedly is wretched, despite the apparent benefits that accure to the supremely wicked man. Thus it is the inherent happiness of the just life that the main body of the *Republic* undertakes to show.

A mainstay of Plato's non-consequential argument for the prudence of virtue is the analogy that he draws between body and soul (cf., e.g., *Grg.* 464a ff.). If this analogy holds good,[48] then, just as there is a health of the body, so there will be a health of the soul.[49] Health in the body is the kind of thing we desire in itself and without further reflection or dispute (*Rep.* 357). If it can be shown that virtue is the health of the soul, the same desirability will attach itself to virtue. Considered not merely for its consequences but intrinsically, it is a good for its possessor.[50] Vice, conversely, will be an evil. As Socrates suggests (*Grg.* 477b ff.)[51] it is the greatest evil that can afflict a man.

The prudential argument of the *Republic* relies upon a new and complex moral psychology.[52] Thus in Book 4, Socrates claims that justice exists in the soul when reason, with the help of the spirited element, is

46. Cf. Mabbott, "Is Plato's *Republic* Utilitarian?" in Vlastos, ed., *Plato: II* (London: Macmillan, 1971); C. Kirwan, "Glaucon's Challenge," *Phronesis* (1965):162–173; and R.C. Cross and A.D. Woozley, *Plato's Republic: A Philosophical Commentary* (London: Macmillan, 1964), pp. 65–68.

47. Problem here: are justice and happiness intensionally or only extensionally equivalent?

48. There are problems, of course, with arguments from analogy. It is not, for example, persuasive to draw an analogy between X and Y and then, on this basis, to assert that X and Y are alike in every respect. Cf. Santas, *Socrates*, pp. 138 ff. and pp. 286 ff.

49. A.J.P. Kenny, "Mental Health in Plato's *Republic*," *Proc. Brit. Acad.* (1969):229–253, considers this to be metaphor only; but for the prudential argument to be effective, Plato may need a stronger and more literal claim. However, cf. below and Ch. 10.c for the effect of a literal "vice is disease" thesis; cf. also Flew, "Crime or Disease," *B.J.S.* (1954):46–62.

50. The analogy with health may perhaps illuminate the notion of an *intrinsic* good. Health is something that we can positively enjoy without reflecting on the rewards—long life, efficient faculties, ease in appreciating pleasures—that it may bring. This, at least, is what Plato seems to suppose, although on further consideration it is difficult to show how much of our enjoyment of good health is strictly non-consequential and not, for example, the anticipation of heightened pleasures.

51. Cf. Appendix I for the argument here.

52. Foreshadowed in the *Grg.* 504a ff. where Socrates initiates the idea of the well-ordered soul.

in control of appetite.[53] Thereafter, he first draws the analogy with health and then argues that virtue is order in the soul. In the first case, virtue is desirable simply because health is desirable, both in itself and in its consequences (cf. 444c ff.). In the second case, Socrates may draw on the notion, admitted even by Thrasymachus (351b ff.), that the well-ordered state benefits its citizens. Because the state is analogous to the soul, the well-ordered soul benefits itself[54] (cf. the series of arguments from 577).

These two arguments are clearly intended to mesh together. As health is the establishment of proper control in the body, so justice is the natural organisation of the parts of the soul to rule and be ruled. Virtue, therefore, is a kind of health, excellence, and good order of the soul, whereas vice is sickness, ugliness, and weakness. It follows, of course, that vice is an undesirable state of soul.

This description of virtue and vice is presented as a metaphor to sum up the preceding argument (441c ff.) in which Plato established the principle of order in the soul. There is no suggestion that we should regard vice literally as sickness. Consequently, Plato is committed neither to the strongest thesis that vice is caused by physical disorders, nor to the more moderate claim that there is a species of disease which exclusively affects the mind.[55] The first of these proposals requires impossible degrees of scientific demonstration; for the second, if vice is a species of disease, we require further information as to its pathology.[56] As a description, therefore, it deceptively tells us very little.

However, if disease is but a metaphor for vice, we may hope for some illumination. The function of the analogy in the argument is to exploit our attitude towards sickness, which we regard as against our interests. Equally, Plato argues, we should avoid having a vicious disposition. But if the analogue holds good, we may suppose that other attitudes we have towards the sick may be carried over into our approach to the wicked. In particular, the question of the culpability of patient and of offender deserves consideration.

The original Socratic position, that vice is ignorance, supposed that the agent had misguided impulses towards what he thought to be in his interests; for his failure we can but pity his intellectual deficiency. It is possible, however, to imagine a situation where his ignorance is wilful

53. The tripartite psychology is discussed in detail in Ch. 10.b.

54. There are obviously problems of symmetry here. Cf. Williams, "The Analogy of City and Soul in Plato's *Republic*," in E.N. Lee et al., *Exegesis and Argument: Studies Presented to Vlastos* (Assen: Van Gorcum, 1973).

55. But cf. Ch. 10.c.

56. This is J. Gosling's complaint (*Plato* [London: Routledge, Kegan Paul, 1973], p.84).

and therefore, even if his actions prove to be against his interests, he is culpable. The new doctrine, that virtue is psychic order, raises this question of culpability with even greater urgency, since we may readily conceive of a man deliberately promoting disorder (although his clumsy counterpart does not).

The idea of virtue as order in the organism, however, is, in Plato's eyes, very close to the idea of virtue as health. It is not a matter of the disposition of one's possessions, but of the care of one's person, less obviously a matter for deliberate failure. Now, Gosling believes that the idea of vice as disease does not carry exculpation with it. For despite Plato's

determination to treat wrongdoing as a form of illness, for which the patient might be pitied and treated, but hardly held responsible, . . . while it would always be sensible to try to cure the illness and for the long term constructive, the appeal to illness need only win sympathy, not exculpation.[57]

Gosling relies on a view of Plato's position whereby the vicious behaviour is but the symptom of the disease; therefore it may be suppressed. For example, a man whose disease makes him prone to unpunctuality may be late for an appointment. We may well understand this yet still blame him for failing to control his symptoms. However, for two reasons this seems to be a faulty view of Plato's analogy.

The first is that Plato himself does not specify the disease, as Gosling's particularised argument requires: Plato does not exclude pathological unpunctuality *or* cancer. On the contrary, he is interested only in our general attitudes to disease—that it is to be avoided, and, we may infer, that it is something we do not actively court any more than we do any other misfortune. On this analogy, therefore, even more than on the original Socratic position over the ignorance of the criminal, we should urge exculpation.

The second reason is that Gosling fails to see that Plato views the vice as the disease itself, not as the symptom. Thus, if unpunctuality is our example, it must not be treated as the symptom, which could be suppressed or otherwise, but as the disease itself, which is either present or absent, despite us. Alternatively, if we insist that unpunctuality is but the symptom of the disease, Plato might complain that the symptoms were not repressed. But he would still argue that the vice itself, that is, the disposition which causes the unpunctuality, is not subject to blame.

Two riders should be added. First, there are circumstances under which a man may be said to court infection, for example, when he deliberately runs the risk of contracting a disease in his pursuit of some other

57. *Ibid.*, p. 83.

object. Under these conditions we may still blame him. Second, even if the criminal is not to be blamed for his original condition, he may well be in a position to seek a cure; failure to do so may equally result in his being blamed. What is more, his avoidance of a cure could result in his disease becoming chronic and incurable; likewise, Plato suggests, the criminal who foolishly avoids submitting to the due process of the law becomes incurably vicious and ultimately subject to execution.

This account of virtue and vice, therefore, will lead to a theory of punishment wherein the criminal is not subject to blame. His crimes should not, however, be ignored as if they were a series of accidents that have happened to him. On the contrary, the thesis that vice is a disorder of the soul provides an account of why the criminal commits crimes: because he has a criminal/disordered disposition. His crimes, therefore, are his, not accidents that happen to him, since they arise from his disposition, and to this extent he is responsible for them. His responsibility then renders him liable not to blame but to whatever action is thought proper to be taken against the disordered psyche.

The prudential argument that Plato offers, moreover, will affect the type of action that will be suitable in this case. For the notion that vice, like disease, is intrinsically undesirable will lead Plato to think of criminals as we think of sick men. I have argued that the Socratic paradox, "No one does wrong willingly," will prompt benevolence towards the unfortunate wrongdoer, for we pity him for his mistakes. How much more do we pity the sick and encourage them to seek the help that medical science can offer?

Our attitude towards the sick, however, undergoes a subtle change from the straightforward benevolence inspired by the idea that the criminal is mistaken. For it might be argued that the pigheaded maker of mistakes should be allowed to continue in his error if he insists, and that our benevolence is strictly limited by the consent of its object. With a medical analogy, however, the situation is more complex. We may allow that the sick man's refusal to be cured, when his treatment would violate some religious principle that he holds, should override the benevolence of his doctor. However, when the sick man withholds his consent to a lifesaving operation simply because he dislikes his doctor's face, then we might feel justified in insisting that surgery proceed.[58] The decision about the limits of benevolence is not an easy one, and if the benefactor is seen in the role of doctor, then the reasons for withholding consent may need to be pretty strong to restrain the medical profession's good intentions.

58. Cf. Glover, *Causing Death and Saving Lives*, p. 75, on the heroin addict.

The consequence, therefore, of explaining the disadvantage of crime in medical terms is that the benevolence that Plato has already encouraged us to feel towards the criminal will slip over into paternalism. And paternalism—inasmuch as it cares less for the choice of the beneficiary and gives priority to the dictum "It's for your own good"—is suspect.

I have suggested that the burden of Plato's prudential argument is non-consequential; that is, it appeals to the intrinsic disadvantage of vice, rather than to the unpleasant consequences that it provokes. The argument is non-consequential, but still it is teleological, in the sense that it appeals to the interests of the agent, to the good, rather than to the right. In such a context, the penal expedients that might be advocated should be teleological too, for Plato, by using such an approach, has left no independent notion of the right in which a deontological theory of punishment might find anchorage.

If this is so, what kind of teleological theory might we expect? For two reasons, I suggest, a humanitarian theory is a more natural consequence of Plato's ethics than a utilitarian one. First, the general tone of Plato's ethical arguments is individualist: he aims to demonstrate—to Glaucon, to Adeimantus, and to me—why wrongdoing is against our interests. His approach, therefore, is individualist and as such tends away from the universalist considerations of utility. Second, and more specifically, the Socratic paradoxes exculpated the individual criminal and hence engendered in Plato an attitude of compassion towards him. This, I have argued, would lead him to feel benevolence towards the criminal and thus to advocate a humanitarian penology.

The non-consequential attitude will also affect the treatment thought proper for the criminal. For the imprudence of vice, if the non-consequential argument holds, will need no further demonstration such as that provided by deterrent penal measures, and indeed, deterrent punishments, imposed on top of the intrinsic disadvantage of vice, will only aggravate the misfortune of the criminal. Yet we already pity him for his disposition; there can be no justification, on benevolent grounds, for unwarrantably increasing the unhappiness he suffers. The justification would derive from a consequential account of the disadvantage of vice. But since a non-consequential account is, apparently, available, then deterrent measures will be superfluous and, as such, unjustifiable.

Benevolence combined with non-consequentialism, therefore, will lead Plato towards a theory of punishment which will benefit the individual criminal by treating his disposition, and away from the invocation of penal measures to deter the criminal from crimes. The function of punishment, paternalist or otherwise, will be to offer a positive means to virtue, rather than a sanction against vice.

d. DISPOSITION AND BEHAVIOUR, AND THE THEORY OF JUSTICE

Non-consequentialism, it seems, does more than recommend the intrinsic advantage of virtue; by concentrating on the dispositions of the
virtuous and the vicious man,[59] it tends to devalue the importance of
their actions. Although originally we may have been interested in the
criminal's tendency simply because it caused crimes—or, more strongly
still, we may have thought of the criminal as having a tendency only
inasmuch as he commits crimes—we now find ourselves thinking of the
disposition as the important thing and the crimes, like the symptoms of
a disease, as mere manifestations of the basic evil. Being, therefore,
takes precedence over doing, and the prudential argument will declare
not that "crime does not pay," but that "criminality does not pay."

Of course the body/soul analogy immediately suggests that we should
be interested in the disposition rather than the behaviour, in health
rather than in healthy actions. But the most striking example of the
non-consequential approach to criminality occurs in the *Republic*, where
Plato discusses justice—as we might think, a behavioural virtue *par excellence*—in dispositional terms, to the extent that he leaves it unclear what
relation he supposes to exist between justice in the soul and just actions
manifested by the just man. This theory of justice has far-reaching implications, as the following chapters demonstrate.

First (441c), justice is explained as the proper order of the three parts
of the soul, whereby the appetitive and spirited (thumoeidic) parts are
subject to the rule of reason.[60] The behaviour of the parts may thereafter be likened to the internal organisation of a just state: each mem-
ber/part will have and do his own.[61] But this state, apparently, has no

---

59. If a man commits crimes, we may regard him as having a *tendency* to commit crimes;
this tendency will simply be an account of the probability of his doing certain actions. By
disposition, however, I mean some further attribute of a person which, although it also
suggests a tendency to commit crimes, describes some morally wrong state of mind, or
character, or soul, which is in turn the cause of wrongdoing. Now it might be thought to
follow from this distinction that there is no such thing as a disposition separate from a
tendency. Plato, however, is clearly interested in states of soul and in their intrinsic wrongness apart from the wrong actions in which they issue. Cf. M.F. Burnyeat, "Virtues in
Action," in Vlastos, *The Philosophy of Socrates*, despite whom I am preserving the term 'disposition'.

60. The argument for the division of the soul will be discussed in Ch. 10.b.

61. Cf. Vlastos, "Justice and Happiness in the *Republic*," in *Plato: II*. The arguments of
Book IV concentrate on 'doing one's own' and, for this reason, it has been thought (cf. n.
65 below) that Plato is not talking about Glaucon's kind of justice ('having one's own') at all.
Two points may be made against this. First, the tradition supposes that justice (the
virtue) is a matter of 'doing *and* having one's own'. Cf. Ch. 7. Second, the first book of the
Republic (which is, as the work stands, connected to the rest, albeit—and, I suspect, delib-

foreign policy;[62] likewise, Plato tells us little about the behaviour of the just man. The analogy suggests that members of the well-ordered state will be happy because justice prevails and they have and maintain what they deserve.[63] Equally, the just soul will be, by its very nature, happy; the account is non-consequential.

The argument to explain justice in the individual (441d ff.), however, supposes that the just disposition will lead to just behaviour:

1. *We call a man just in exactly the same way as we call the state just.*[64]
2. *The state* [it was agreed from 433a] *is just when each class does its own.*
3. *Therefore each man will be just when each part of him does its own.*
4. *And he will do his own.*

The move from *3* to *4* is notorious.[65] Both Sachs and Vlastos[66] argue

---

erately—Socratic in tone) focuses upon the distributive notions of *having* one's own (cf. e.g., 335c7; 343d3) as well as on the just man's activity. 'Having' is associated with 'doing' (by equivocation on Socrates' part) from 349b6 ff.

62. Contrast the discussion in Book I, 351c ff., of the gang of thieves, effective only in its nefarious activities when it is internally just.

63. Cf. the earlier anxiety that manifest unfairness should not prevail, Ch. 7.c.

64. This is the *univocity thesis*, described by Vlastos, "Justice and Happiness," p. 128 as a "fundamental Platonic principle." It is supported by the theory that claims that for each instance of a quality there exists a corresponding and unique form which accounts for the quality; univocity is guaranteed from the uniqueness of the form. Cf. C. Strang, "Plato and the Third Man," in Vlastos, ed., *Plato: I*; Kahn, "The Meaning of 'Justice' and the Theory of Forms," *J. Ph.* (1972):567–579. Univocity is also recommended by the principle of non-contradiction (436b; cf. Ch. 10, n. 10), since ambiguity will give rise to apparent contradictions. The principle of non-contradiction, of course, is well founded in the philosophical tradition. It is brought out, for example, in Heracleitus' paradoxes (cf. e.g., DK22B60), and it is a premise in Parmenides' argument (cf. DK28B6, 8–9).

A problem attached to univocity, however, is how well it survives the criticism of the theory of forms at *Parm.* 130 ff. Within that dialogue it is maintained; cf. 147d5. Later, however, the principle is explicitly dropped, cf. *Sophist* 259c7 ff.

65. Apart from the objection discussed in the text, there are, it seems, two major criticisms levelled at Plato's logic, which may be mentioned briefly here.

a. D. Sachs ("A Fallacy in Plato's Republic," in Vlastos, ed., *Plato: II*, inadequately countered by R. Demos, "A Fallacy in Plato's Republic?", *Plato:II*) complains that there is a hiatus between conventional or vulgar notions of justice and Plato's own, to the extent that Plato's redefined account of justice fails to correspond to the original question, "What is justice?" This objection may be rebutted by the observation that Plato is entitled, by the tradition in which he lives, to claim that justice consists in 'doing and having one's own'. Cf. n. 61 above. Platonic justice, therefore, is the same thing as conventional justice, at least within the formal structure of the argument.

b. Vlastos, "Justice and Happiness," suggests that there is a general slipperiness about the use of "just" in that Plato interchanges two senses of the word without warrant (cf. Ch. 3.b for a discussion of the ambiguity of "just"). To this, as Vlastos himself observes (p. 128), Plato would counter either that "just" is univocal, and therefore there can be no shifts from one sense to another, or that there is an essential relation between "just" in the state and "just" in the individual (between these two senses the shift comes), inasmuch as the state is just because its members are just; therefore the senses are the same. But, as Wil-

that, although Plato defines justice as psychic harmony (as the argument above aims to establish at 3) and refers it to our internal disposition, he fails to demonstrate either that the man who has psychic harmony will in fact behave justly towards others (i.e., the connection between 3 and 4) or that just behaviour will contribute to our having psychic harmony. Plato must explain, therefore, on the one hand how the practice of vulgar justice leads to psychic harmony and on the other how psychic harmony leads to the practice of vulgar justice.

Plato himself argues against the second arm of the criticism on the basis of the medical analogy. For, he claims at 444c, as healthy activities promote health, so just activities promote justice in the soul. If we were to question further the connection between just activities (vulgar justice) and psychic harmony (Platonic justice), he could reply that justice is univocal (as was asserted at 441d5) and therefore there can be no hiatus; he could respond further that Platonic justice is founded upon the conventional notion of "having and doing one's own." The implication of this is that virtue is at least in part derived from the practice of virtuous activity.[67]

To the first arm of the objection—that having psychic harmony does not entail behaving justly—Plato himself presents a weak answer, by assessing examples of the various types of virtuous and vicious character (442e ff.) and of the kind of behaviour we expect from each. To supplement this, both Vlastos and Kraut argue that when a man has psychic harmony, his reason will be in control, and he will therefore necessarily act justly. The reason for this, we may assume, is that the rational man will know that virtue is in his interests[68] and will also recognise which course of action is virtuous. Therefore he will follow the right course

---

liams, "Analogy of City and Soul," points out, the latter principle conflicts with a straightforward state/soul analogy and generates a regress.

66. "Justice and Happiness"; cf. also Burnyeat, "Virtues in Action"; R. Kraut, "Reason and Justice in Plato's *Republic*," in Lee *et al.*, *Exegesis and Argument*; and, most recently, Irwin, *Plato's Moral Theory*, pp. 205 ff.

67. The notion that virtuous behaviour leads to the having of a virtuous disposition will be influential in the theory of punishment.

68. As the work as a whole is designed to show. But here, of course, the danger is that "virtue" may mean either a virtuous disposition or virtuous behaviour. It still remains to be proven that although the disposition be accepted as prudent, the behaviour also is in our interests. Kraut suggests that virtuous behaviour, inasmuch as it promotes the rule of reason, is the goal of the rational part, and therefore the reasonable man will pursue just actions.

The problem in all these interpretations (which is avoided by Irwin's more compelling argument) is that the connection between just souls and just actions appears to be merely contingent, because just acts happen to promote just activity. There is no account, for example, to be given on this interpretation for the rational man's choosing supererogatory just acts.

and act justly. Irwin offers a more positive suggestion:[69] that the just man will, like the lover of the *Symposium*, love and long to promote justice, both in others and in his own actions.[70] He will therefore actively pursue justice not only in his own disposition but also in his behaviour.[71]

Each of these attempted rebuttals of Sachs' objection carries weight. However, the fact that the rebuttals need to be made at all is significant. For Plato, in his discussion of justice, is apparently not interested primarily in the behaviour of the just man—which he seems to take for granted as following from the disposition, and takes for granted in a way that suggests that this is a secondary concern—but in the state of soul which we may designate just, and which is psychic harmony. The argumentation of Book IV concerns the nature, and the prudence, of justice. Both are argued for from the analogy with the state; both, as Plato's own arguments and the anxieties of the commentators make clear, are a matter of the internal disposition of the just man, however it is manifested in his actions (this will be a matter of opportunity as well as logic).

A similar emphasis upon the disposition rather than the behaviour of the virtuous or the vicious man is to be detected in other contexts. In the *Protagoras*, for example, where the argument is designed to demonstrate an extreme intellectualist thesis,[72] the analysis of the virtues is largely dispositional. Cowardice, for example, is seen not as the consequence of ignorance (i.e., ignorance manifested in action) but as the same thing as ignorance (e.g., 360d5).[73] Similarly, a vexed passage of the *Gorgias* (460b ff.)[74] analyses the dispositional aspect of the knowledge that is virtue (analogous to the technical qualification, rather than the

69. *Plato's Moral Theory*, pp. 205 ff. Cf. R. Kraut, "Egoism, Love and Political Office in Plato," *Ph. Rev.* (1973):330–344.

70. This will be important when we come to consider the benevolent—or paternalistic—activities of the just legislator. Cf. Ch. 12.d.

71. Irwin's interpretation is attractive. It makes the assumption (recommended, of course, by the univocity thesis) that just acts are just in the same way that the just man's soul is just—in other words, that the justice he loves will indeed be embodied in vulgarly just actions. However, the great disadvantage of Irwin's approach is that although the terminology of the ascent of love may be found elsewhere in the *Rep.* (e.g. at 490a, 496a), it is missing from the vital passage in Book IV. This suggests—in favour of the point I am making here—that although Plato could assemble a defence against Sachs' objection, in the initial discussion of justice he is interested in the disposition, not the behaviour.

72. Cf. Ch. 10.a.

73. Cf. T. Penner, "The Unity of Virtue," *Ph. R.* (1973):35–68: cowardice and ignorance are "states of soul". Socrates' approach to the explanations of virtuous or vicious behaviour is devalued by Vlastos' Pauline account ("The Unity of the Virtues in the *Protagoras*," in *Platonic Studies* [Princeton: Princeton U.P., 1973]), where "cowardice" is thought to stand in for the class of cowards.

74. Discussed in Ch. 10.a.

activity, of the carpenter, the doctor, the musician) before adding the (logically questionable) rider that this disposition will result in virtuous behaviour (460b8). The *Laws* makes explicit the distinction between the damage done by the criminal—or by the clumsy man—and the vicious disposition from which he suffers (863e6 ff.).[75]

All of these passages suggest, therefore, that Plato's first concern is to explain and to recommend the state of the soul that is called virtue, and to argue the intrinsic imprudence of possessing a vicious disposition. As I have argued, the prudential aspect of the argument will suggest that benevolent action towards the criminal should aim to remove the disposition. The view that the disposition may be considered apart from its criminal manifestations as the primary disadvantage reinforces the non-consequential approach. This will remove any justification that might be thought possible for deterrent penal action. Humanitarian motives will suggest that the criminal should be reformed, not that he should be made to suffer further at the hands of utilitarian or deterrent (albeit to deter himself) legislation.

Now, however, the view that criminality does not pay will place further restrictions upon the operation of a penal system. For if it is the disposition that matters, then merely repressing its symptoms will not be a benevolent but rather a malevolent action (inasmuch—as Socrates argues in the *Gorgias*—as this unfortunate criminal will escape detection and reform). So repression will be both ineffective and unjustifiable. Consequently, the humanitarian, already activated by the notion that criminality is involuntary, will need to employ means to reform that genuinely improve the disposition of the subject.

e. MORAL THEORY: ITS EFFECTS

In this chapter I have argued that Plato's moral theory will lead him to adopt certain attitudes towards the criminal or the vicious man. He thinks of the criminal as the possessor of a vicious disposition, rather than as the agent of crimes, and he considers him to be disadvantaged thereby. The criminal is what he is and does what he does against his best interests and therefore against his true desires. Thus he is criminal involuntarily. Accordingly, although he should still be held responsible for both his disposition and his behaviour since they are both *his*, he should not be blamed, but rather pitied, for them.

What then should be done about the criminal? Plato clearly feels benevolence towards him, hence the pity. This benevolence—or paternalism—will suggest that the criminal be saved from himself and that the

75. See Appendix II for a detailed discussion of this passage.

judiciary should attempt to improve his disposition. At the same time, the intrinsic good fortune enjoyed by the non-criminal members of the community will militate against Plato's adoption of a utilitarian ethic. Rather, his benevolence will be concentrated upon the individual who excites his pity, just as his arguments focus upon the individual who threatens to do wrong. Thus his penology should be humanitarian.

CHAPTER
10

PLATO'S
MORAL PSYCHOLOGY

For a penologist to have humanitarian purposes is not enough. He needs to know not merely why he should reform the criminal but also how this may be done. To that end, he must give a comprehensive account of moral psychology. And Plato does.

a. THE IGNORANT SOUL

Plato tells us, then, that vice is a state of soul. But what state of soul is it? Several answers to this moral psychological question may be discerned in Plato's work, as his account of the nature of the soul evolves and gains in complexity.

The first, Socratic, position that he holds is intellectualist, and the *locus classicus* of intellectualism is the *Protagoras*. In this dialogue Plato argues for the thesis that:

Knowledge is necessary and sufficient for virtue; ignorance is necessary and sufficient for vice.[1]

From 351b–357e Socrates has argued that no one fails willingly.[2] Knowledge, from this thesis, necessarily and always leads to right choices, whereas ignorance, the contradictory of knowledge (350a–b), is both necessary and sufficient for failure. It remains to tie this in with the discussion of virtue, the true target of the dialogue. To this end Socrates must demonstrate the identity of "good for me" (prudential; "success")

---

1. It will transpire, particularly in the discussion of the *Republic*, that the relation between knowledge and ignorance is vital to the logic of these entailments. Cf. Ch. 9, n. 1.
2. Discussed in Ch. 9.a.

and "good done by me" (moral; "virtue"). This, perennially, is his hardest task.

He considers courage:

    i. *Cowards go reluctantly into battle; brave men go willingly.*

    ii. *Going willingly into battle is noble.*

    iii. *Therefore going into battle is good and pleasant.*[3]

    iv. *Cowards, going into battle, cannot know, since they avoid what (truly) is noble, good, and pleasant.*

    v. *Cowards are cowards by virtue of what is called cowardice.*

    vi. *Cowards are cowards by virtue of their ignorance of what is terrible* [from *iv*].

    vii. *Therefore cowardice is ignorance.*

    viii. *Courage is the opposite of cowardice.*

    ix. *Knowledge is the opposite of ignorance.*

    x. *Therefore knowledge (of what is terrible) is courage.*[4]

Statements *iv* and *vi* are deduced from *ii* and *iii* on the grounds that, since going into battle genuinely is noble, good, etc., it must be a matter of intellectual error on the part of the cowards to fail to recognise their best interests. Knowledge leads us invariably to pursue our interests, and *ii* claims that in fact our interests lie in the practice of virtue. Conversely, failure to act virtuously is imprudent, and therefore it must be a matter of ignorance. This relies, of course, on the conclusion of the previous argument that nothing but intellectual error accounts for failure to pursue our interests.

The intellectualism, therefore, of the *Protagoras* claims that virtue is knowledge, vice is ignorance. At the same time, Socrates denies the possibility of other factors influencing behaviour;[5] thus his thesis is the strongest version of intellectualism possible: that there is no other source of vice than ignorance, no other source of virtue than knowledge.

The *Gorgias*, written later than the *Protagoras*, has been described as

3. Statement *ii* appeals to the convention that going into battle is noble, and if, as the preceding argument established, all values may be reduced to a single currency, we may translate 'noble' into 'good', 'pleasant', or whatever else we desire, and therefore *iii* follows. However, although the vital claim thus has some formal plausibility, it must still be accounted dubious. For although we may admit *ii*, it does not follow, without exploiting the prudential/moral ambiguity of 'good', that going into battle is good *for the man who does it*. Indeed, we might argue that the nobility of going into battle resides precisely in the fact that it is not good for the man who does it, but good for others. This proposition, then, fudges the central question of the identity of good for me and good done by me. But cf. Santas' defence of Socrates' argument, *Socrates*, p. 172, on the grounds that going to war is better than the alternative—being overrun by the Persians, etc.

4. Cf. Ch. 9.d. on cowardice as a state of soul.

5. I exclude 'accidents' from 'behaviour'; cf. Ch. 9.a. and Ch. 11.d.

pessimistic, distinguished "by the tragic tone of its later pages and by the direct and bitter criticism which it levels against Athenian politics and politicians."[6] But if we were to judge by the moral theory of the first half of the dialogue, where Socrates confronts Gorgias and Polus, we might be forgiven for thinking ourselves still with the strong intellectualism of earlier dialogues.

At 460b ff. Socrates offers the following chain of reasoning:

1. *The man who has learned carpentering will be skilled at carpentry* [tektonikos], *the man who has learned medicine will be a medical man, the man who has learned music will be musical.*
2. *Therefore the man who has learned is such as his knowledge makes him.*
3. *Therefore the man who has learned just things will be just.*[7]
4. *And he will do just things.*
5. *He will want to do just things.*

This argument is notoriously problematic. For there is no reason to suppose that the man who knows will act on his knowledge, and no guarantee that moral qualities may be assigned and exercised in the same way as technical expertise.[8] Even if we admit the analogy with the skills, we should not therefore allow that being skilled leads to just action.

Yet this exposition reveals the function of the analogy, since it illustrates the deficiency of popular moral thinking (exemplified by *4* and *5*). The popular view is inadequate because it only evaluates activity and

6. Dodds, *Plato: Gorgias*, p. 19.

7. This move is warranted by the linguistic apparatus of the induction.

8. Thus on the one hand Dodds tries to explain the apparent fallacy in the context of traditional Greek values:

"From Homer onwards moral conduct had been explained in terms of knowledge, not in terms of will—a concept which is completely absent from early Greek thought. . . . The *agathos* was the man who did things well, and doing things well involved knowing how to do them . . ." (*Plato: Gorgias*, p. 19).

On the other hand, R. Bambrough attacks the analogy with the skills on the grounds that moral behaviour is simply not analogous to technical activity ("Plato's Political Analogies," in Vlastos, *Plato: II*).

We should be wary, however, of both the force and the complexity of Plato's argument. First, he is right to observe that we accord a man a title when he possesses a certain body of information; thus the man with a medical degree is called 'doctor' irrespective of whether he practises. So it would be possible to delineate a sense of 'just' which would work in the same way: a man who has a 'degree in justice' will be a just man. Thus the move from *1* to *3* may be defended.

Second, it is true that the man who is just, in the commonplace sense of the word, acts justly; indeed he is probably so described exactly because he acts justly. Therefore *4* and *5* are protected by conventional usage. But it does not follow that the man who is just in the sense newly defined (at *3*, he has a degree in justice) will act justly (*4* and *5*, conventional). There is a hiatus, therefore, between *3* and *4*, since 'just' newly defined should not be conflated with 'just' conventionally used—unless Plato can defend univocity.

fails to give an explanation of that activity. Plato suggests, therefore, that the source of the just man's behaviour is the skill he possesses; this, we may infer, is the primary sense in which he is just.[9]

This argument claims first of all, therefore, that knowledge is sufficient for right action, since the knower (skilled man) will behave justly. Furthermore, we may cite the conventional view, to which the new explanation is harnessed, that only just men do (genuinely) just acts. It follows that knowledge (which is equivalent to a just disposition) is necessary for just behaviour. And that knowledge is not only sufficient but also necessary, for just behaviour is ensured by the analogy with the skills, since only a skilled man will act in a skilled way. If anyone else achieves the same results we will have no hesitation in ascribing this to luck or accident[10] and therefore not to genuinely skilled activity at all.

There follows the analysis of the nature of choice,[11] which again rests on a strongly intellectualist moral psychology. The distinction between "what I think I want" and "what I truly want" ensures that choice will be intellectual, such that bad choice is a matter solely of mistake, good choice of correct judgement. This appears to be the function of both this argument and the one which precedes it: to establish the intellectualist thesis that knowledge is necessary and sufficient for success against the idea that power is not a matter of knowledge. The prudential argument which follows (473 ff.)[12] claims that success should be correlated with virtue, failure with vice. Ignorance is the contradictory of knowledge.[13] Therefore ignorance is both necessary and sufficient for vice.

The two early discussions of virtue and vice in the *Gorgias*, therefore, suggest that Socrates is committed to an intellectualist thesis as strong as the account of a measuring skill in the *Protagoras*. However, Callicles' appearance on the scene (from 481) marks a new approach to the account of virtue and vice. Intellectualism, we discover, does not tell the whole tale.

At 493 Socrates sets out to rebut Callicles' immoralist thesis: he needs first to show that indulgence is not happiness and second to repudiate the immoralist redefinition of virtue as the power to maximise desires and their fulfilment. In response, he suggests the image of the leaky

9. Cf. Ch. 9.d. The notion that the just man is skilled is, in the present argument, primarily dispositional and only secondarily—witness the weakness of the move to 4—to do with behaviour.

10. Accidents are explicitly excluded from consideration at *Prot.* 352d7, where the supposed akratic must be *able* to follow the better course instead of the worse.

11. Discussed in Ch. 9.a.

12. Discussed in Ch. 9.b.

13. Cf. the opposition of *epistēmōn/anepistēmōn* and *eidōs/mē eidōs* at 459.

soul: a soul whose appetitive part is unreliable, unpredictable and insatiable. But the man who lives an orderly life, satisfied with what he has, is happy and contented (493a).

Intellectualist elements in this passage are unmistakeable. Socrates describes the intemperate and mindless, *anoētoi*, and accounts for their insatiability by their intellectual deficiency: they lack conviction and memory. But a new element appears, for Socrates has marked off the appetitive part of the soul (where the desires reside, 493b1) from the intellect. If the appetite is distinct from the reason, there is, to begin with, a move away from the reduction, in the *Protagoras*, of all impulses to the pursuit or avoidance of a single type of value. This, in turn, will disrupt the simple analysis of desire which succeeds or fails according as the agent knows or is ignorant.

Now there is the possibility that a man's judgment may be overruled by his appetites, and therefore both the ignorant man may, under pressure from his desires, succeed and the knowledgeable man may, for the same reason, fail. Psychological conflict, therefore, is no longer ruled out, and *akrasia* can no longer be denied on the grounds that intellectual error alone accounts for vice. In short, the notion that the soul may have parts opens the door to a complex theory of action denied by the strong intellectualist thesis.

However, this does not mean that Plato needs to abandon intellectualism altogether. Indeed, the pages that follow suggest that he wishes to combine a version of intellectualism with the idea that the soul is complex. Now although this theory is neither fully explicit nor clearly resolved until the *Republic*, it begins to develop in the discussion between Socrates and Callicles on the nature of *sōphrosunē*.

After presenting some dialectical arguments to demolish Callicles' view of hedonism, Socrates develops his own view of the good life. At 504a (recapitulated at 506c ff.) he describes the activity of the skilled legislator, who improves his subject's soul to make it well-ordered (*tetagmenon kai kekosmēmenon*). By conformity with the law, men become law-abiding and hence orderly in the same way as they become healthy by obeying the instructions of their doctor. The law-abiding man has justice and temperance and he is skilled.[14]

14. As we know from 460b ff. But cf. Ch. 12.d on the skill of the legislator. *Prima facie*, by *technē* here we understand the skill of the legislator who makes his subjects virtuous. However, the list at 506d of the factors influencing a man's character ("order, correctness and skill") seems asymmetrical, since "order" is a quality ascribed to his soul, and he has only been argued to be the product of the skill, not its possessor. Yet there is no indication in the Greek that *technē* is not a correlate of *taxis*, nor that the former is associated with the virtuous man only because he is the object of skill. It seems, therefore, that Socrates is equivocating between the skill of the legislator and the skill of the moral agent, and therefore the moral agent is no longer the pupil, but himself a *technikos*.

The argument continues with a demonstration of the unity of the virtues (507a ff.).[15] But here the cardinal virtue is self-control, *sōphrosunē*.[16] One view, therefore, might be that intellectualism, instantiated in the thesis of the *Protagoras* that knowledge (or wisdom) is the superordinate virtue, has now been dropped; hence, it could be argued, the striking omission of the intellectual epithet at 507c2 and the description at 504 ff. of the moral agent as the product, rather than the exponent, of a skill.

This, however, is but a superficial view, for on reflection we see that temperance now incorporates the reasoning faculty.[17] Hence, throughout the argument for the unity of virtue, reason is only apparently missing, since it is now part of self-control. Moreover, it is a notable implication of this last argument that if virtue is a matter of determining what is appropriate, we need some kind of measuring ability to determine precisely what is appropriate in various cases; what will perform this function better than reason? In short, the account of virtue at this point relies on the intellectualist idea that knowledge of the good is essential for virtue.

However, intellectualism is diminished, inasmuch as it is apparently not the sole account to be given of why men are virtuous. Thus, although one opposite of 'temperate' is 'foolish', there is another, namely, 'unrestrained'. Indeed, the whole passage, from 504 on, emphasises the

15. This reminds us, of course, of the *Protagoras*.

16. A. *The ordered soul is temperate and therefore good.*
   B. *The opposite soul, which is* aphrōn *and* akolastos, *is bad.*
This claims we should observe that "temperate" has two opposites (cf. a similar claim at *Prt.* 333), of which one, *aphrōn*, is strikingly intellectual.
   C. *The temperate man will do what is appropriate (*ta prosēkonta).
This proposal is, we may suppose, sanctioned by conventional usage, that self-control is a matter of restraint and of staying within one's own proper limits.
   D. *Thus the temperate man will behave properly towards gods and men.*
   E. *Therefore he will do just things and holy things, he will be just and holy.*
   F. *He will also be brave, pursuing and avoiding what he ought.*
This sequence looks like the ruthless exploitation of the wide possibilities of 'what is appropriate'. Doing what is appropriate towards the gods is certainly piety, at least to a Greek, and doing what is appropriate to men is, at least on a distributive ideology, justice. But the man who does what is proper in these respects will not necessarily act appropriately in respect of his own interests. The latter would be courage, the proper pursuit and avoidance of benefit and harm.
   G. *Therefore the temperate man will be just, holy, brave and completely good.*

17. Thus, first, at 506d7 the asymmetry must be explained by the fact that the skill is being transferred from the teacher to the pupil (n. 14); this, of course, was the purpose of the educative process (cf. the dispute with Gorgias, 454, 459). Second, Socrates explicitly incorporates the intellectual aspect into his account of temperance (n. 16), by explaining that it has two opposites, lack of restraint and folly; 'folly', of course, reminds us of the men who have no *nous* at 466 ff.

importance not of knowledge but of order and control. If the cardinal virtue, therefore, is temperance, the cardinal disposition will combine order with rationality. The idea of order conforms with the suggestion at 493 that the soul is a complex entity wherein desires may conflict with reason. At the same time the power of reason is essential for the proper assessment which will lead to prudent choice.

The unification of these two aspects of the virtuous soul in the single virtue of temperance, however, ensures that knowledge will be necessary for virtue. For now virtue is conceived as the ordered state of soul (the behaviour which stems from it seems almost incidental), and the ordered state of soul necessarily incorporates knowledge. Moreover, the virtues are unified, inasmuch as the virtuous man does what is appropriate in all circumstances, whether he has to do with gods or men. Since knowledge (wisdom) is thought of as a virtue, then the presence of knowledge entails the presence of the other virtues. The reason, therefore, which will show a man how to do what is appropriate, presupposes that he has the requisite ordered disposition. This combination is virtue; knowledge, therefore, is also sufficient for virtue.

Conversely, if ignorance is the contradictory of knowledge, and vice is construed as the absence of a virtuous disposition, then ignorance will be both necessary and sufficient for vice. Otherwise, ignorance may be seen as the failure of but one part of the soul, the reason. Then ignorance will be necessary for active vice, but it may not be sufficient. For it is now disjoined from psychic disorder, and wrongdoing may be prompted not only by mistake but also by the unruly behaviour of the appetitive part of the soul.[18]

Finally, a short passage at 509d ff. discusses how we may avoid wrongdoing. Is the desire to refrain from vice enough, Socrates asks, or do we need additional protection? But the desire to avoid wrongdoing is im-

---

18. Treating vice variously as the absence of virtue or its positive contrary, and ignorance variously as the contrary and the contradictory of knowledge, ignorance and vice may be related in four different ways:

1. ignorance $\equiv$ $-$knowledge   (contradictories)
    vice $\equiv$ $-$virtue   (contradictories)
    knowledge $\equiv$ virtue   (conclusion of the argument from *Grg.* 504)
    knowledge $\equiv$ virtue. $\supset$.vice $\equiv$ ignorance
$\therefore$ vice $\equiv$ ignorance

2. ignorance $\equiv$ $-$knowledge   (contradictories)
    vice $\equiv$. $-$(virtue v tertium quid)   (contraries)
    knowledge $\equiv$ virtue
$\therefore$ ignorance $\equiv$ $-$virtue
    $-$virtue $\equiv$ .vice v tertium quid
$\therefore$ ignorance $\equiv$ .vice v tertium quid
$\therefore$ vice $\supset$ ignorance
NOT ignorance $\supset$ vice

plicit in every man's activity, since we never desire the greatest of evils; no one does wrong willingly. Therefore we need further resources against becoming criminal, namely, *dunamis kai technē.*

This passage suggests, therefore, three prerequisites for the avoidance of wrongdoing: *boulēsis, dunamis* and *technē.*

Boulēsis was discussed in detail from 466 and redefined to cover our desire for goods but to preclude our mistaken choice of evils. Thus all desire is of goods, and therefore when we actually obtain evil, we have not desired it but have only obtained what seemed best to us. Here, then, the Socratic paradox is derived from the same thesis. If wrongdoing is against our interests, we cannot desire to do it; therefore no one does wrong willingly. But despite the universality of this desire, men do in fact do wrong; hence the specification that there must be other factors involved.

These other factors are *dunamis kai technē. Dunamis,* I suggest,[19] refers

---

3. ignorance ≡ . − (knowledge v tertium quid)   (contraries)
   vice ≡ − virtue   (contradictories)
   knowledge ≡ virtue
. ˙. vice ≡ − knowledge
   − knowledge ≡ .ignorance v tertium quid
. ˙. vice ≡ .ignorance v tertium quid
. ˙. ignorance ⊃ vice
NOT vice ⊃ ignorance

4. ignorance ≡ . − (knowledge v tertium quid)   (contraries)
   vice ≡ . − (virtue v tertium quid)   (contraries)
   knowledge ≡ virtue
. ˙. ignorance v tertium quid.≡.vice v tertium quid

The present passage, I have suggested, employs arguments 1 or 2. Argument 3 will come into play in the *Republic,* where ignorance is treated as the contrary of knowledge at 477 ff. Cf. below, b, and n. 32. Argument 4 is inconclusive as an account of how ignorance is a condition of vice. However, both 2 and 4 are rendered suspect by the fact that Plato does not, in this dialogue, present the (plausible enough) possibility that vice is the contrary of virtue. Rather, as he conceives the relation of success and failure to be one of contradictories, such that any falling short of success constitutes a failure, so he will shift quite happily from 'not being virtuous' to 'being vicious'. This is exemplified in his treatment of *kalon* and *aischron,* 474 ff. The conclusion is that the present passage may well present a strong case for ignorance as both necessary and sufficient for vice.

19. The context does not make it clear whether *dunamis* and *technē* are two separate faculties, or whether *technē* is introduced to amplify *dunamis.* Dodds separates them:

"The *dunamis* is not material power but the capacity to understand our true interest; the *technē* is the Platonic "moral science" which enables us to distinguish "good" and "bad" satisfactions" (*Plato: Gorgias,* p. 343).

The difficulty attached to this view is that there is no evidence to tell against the views of the *Protagoras* that the "capacity to understand our true interest" is but a part of the intellectual process of "distinguishing satisfactions." If the former is *dunamis,* then Dodds' explanation in fact conflates it with *technē,* with the result that the phrase as a whole is

to the capacity to avoid external coercion or inhibition,[20] such as the physical power to resist being pushed (into someone else in a crowd) or possibly the moral power to withstand blackmail. Even this, however, is insufficient against doing wrong; therefore we need the skill at judging what is right and what is wrong which was introduced in the very earliest pages of the dialogue. Freedom from coercion does not ensure that we act virtuously; nor does our universal desire to avoid the greatest evils. Thus choice is an ineffectual distinguishing mark of the wrongdoer, who, like everyone else, really wishes to do right. However, if we are coerced, we can hardly be said to do either right or wrong, since our actions are, at least to an extent, beyond our control. Therefore, the positive factor that contributes to our behaviour is our moral skill. This is the efficient cause of virtue, and it is, as the early exchanges with Polus made clear, intellectual.

Does this mean that the hints of a complex psychology in the discussion of *sophrosunē* have now been dropped? At first glance, this seems to be the case, and we seem to have returned to a strong intellectualist thesis whereby the efficient factor in virtue is knowledge, in vice is ignorance. However, neither the account of *sophrosunē* nor that of *technē* is detailed or clear enough for one to be justified in holding that either is incompatible with the other. Moreover, the proximity of the two accounts suggests that they should be reconciled. The complex approach may be upheld in the notion of *dunamis*, a psychological ability (as I have suggested, the power to withstand blackmail) whereby our lower impulses may be restrained. We need *dunamis* in addition to *technē*. Thus, the intellectualist position of the Socratic period begins to admit a complex view of our moral character.

By the end of the *Gorgias*, therefore, Plato has explored the thesis that the cause of vice is ignorance, and the consequence of his view of knowledge will be that virtue cannot occur in the ignorant man. The strong intellectualist position, however, is eroding under the pressure of a complex moral psychology, which suggests a different view of vice.

b. THE DISORDERED SOUL

The ethical theory of the *Republic* centres upon the new tripartite psychology proposed formally in Book 4. This amplifies the suggestions

---

equivalent to the measuring skill of the *Protagoras*. However, *dunamis* at 509d4 was used to mean the material power to avoid victimisation (exemplified in the [temporary] immunity to misfortune enjoyed by the friends of tyrants); therefore here it might refer to the material power to avoid doing, rather than suffering, wrong.

20. Echoing *exon autois* at *Prot.* 352d7, and anticipating *Laws* Book 9. Cf. R.M. Hare, *Freedom and Reason* (Oxford: Clarendon, 1963), Ch. 5, § 8.

of the *Gorgias* that moral dispositions require complex explanations, and it moves away from the stark intellectualism of the early dialogues. The vicious soul, Plato suggests, is disordered. At the same time, the problem of *akrasia*, which was denied by Socrates in the *Protagoras*, receives renewed attention, as Plato offers a more sensitive account of moral failure.

Socrates had supposed [21] that internal conflict denies the principle of non-contradiction; thus he repudiated the possibility of *akrasia*. Plato, however, observes that both *akrasia* and internal conflict do in fact occur and concludes that they must be explained by a parts-of-the-soul theory in order to accommodate non-contradiction.[22] Thus attraction towards a particular object may be attributed to one part of the soul, repulsion from the same object to another, and coherence may be maintained.[23] The situation where a man is thirsty (he wants to drink) and does not

21. Cf. Ch. 9.a,e.

22. Non-contradiction:

NC. *The same thing cannot act or be affected in opposite ways in the same respect and the same relation at the same time* (436b).

This principle will apply to any contradictory predicates. It will be true, for example, of motion and rest (436c). Thus when a man is said to be both in motion and at rest, *NC* requires that different parts of him must be either in motion or at rest, and not the same part at the same time. Then:

A. *Attraction and repulsion are opposites.*

It will follow, of course, that if a man is both attracted and repelled by the same thing in the same respect, etc., he must be so in respect of different parts of himself (cf. Penner, "Thought and Desire in Plato," in Vlastos, *Plato: II*, pp. 96–118).

B. *Thirst is for drink, hunger for food, rather than for good drink or good food.*

C. *Thus each desire is for its natural object, unqualified.*

Take the test-case of the man who both wants this drink (because he is thirsty) and does not want it (because he knows it is poisonous). *B* and *C* deny that we can explain this contradiction in terms of his having two distinct desires (one for drink, and the second for good drink, and therefore for avoiding harmful drink). *NC*, however, prevents us from saying that the man both desires and does not desire, is both attracted and repelled, *tout court*. On the analogue, therefore, of the man who is both in motion and at rest, we must conclude that our test-case experiences attraction in one part of himself, repulsion in another. His desire for drink is simple, as *B* and *C* claim, and it stems from the appetitive part of his soul (*to epithumētikon*). His simultaneous determination not to drink must have a different source.

D. *Knowledge itself is of learning itself, but a particular knowledge is of a particular learning* (438d).

This rather obscure claim has the effect of enabling a comparison to be made between a particular knowledge and a particular desire (439a). Thus involing *NC*, Plato may conclude that in the case of psychological conflict, there is a second element comparable to desire, to which the opposite impulse may be attributed; this is reason, *logismos*, 439d.

23. The continuing popularity of this kind of solution to the problem of *akrasia* is exemplified in G. Watson, "Free Agency," *J. Phil.* (1975):205–220; in Ginsberg, "The Nature of Responsibility," p. 90; and, of course, in Freud. Cf. Kenny, "Mental Health in Plato's Republic," and B. Simon, *Mind and Madness in Ancient Greece* (Ithaca: Cornell U.P., 1978).

want to drink may, as a result, be relieved of contradiction. He is impelled towards the drink by his appetites (which are supplied, Plato tells us, by our dispositions and sickness, *pathēmata kai nosēmata*), but repelled by his reason, which tells him that the drink is poisonous. That he does not drink, therefore, may be attributed to his reason's mastery over his desires.

The first part of the soul under consideration is simple, desiring only its natural objects.[24] The qualification of the object (good, bad, indifferent, poisonous or health-giving) will be a matter for a more complicated faculty capable of making evaluative judgements.[25] Effectively, therefore, the original distinction between attraction and repulsion provokes a new contrast between uninformed appetite and informed judgement, between irrational and rational. This will allow the possibility of *akrasia*, the conflict between desire and reason, which Socrates denied on the basis that all desire could be reduced to reasoned judgement.

But now, in contrast to the Socratic doctrine, we cannot even predict that reason, even if right, will be victorious in its struggle with desire. So far, therefore, knowledge is neither necessary nor sufficient for right choice.[26] For example, desire might fasten upon a beneficial natural object by accident (e.g., the drink to hand might happen to be milk rather than hemlock), in which case knowledge is not necessary. Or desire might overrule the right decision of knowledge and lead to the wrong choice; thus knowledge will be insufficient for success. Mistake, conversely, may be a factor in wrong choice, but it will neither determine it nor wholly account for it.

Next, Plato postulates the existence of a third element in the soul, the *thumoeides*, which corresponds to the military class in the state. At first it appears that the introduction of a third element is otiose, dictated solely by the political analogue which introduces the tripartite theory.[27] For Plato has already given us a rational/irrational dichotomy, into which the

24. As *B* and *C* declare, n. 22.

25. This, of course, will confuse any straight parallel claimed between a particular desire and a particular knowledge or judgement.

26. Although, in fact, Plato does not believe that knowledgeable reason is susceptible to *akrasia*.

27. The analogy itself is problematic, if Plato is merely asserting, as a factor in his proof, that the state is a suitable analogue for the soul. He would claim, in his defence, that, first, 'just' is used of both state and soul, 'just' is univocal (cf. 441d5), and therefore there must be a significant parallel between the structure of the state and the structure of the soul. Second, he would claim that he supposes the justice of the state stems from the justice of its members (435e), and therefore they are structurally related, since one is derivative from the other. That it is the analogy which explains why the *thumoeides* is introduced, is suggested, e.g., by Williams, "Analogy of City and Soul," p. 206.

notion of the spirited part of the soul fits uneasily. But it seems that this psychological complication is intended to account for a phenomenon which Plato felt to be non-rational but which, nevertheless, urges rational, and hence moral, behaviour.[28] "Plato . . . is using the word *thymos* technically to isolate a phenomenon for which there is no term readily available, but a salient characteristic of which this word catches . . ."[29]

And yet the spirit is not always on the side of reason, for at 441a Plato enters the proviso that it may be corrupted by upbringing so as to support desire. This possibility is quickly passed over, but it paves the way for the suggestion that the irrational parts of the soul should be trained (conditioned) to obey the commands of the rational part. The desires will then be trained to remain suppressed, whereas the spirited element will be encouraged to be active on behalf of the commands of reason. It should further be observed that the account of the *thumoeides* suggests that, as in the case of children, the training of the spirit should *precede* the education of the intellect.[30]

At 441c Socrates offers a schematic analysis of the four virtues of the tripartite soul:

  i. A man is wise because his reason is wise.

  ii. A man is brave because his thumoeides *is brave and obedient to the dictates of reason* (442c1).

  iii. A man has the virtue of sōphrosunē *when the better part rules and the worse part agrees to be ruled; here again, the dictates of reason must be obeyed.*

  iv. A man has the virtue of dikaiosunē *when his reason rules and each part has and does its own.*

This analysis presents two vital corollaries to the tripartite psychology. First, the fact that there are three parts, rather than only two, enables Plato to explain not only the difference between virtue and vice but also the difference between different virtues and vices, which the Socratic analysis was unable to do for the simple reason that it was unitary. Sec-

---

28. Plato himself offers two arguments in support of this variation on the original psychology. The first is the story of Leontius, whose desire conflicts with his spirited element (439e), and who shows *akrasia* when his desires win the battle. Leontius' impulse away from what is shameful is presumably classified as 'angry' rather than as rational because the attitude he displays towards his own debased desires is anger, rather than reasonability.

The second argument adduces the spirited behaviour of children who, Plato supposes, lack rationality. The *thumoeides* apparently takes the side of reason when rational/irrational conflict occurs (compare the behaviour of the spirited horse, *Phaedrus* 246 ff.); therefore its function is either to replace reason, in situations in which reason cannot operate, or to supplement it and to create righteous indignation in the soul concerned.

29. Gosling, *Plato*, p. 41.

30. Cf. 441a8; 522a; 582b; 589a; 590a ff.

ond, although at first it appeared that Plato was forsaking knowledge as the supreme factor in a man's moral constitution, knowledge now comes into its own.

Knowledge is necessary for virtue because that reason rules is specified as the condition for each virtue. Knowledge is sufficient for virtue, because reason can only rule after the other elements have been repressed.[31] Knowledge therefore entails control and is thus equivalent to virtue. However, ignorance, now officially conceived as the contrary of knowledge (476 ff.), will be sufficient but not necessary for vicious behaviour, since ignorance is now but one of the three possible causes of vice: mistake, inflated desires, or perverted spirit. But, at the same time, it follows from the account of knowledge that wrongdoing cannot take place unless knowledge is absent and, in this sense, the agent is ignorant.[32] At this juncture, therefore, the ethical theory of the *Republic* moves away from the strong intellectualism of the *Protagoras*, since, although true virtue requires that knowledge should control the appetites, vice may be explained by inflated desires superseding the failure of reason.

In the analogy of the Ship of State in Book 6 (488 ff.), by comparing the art of politics with the art of navigation, Plato makes three important claims about politics and thence about morals in general. First, he insists that our job is to determine the means to the good ends which are universally desired.[33] Second, the image shows that politics is a skill, a

31. This view of the repression of desire preceding the proper exercise of the intellect is presented not only in the *Republic* but also in other works, e.g., *Phaedo*, 66 ff.; *Tim.* 44b.

32. Cf. above, n. 18.

1. Any virtue $\supset$ reason rules
$\therefore$ virtue $\supset$ knowledge
   rule of reason $\supset$ control   (chronological priority)
   knowledge.control. $\supset$ virtue   (by definition)
$\therefore$ knowledge $\supset$ virtue
$\therefore$ knowledge $\equiv$ virtue
   $-$ knowledge $\equiv$ $-$ virtue   (the agent is ignorant in a mild sense)

2. If ignorance is the contrary of knowledge and vice is the contradictory of virtue, ignorance v inflated desires v perverted spirit. $\equiv$ vice
$\therefore$ ignorance $\supset$ vice
But *not* $\therefore$ vice $\supset$ ignorance (n. 18.3)

3. If ignorance is the contrary of knowledge
If vice is the contrary of virtue
And if ignorance means necessarily making mistakes (cf. 477a ff.)
If vice is a mistake (imprudent)
$\therefore$ ignorance $\supset$ vice
But *not* vice $\supset$ ignorance (since mistakes may result from false belief as opposed to ignorance) (a resolution of n. 18.4).

The present passage, I argue, suggests 1 and 2.

33. Bambrough, "Political Analogies," implausibly imagines that Plato has made a mis-

technē, to which there corresponds a body of knowledge which, once acquired, is practically effective, since it ensures the proper choice of means to the maximisation of happiness. This picks up the theses of both the *Protagoras* and the *Gorgias* and must extend beyond politics to moral ability in general; further, it presents a strong intellectualist case for an art of being just which leads directly to the desire to be just and thence to just activity.[34] Third, although Plato has been criticised[35] for conflating "knowing that" with "knowing how" in his moral analysis, he may reply by offering a moral syllogism:[36] The man who knows just things will be able to identify them wherever they occur (minor premise); if just actions are desirable (from the point of view of the agent), and the prudential argument claims that they are (major premise), the man who knows just things will complete the practical syllogism and pursue just things or act justly.[37] This evidence,[38] therefore, suggests that reason is still the supreme factor in our moral constitution.

Yet the stark intellectualism of the early dialogues has indeed lapsed, to be replaced by a complex description of virtue and vice. For virtue, as Plato now conceives it, is a matter of an ordered disposition within which reason operates, whereas vice will result from the improper prevalence of any of three factors: ignorance, inflated desires or a perverted spirit.

The complex psychology appears to be upheld in the middle period—in the *Phaedrus*, for example, the image of the charioteer (246a

---

take in his choice of analogue and has failed to notice that the navigator, unlike the politician, chooses the route to a destination but not the destination itself. But this, surely, is Plato's point: that in politics also, the end is predetermined (it is happiness, which we all desire), and the politician's job is to steer the state towards this goal.

34. Irwin argues that the *technē* analogy (in his flood of acronyms, "CA") lapses after the Socratic period. But he dismisses this passage in too cavalier a note (*Plato's Moral Theory*, p. 334).

35. E.g., by J. Gould, *The Development of Plato's Ethics* (Cambridge: C.U.P., 1955), or Bambrough, "Political Analogies." The *Grg.* analysis of choice suggests the interpretation I offer here: the moral agent will be impelled by his moral knowledge directly to just actions, inasmuch as he knows that doing right is in his interests, doing wrong against them.

36. Cf. D. Wiggins on constituents of happiness in Aristotle, "Deliberation and Practical Reason," *Proc. Ar. Soc.* (1975–76):33.

37. That this is Plato's interpretation of the "knowing that"/"knowing how" dichotomy is suggested first by the *technē* analogy itself, which is startling enough to suggest that Plato understood at least some of its complex implications. Second, we might adduce the prolonged discussions of how we are to attribute moral labels, e.g., at *Rep.* 479a, cf. *Symp.* 211a.

38 To which we might add the account of the choosing ability of the philosopher at 580, the importance of the intellect in the choice of lives, 618b, and also the supposition that the knower, returning to the cave, will be the philosopher-king (519).

ff.) echoes the account in the *Republic*. A brief passage in the *Timaeus*, however, suggests strong intellectualism, coupled with a physical explanation of vice.[39] By the time we reach that late work, the *Laws*, how far has Plato moved away from the account of virtue and vice he gave in the *Republic*? It is, of course, in the *Laws* in particular that Plato will implement the moral psychology with a detailed theory of punishment.

Two passages will especially concern us here. The first is in Book 3 (supplemented from other contexts in Books 5 and 9) where, amid a discussion of the problems of legislation, Plato returns to the nature of virtue and its relation to happiness. The second is, by contrast, a formalised account of the causes of vice, which appears in Book 9 immediately after the theory of punishment.

Superficially, the moral theory of Book 3 reverts to a strong intellectualism.[40] Thus Plato reintroduces the amount of choice first argued for in the Socratic period.[41] At 689a the ascription of failure to ignorance[42] prompts the Stranger to further explication. Sometimes a man recognises the noble and good, but hates it, or recognises the shameful and unjust, but rejoices in it. Then his feelings of pleasure and pain are at odds with his reason.[43] This is the greatest ignorance (*amathia*), because it involves the greatest part of the soul, namely, the appetite. Accordingly, whenever the soul quarrels with its sovereign, reason, this must be called folly (*anoia*), and the *kaloi logoi* (excellent principles?) in a man's soul are worse than powerless.

This argument seems to present firmly intellectualist overtones. Folly is described as ignorance which leads to positively bad judgement; the mention of reason and of the *logoi* in the soul is emphatic. However, it is not clear why this state of soul should be described as ignorance at all, when the substance of the passage suggests psychic conflict rather than mere intellectual failure. In part, this may be explained according to the model I have suggested of the moral syllogism.[44] The foolish man described here has difficulties not with recognising which course of action is virtuous (the minor premise) but in realising that it is in his interests

39. Cf. below, c.

40. I.M. Crombie argues that: "The general impression from the *Laws* is that Plato is much more conscious of the importance of non-rational factors than he once was . . . ' (*An Examination of Plato's Doctrines*, Vol. 1 [London: Routledge, Kegan Paul], p. 270). This seems to me to be no more true of the *Laws* than of the *Republic*.

41. Cf. Ch. 9.a.

42. E.g. 688d, the failure of the Peloponnesian kings came about through their ignorance of the greatest concerns.

43. It will be important subsequently (864a) that Plato uses *doxa* here for a *correct* apprehension of right and wrong, here overwhelmed by the appetite. Cf. also the assimilation of *doxa* to *phronēsis* at 688b3.

44. Cf. Santas' account of the relation between the prudential and moral paradoxes in the Socratic dialogues; *Socrates*, pp. 183 ff.

(the major premise). Consequently, he hates what is noble and fails to pursue it.

A similar interpretation may be derived from the evidence of 727 ff., where although the agent has been told by the legislator what is right and what is wrong, he has difficulties in realising that virtue is in his interests. The man with excessive self-love, however, fails on the minor premise, since his intellectual blindness prevents him from determining what is right and what is wrong. The job of the legislator, therefore, as the Stranger suggests in Book 9 (858d5 ff.), is to advise on both parts of the syllogism: on the one hand he must explain what is just, and on the other he must show how happiness is to be achieved. Failure to understand both elements may be described as ignorance and necessarily, according to the evidence of Book 3, results in failure.

This interpretation, however, concentrates on the language of the argument, which gives it the appearance of strong and Socratic[45] intellectualism. Yet the theory of psychic harmony, although not formally set out, retains its power. Thus at 688e, though folly is described as the greatest ignorance, it is actually explained by the conflict of the appetite with the reason. This thesis is foreshadowed at 687e, where the Stranger stipulates that our desire should follow our reason. Here again the surface is intellectualist, but the underlying psychology is complex. Thus, not only should reason be sovereign, but we need obedience from the irrational parts (688b3). The truly wise, therefore, are those who have psychic harmony and who lead their lives according to reason (689d). Psychic harmony, it appears, is the prerequisite of correct choice, and it is brought about[46] when reason is in control.

A similarly complex account may be derived from 734b, where the Stranger concedes that wickedness may be caused by ignorance or intemperance or both, whereas the life of *sōphrosunē* is the life of happiness and maximised pleasure. Here again, therefore, it is only the overtones that take us away from the *Republic* account of virtue and vice in terms of psychic harmony. In both contexts knowledge is both necessary and sufficient for virtue: necessary because reason controls the temperate soul; sufficient because the control of reason leads to psychic harmony. Ignorance, however, is the contrary of knowledge.[47] Accordingly,

45. We are reminded of the *metrētikē technē* (*Prot.* 351 ff.) from the discussion of how we should compute pleasures and pains at 733d.

46. But the relation between psychic harmony and intellectual control is confused. At 689a8, they appear to be the same thing; at 689b3 the rule of the intellect is presented as the cause of harmony, its failure the cause of disharmony; whereas at 689d4 harmony seems to be the precondition of *phronēsis*. This is but an indication of the confusion generated by Plato's attempt to reconcile a superficial but strong intellectualism with the theory of psychic harmony.

47. Hence the disjunction of ignorance and intemperance at 734b5.

the lapse of knowledge will be necessary for vice, but ignorance or mistake will only be sufficient for vice, since there may be other causes of wrongdoing, notably the disruptive effect of inflated appetites. As in the *Timaeus*, therefore, the terminology of intellectualism is prominent; but in the *Laws* the moral theory to be discerned beneath remains faithful to the *Republic*.

Book 9 suggests that understanding the criminal's disposition is essential to evaluating his behaviour. Accordingly, the Stranger follows the theory of punishment with a detailed account of the disposition of the vicious man.[48] He offers three causes of vice: anger, pleasure and ignorance. Of these, anger and pleasure are positive impulses towards wrongdoing, whereas ignorance signifies a man's lack of knowledge[49] and lack of the rational power to resist his emotions. All three causes, however, pervert a man from his true objectives to their opposite; thus he acts involuntarily (cf. 863a5–6). This may happen in a variety of ways, either because he mistakes this action for the right one[50] or because he is overcome (by the effects of emotion).

As a consequence, this account of the causes of vice combines the intellectual explanation of involuntary wrongdoing with the admission of *akrasia* (being overcome by anger or pleasure). In the case of ignorance, wrongdoing arises from intellectual deficiency; in the case of emotional impulses, the *akratic* is overcome by a positive force.

The Stranger goes on to divorce the damage done in a crime from the criminal disposition itself. The disposition is internalised, as in the *Republic*, and explained in terms of the politics of the soul. When the lower emotions are in control, then the man is necessarily unjust, irrespective of the way he behaves. As far as his behaviour is concerned, any deliberate damage that he does will be called an injustice, since it was prompted by his unjust disposition, that is, by the tyranny of emotions in his soul. But if the damage is done by accident, the act will not be an injustice, although the agent will still be described as vicious, in view of his disposition. And even if he does no damage at all, his disposition is vicious, albeit not manifested in injustices done to others.

The good man, however, is controlled by his belief in the best; he and

48. The interpretation of this passage is vexed. I offer my own version below in Appendix II.

49. In other words, ignorance is seen here as the contradictory of knowledge. As such, although knowledge is both necessary and sufficient for virtue—as, I argue, 864a1 suggests—ignorance is necessary for wrongdoing. It is not sufficient, however, as the whole passage suggests. Consequently, cf. above n. 18, vice must be seen here as the *contrary* of virtue.

50. This suggests a different view, that ignorance is the contrary of knowledge, and thus sufficient but not necessary for vice. All in all, in the *Laws*, Plato equivocates hopelessly as to whether he views ignorance as the contrary or the contradictory of knowledge.

all his actions, damaging or otherwise, will therefore be called just. He may, indeed, make mistakes, but these will not be errors of moral judgement; rather, they may be inaccurate assessments of the situation confronting him, or bad predictions of the results that will follow from his actions. Such mistakes, being of a practical nature, will not affect our evaluation of him as a good man, although they will affect what happens; thus some injury might follow as a consequence.

In the *Gorgias*, Socrates claimed that, in addition to the determination to avoid wrongdoing, we need both *dunamis* and *technē*. The moral skill, I have argued, is invariable both here and in the *Gorgias*, it is complete and not subject to mistake. However, I have suggested that the vaguer *dunamis* covers the ability to resist external coercion or interference. Both of these may be caused by physical necessity or by the mere limitations of being human, so that we can never predict or even itemise all the circumstances affecting our behaviour. The man who believes in the best, therefore, is prone to various kinds of mistake, but his belief or his knowledge remains intact, and this is what determines our assessment of his intentions and of his entire moral character.

Thus Plato's formal position has not changed from the *Republic*. He retains the tripartite psychology, although the *Laws* is notable for its intellectualist vocabulary. He still believes that knowledge is the controlling element of the soul, without which the many-headed beast of appetite and emotion can take over. What the *Laws* does contribute is a complex analysis of the interrelation of the causes of vice, suggesting that both the positive forces of anger and pleasure, and the deficiency that is ignorance, are such that we must still insist that the criminal is so involuntarily.

c. THE DISEASED SOUL

Plato's moral psychology develops, then, from the intellectualist position put forward by Socrates in the early dialogues to a conception of virtue as order in the soul. Alongside this development, however, a different view of the soul persists. This arises from the analogy drawn, from the earliest period, between the body and the soul, and it regards the virtuous soul as healthy, the vicious soul as diseased.

To begin with, the idea of the "disease of the soul" is metaphorical. At *Grg.* 464a ff., for example, the health of the body, which is created and preserved by medicine and training, is kept strictly separate from the health of the soul, subject to the skills of the lawgiver and the judge. The prudence of virtue, therefore, is urged on the basis of the analogy, and not on the basis of a direct connection between physical wellbeing and a man's moral disposition.

Similarly in the *Republic*, where the analogy assumes a great deal of importance,[51] Plato still resists the temptation to recommend virtue on the grounds that it is physically healthy, and sticks to his analogical argument (444c ff.). Vice is described as sickness, therefore, as the product of a metaphor. The purpose of the metaphor is not to offer the pathological detail of wrongdoing. This, indeed, Plato does not do. Rather, he wishes to claim that our attitudes towards sickness, including our avoidance of it, should operate also for vice.[52]

The weakness of this position is that it is both inexplicit and metaphorical. Thus first, although the idea of vice as disease may be informative about the attitudes we should adopt towards the vicious man, it tells us little about his actual disposition. Second, Plato must face the criticism that sickness is merely a metaphor and that the relation between vice and disease, to be philosophically effective, requires rigorous demonstration, rather than assertion.

In a short and considerably vexed passage in the *Timaeus*,[53] Plato counters these and similar objections with the thesis that vice is an effect of physical disorder; thus "vice is disease" literally.

Diseases of the soul occur through the disorder of the body (86b1).[54] We may classify psychic disease, or folly, as either madness or ignorance,[55] and the physical disorder which accompanies madness or ignorance is itself a disease. The excessive sensation of pleasure and pain, therefore, should be recognised as the greatest disease of the soul, for the man who suffers in this way makes inopportune choices, as his faculties are impaired and his reason blinded. For example, overflowing bone marrow leads to excessive sensation and thence to madness, whereupon the man is described as criminal.[56] Hence sexual intemper-

51. Discussed in detail in Ch. 9.c.

52. Cf. Mourelatos, *The Route of Parmenides* (New Haven: Yale U.P., 1970), p. 38. Plato's argument suggests that this is a metaphor of "interaction" in Black's terminology.

53. The evidence here discussed seems to show affinities with the pessimism of the *Laws* rather than the moral theory of the *Republic*. But note the Socratism of both the intellectualist thesis here and the analysis of "genuine" choice. Cf. ch. 9, n. 26.

54. It is possible to read this as "Some diseases of the soul take place through the body." But this weak reading is militated against by the rest of the passage. For, at 86d6 and at 87b3, Plato explicitly claims that this analysis of why men are involuntarily evil is exhaustive. Correspondingly, we must suppose that his analysis of what it means to be evil in the first place is equally comprehensive. Thus both here and at other dubious points in this compressed passage I have adopted a strong reading.

55. Here again, it is possible (just) to take this sentence as only offering a partial list of the species of folly; I have not done so. "Ignorance" seems to mean a disability rather than merely the lack of knowledge. Cf. above, nn. 18, 32, 49, 50.

56. But he is so characterised descriptively rather than prescriptively. Hence to call him criminal does not require that we ascribe blame to him, for this Plato denies. Cf. Ch. 9.b.

ance is a psychological disease caused by a physical disturbance (generally in the bone marrow). Equally, physical pain attacks the three parts of the soul[57] to cause all kinds of discontentment, of foolhardiness or cowardice, of forgetfulness or ignorance.

This analysis claims that those psychological disorders which we regard as vicious have, in every case,[58] a physical source. Bodily disorders lead to distorted perceptions, particularly of pleasures and pains, and this alone gives rise to vice. This thesis has three immediate effects. First, it strengthens the appeal to prudence which originally prompted the formulation of the body/soul analogy, for if wrongdoing really is the product of disease, it must be against our interests. Second, Plato now has an answer to Gosling's complaint[59] that on his former "vice is disease" theory, he failed to supply a pathology of vice. Here the pathology of vice will be the same as the pathology of normal physical disorders, subject, no doubt, to the same difficulties and limitations that beset any scientific discipline, but nevertheless capable of analysis from observation and experiment. So vice, like measles, can not only be diagnosed, but explained and also cured. Third, then, vice should be treated by medical means. Drugs and surgery will be no less effective against sexual intemperance than they will against tuberculosis or cancer, and the legislator should no longer be analogous to, but identical with, the doctor.

Yet the passage as a whole contains some striking intellectualist overtones. For example, although the explicit theory is that psychological disorder is to be attributed to physical sickness, the vice itself has an intellectual title—*anoia*, folly—which may be classified as madness or ignorance. It is surely no coincidence that madness and ignorance were the two intellectual disorders prominent in the *Protagoras* (349 ff.), the *locus classicus* of intellectualism. Equally, an overflowing bone marrow is said to result in distorted judgement, which leads to the making of bad choices (86c1 ff.). Again the effect is felt primarily in the intellect. Thus, although Plato nods in the direction of the theory of psychic harmony (physical pain affects the three parts of the soul in different ways, 87a5), the general tenor of the passage is to present a strong intellectualist thesis and to explain this thesis in terms of physical disturbance.

This, we may suppose, is intended to reconcile the "vice is disease" theory with intellectualism. Thus Plato attempts to explain the irrational (those impulses of the soul which go against our better judgement and cause *akrasia*) in terms of the physical, reducing psychological conflict to

57. It is a mark of the oddity of the passage, and of the dialogue as a whole, that the tripartite soul is conceived as physically located. Hence Plato here speaks of the three "places" (*topoi*) of the soul. Cf. 69e ff.

58. Again, as I have argued, the account is exhaustive.

59. *Plato*, p. 84.

a dichotomy between the impulses which come from the body and those which come from the soul. Effectively, then, we are back with the unitary Socratic account, whereby conflict internal to the soul was denied; it must be explained in terms of external factors. Unfortunately, the explanation that Plato comes up with this time is unsatisfactory on two counts. First, because it is difficult to envisage any common ground on which the two impulses, physical and psychological, might do battle. Second, this explanation debases the complex, and correspondingly convincing, account of our psychological make-up which was offered in the *Republic*.

The odd experiment of the *Timaeus* with the thesis that vice may be explained in terms of physical disease is, in the end, a failure. Nevertheless, the body/soul analogy is influential throughout Plato's work, and, as the next chapter will show, it exercises considerable influence directly upon his penology. Indirectly, the idea that vice is disease has a strong effect upon Plato's attitude toward the criminal.

First, if the criminal is diseased, he is to be pitied. The introduction of disease strengthens the possibility that benevolence—urged by the Socratic paradoxes—will tip over into a paternalistic attitude towards the criminal. For, after all, it is to explain our good—and paternalistic—intentions that we exclaim, over the spoonful of vile medicine: "It is for your own good."

Second, if the criminal is diseased, the appropriate treatment will be medical, provided, that is, that his disease is curable.

Third, if the criminal is diseased, he may well be infectious (cf. *Rep.* 552c). With regard, therefore, to the other members of the community in which he lives, benevolence will urge the judiciary to protect the many. Thus benevolence, in this case, may well lead to utilitarianism.

Plato offers three different analyses of the criminal disposition: that it is ignorance; that it is psychic disorder; that it is disease. If he were to advocate only one of these various accounts, then the treatment that he should propose for the criminal would be easy to predict. But, as we have seen, he is neither clear nor definite about when, or whether, one moral psychology takes over from another. This has its inevitable effect on his penology.

CHAPTER
11

PLATO'S
THEORY OF PUNISHMENT

a. THE *GORGIAS*[1]

The unjust man who gets away with it is worse off than the man who
is punished for his wickedness. With this paradox, Socrates launches a
theory of punishment whereby the criminal, made unhappy by possessing an intolerable disposition, derives a positive benefit from his punishment. In the *Gorgias'* analysis of the prudence of virtue, punishment,
commonly thought of as an evil, is startlingly presented as, in fact, a
benefit. Despite the prudential context of the arguments of this dialogue, Plato does not recommend deterrent penal measures. On the
contrary, he proposes first that virtue is in our interests and second that
punishment is the means by which we may acquire the good fortune of
a virtuous disposition. Thus, as his general moral theory had foreshadowed, Plato produces a humanitarian penology in a theory of reform.

The Prudence of Submitting to Punishment

From *Gorgias* 474 ff. Socrates demonstrated that doing wrong is
worse than suffering it. This argument rested upon the difficult principle that we may measure what is fine according to the pleasure or the
benefit that it confers, and what is shameful according to the pain or the
harm that it causes.[2] From 476a the same principle is exploited to show
that wrongdoers who escape punishment are more wretched than those

---

1. I treat the *Gorgias* before the *Protagoras* to clarify my argument. The rationale behind my method will appear in the following section, where I consider the *Protagoras* in
relation to the *Gorgias'* penology. But I am certain that the *Protagoras* was written before
the *Gorgias*, for reasons of Plato's development that will have become clear in the preceding
chapter.

2. Cf. Appendix I and Ch. 9.b.

who undergo punishment—to show, in short, that punishment is a benefit *to the punished.*

1. *Paying the penalty* [dikēn didonai] *is the same thing as being punished justly* [dikaiōs kolazesthai].
2. *To every agent there corresponds a patient.*
3. *The patient will be such as the agent makes it.*

Thus, as for any transitive verb, if someone hits, something is hit.

4. *The effect on the patient may be qualified in exactly the same way as the act is qualified* (476d3).

If someone hits violently, something is hit violently. For straightforward examples, this principle holds. It becomes highly suspect, however, when the adverb is evaluative, relational or psychological. For example, from "I did this to you well" (describing my performance) does it follow that "you suffered it well" (describing your forbearance)? If I hit you voluntarily, were you hit voluntarily?[3] We should beware of too ready a shift from active to passive.

5. *The man who punishes rightly* [orthōs] *punishes justly.*
6. *So the punisher does just things, and the punished suffers just things* (from 5 and 6).
7. *All just things,* qua *just, are fine* (476b1).

This move paves the way to the renewed use of the principle for analysing the fine and the shameful established in the preceding argument in Chapter 9 (474 ff.).

E. *Of two fine things, that one is finer which exceeds the other in pleasure or benefit or both. Similarly, of two shameful things, that one is more shame-ful which exceeds the other in pain or harm or both.*

8. *It would be absurd to suppose that he who suffers a just, and so fine, punishment enjoys a pleasure.*[4]
9. *So the just punishment is fine because it confers a benefit.*
10. *Therefore the victim of punishment benefits from it.*

This argument is superficially sound up to the move from *8* to *10.* For until that point, the shift from active to passive is not illegitimately exploited. We might admit that just punishments are fine, for the judge, and are claimed to be so by him—perhaps because he enjoys some bene-
fit they confer upon society at large, or because they assuage his feeling that justice has been outraged. It does not follow from this, however, that his victim would agree that his punishment was fine, because beneficial to himself. Indeed, as I have argued,[5] Plato's use of the modal

---

3. Cf. Aristotle, *E.N.* 1135a15 ff.
4. That punishments are painful to the punished is, of course, true by definition. Cf. Ch. 1.c.
5. In Appendix I.

principle (*2–4*) is supposed to obviate the need for the convict to agree to the vital steps from *8* to *10*.

More fundamental objections, however, are raised by the apparatus of this argument. These objections centre upon two major ambiguities which Plato seems to exploit, or to ignore, in reaching his conclusion. The first ambiguity concerns "justice": by "just punishment" does Plato mean what is exacted in accordance with the law, or in accordance with our moral intuitions? Clearly the two need not be the same. Second, derivative from this is an ambiguity about what is legal: if Plato is discussing legality, does he refer to actual laws, as he obeyed them, or to an ideal legal or penal code?

At *1* the move from "paying the penalty" to "being punished justly" may be understood in one of two ways. Either the penalty is paid according to the law and *as such is just*; or paying the penalty, according to the law, *is fair and therefore just*. In the first case, the punishment is merely legal; in the second it is also morally right. So either Plato uses "just" as "legal" throughout, or else he shifts from "legal" to "moral" in the course of the argument. If "just" is used in a legal sense throughout, then the invocation of the principle of moral analysis (*E*) would be inappropriate, and the argument would fail. But if there is a shift from the legal to the moral usage, notably at *1* and at *5*, how may it be legitimised?

A justification of the shift lies in the second ambiguity of the argument, namely, the status of the laws in question. For Plato may be referring to an actual legal system or to an ideal one where Platonic justice ensures that punishments benefit.

That he is not referring to an actual penal system seems clear. He would hardly come out in favour of the system, or its near relations, that was responsible for the murder of Socrates. Furthermore, the illegitimacy of Plato's argument is at its most extreme in this interpretation of what is legal. Plato would be claiming that current retributive systems do in fact have the effect of reforming the criminal, a claim which appears particularly improbable in a society where the majority of punishments were fines, exiles or executions, none of which suggest any benefit accruing to the convict. Indeed, the great speech of Protagoras, which, I shall argue,[6] foreshadows many elements of Plato's own penology, contains an explicit attack on contemporary retributive systems. This suggests that Plato, as a penologist, would not acknowledge the claims of retributivism—whether real or ideal.

The penalty paid by the wrongdoer must be prescribed by some ideal legal or penal code. At first, this seems a plausible solution to Plato's difficulties. For some ideal legal system could indeed embody all the

6. Below, b.

attributes that morality would demand, and thus the shift from legal to moral could be achieved without raising the spectre of naturalism, or worse.

However, there are still problems, some of which will shortly inflate into full-scale objections.

First, if Plato is speaking of ideal penal systems, which conveniently mesh with his moral ideals, his attempt to saddle Polus and his like with a contradiction will not do. For Polus' idea of punishment as an unequivocal evil is based on current retributivism, and it is this type of punishment that Plato must show to be, in fact, a benefit. All that the argument has done, unfortunately, is to change the subject.

Second, if Plato repudiates contemporary retributivism, albeit not *in propria persona* in the *Protagoras*, how are we to explain the apparently retributive discussion of justice here? To this objection the answer must partly lie in the linguistic apparatus of the argument. "Paying the penalty," although sounding retributive, simply means "being punished," according to whatever system is in question, as *1* claims. The passive "being punished" is vital for the invocation of the modal principle at *6*. "Paying the penalty," however, is a helpful expression later (478), when Plato wants to suggest that by so doing the criminal will "give up" the evil in his soul. The punishment is just, I suggest, inasmuch as it is ideal and morally right (hence fine and beneficial). "Justice" is the commonplace moral notion to accompany punishment, but it need not, here, carry any retributive overtones, which might engender a conflict with the reformative policies to be outlined later in the dialogue.

Santas has argued[7] that Socrates is trying to establish a new criterion for what constitutes just punishment, a criterion which will supplement other, more commonplace ones. On my interpretation, however, the criterion will supersede all others and will produce a theory of punishment which bears only a tenuous relation to justice. The punishment is just inasmuch as it is morally right, but not just when examined in retributive terms.

Thus the talk of justice in the argument at *Grg.* 476 possesses a multiple equivocation between what is legal and what is moral, between what is ideal and what is actual with regard to legality, and between what is specifically retributive and what is generally right with regard to morality. On the interpretation I suggest, Plato is thinking of an ideal legal/penal system, which would embody not strict retributivism but a more powerful morality, the morality of benevolence.

Third, why should punishment be the best means to convey this benevolence? A major objection to this account of punishment is that Plato begs the institution; he assumes that

7. *Socrates*, p. 293.

. . . punishment is a necessary institution in all societies; but it can be morally justified only if it is remedial, therefore it must be remedial. This confuses what is with what ought to be.[8]

Does Plato fail to think radically and critically of the institution of punishment itself? This objection will be taken up further in the next chapter.

Fourth, if punishment is a benefit to him who suffers it, what exactly is that benefit?

Punishment as a Benefit

At 478a Socrates recalls the classification of arts established at 462.[9] The art of financing disposes of poverty, and the art of medicine cures ill health. The worst evil that a man can suffer, however, is neither material nor physical misfortune, but psychological disorder, which is corrected by the art of justice (*dikaiosunē*).[10] As we take men to the doctor to seek a cure, so we should take the wicked to a judge so that they may pay the penalty. For justice (*dikē*) rids a man of wickedness and injustice. According to the body/soul analogy, punishment is the medicine of wickedness—painful, but useful to effect a cure; when it succeeds, it makes us more temperate and just. We should not, therefore, avoid punishment, as is commonly advised; on the contrary, we should seek it out, just as we consult a doctor.[11] In this way, we will rid ourselves of the supreme wretchedness of an unhealthy soul, which, if ignored, may become chronic and incurable. Avoiding punishment is the action of the ignorant man, who does only what seems best to him and fails to achieve happiness.[12]

Thus Plato argues for reformative punishment. He does so by the use of two principles:

i. Virtue is happiness.

ii. An analogy may successfully be drawn between body and soul.[13]

Then he makes a further assumption which will give him trouble later on:

8. Dodds, *Gorgias*, p. 254.

9. Santas, *Socrates*, p. 289, discusses this classification in detail.

10. The virtue displayed by judges is conflated, throughout the dialogue, with the general virtue possessed by the just man, and imparted to him, perhaps, by the just judge. Cf. Ch. 10.a for this ambiguity in *technē* and Ch. 12.d for the advantage that such a conflation will confer on Plato's penology.

11. Note the ambiguity here between ideal and actual penal systems.

12. The model for this argument is discussed in Ch. 9.a.

13. It should be remembered that this analogy would be more plausible to Greeks than to ourselves. To most Greeks, after all, shades were pale imitations of the embodied individuals, possessed, not only of emotions, but even perceptions. Cf. *Od.* Bk. XI, Clytemnestra in Aeschylus, *Choephori* and Plato's own account, *Meno* 81.

iii. To be criminal in disposition is both necessary and sufficient for behaving in a criminal way, that is, committing crimes.

It will be remembered that Plato is more interested in criminality than in crimes.[14] Nevertheless, his argument here, in order to make effective the paradox about punishment, requires that the man with the disordered soul *be punished for his crimes* (committed because of his disordered soul) *and thereby reformed.* Now ideally perhaps he should be reformed with respect to his disposition, and actually he will be punished for his crimes. But not only is Plato changing the subject from actual to ideal penal situations, he is begging the question that a legal process, which by definition concerns itself with crimes, will thereby be operative against criminality. Two questions then arise: What is the connection between criminality and crimes? What renders a man liable to Platonic punishment? The first question has an approximate, but unsatisfactory, answer from *Rep.* IV.[15] The second still requires a reply.

The Methods of Reform

Punishment ideally, and when carried out correctly (478a7), acts as a psychic health service. Its function is to cure the patient and to rid him of his moral disease. However this is achieved, it must affect the disposition of the criminal and not be directed only against the crimes he has committed, as a penalty would be. The justification of punishment cites the obvious prudence of consulting the medical profession in order to cure physical illness. It claims that the same prudence obtains with the analogue, namely, submitting to treatment for psychological 'disease'— provided, of course, that the criminal proves curable.

However, therapy of this kind need not be carried out by doctors, or achieved by means of drugs. 'Therapy' and 'disease' are metaphors applied to the soul. How may the metaphor be cashed? And how does Plato suppose that reform is actually achieved? We are told that the criminal will become more *sōphrōn*, self-controlled. *Sōphrosunē* is the virtue of restraint[16] imposed from outside so this would be a matter of control or inhibition. Self-control may be achieved by enforced practice or habituation or, in an extreme form, by conditioning, where the responses of the subject are manipulated[17] in order that he will behave in the recommended way.

Certainly restraint, however etiolated a form of conditioning it is,

14. Cf. Ch. 9.d.
15. Discussed in Ch. 9.d and below, c.
16. Cf., e.g., *Grg.* 491d; *Rep.* 432a, 442c, where *sōphrosunē* is the virtue whereby the lower elements, in state or soul, are kept under control.
17. Again, compare the language of force and control of the *Republic* or the *Phaedrus*: *Rep.* 431d4, *Phaedr.* 253e4, etc.

may be contrasted with education, since the former works by compulsion, the latter by persuasion and with the consent of the subject. Yet education too is suggested in these passages, since the criminal will apparently become more just. This means that he will acquire a moral skill,[18] which is knowledge and is thus imparted by educative means. The process whereby a man becomes more self-controlled and more just, therefore, must combine restraint and education. Plato describes this process as analogous to remedial treatment.

In the discussion with Callicles, Socrates returns to the subject of punishment. At 504 he is trying to establish the prudence of having a well-ordered soul. In the process he suggests that the satisfaction of bodily appetites is often less useful than abstention, particularly when abstention promotes health. For health is desirable; sickness makes life wretched. So it is with the soul, that when it is evil, its appetites should be restrained, and it should do only those things which improve it.[19] This, of course, is in its own interests, just as medical treatment benefits the body. Since restraining the soul from its appetites is punishment,[20] punishment is better for the soul than indulgence.

Again the medical metaphor is prominent here: the prudence of submitting to punishment is urged on the basis of the body/soul analogy, although the discussion does not refer explicitly to the possibilities of cure. The practical detail recommends that punishment should combine restraint with encouragement (the soul should actively do what improves it: it should pursue virtue, 507d1). Neither restraint nor encouragement necessarily implies anything more than habituation, that is, learning a response by practice. Restraint or conditioning may readily be assimilated to conventional methods of punishment, where encouragement is more novel, since a penal system tends to inhibit rather than to promote activity. Clearly Plato supposes that practice will make a man virtuous,[21] and here it is suggested that punishment will provide the opportunity, or even the necessity, for such practice.

However, the passage also displays an intellectual slant, which cannot be ignored. The vicious man is ignorant, in contrast to the legislator who possesses the moral skill of *dikaiosunē*. This skill is transmitted to his subject, the moral agent, and skills are taught by educational rather than habituative processes. Thus at 505c4 Socrates jokingly suggests that dialectic is a form of punishment. Although this is facetious, the train of

18. Intellectualism in the *Grg.* (e.g., at 460) is argued for in Ch. 10.a.

19. Cf. also the pursuit and practice of self-control at 507a1.

20. Here Plato attempts a definition and once again runs into difficulties as to whether he is talking of ideal or actual punishments, and whether, in the end, he is institution-begging. Cf. Ch. 12.f.

21. Cf., e.g., *Grg.* 509e2, *Rep.* 444d.

his thought is clearly intellectual or educational. Correspondingly, the passage as a whole suggests that punishment should combine practice (conditioning in a weak version) and education.

A similar account appears at 517b, where Socrates is defining the proper activity of the good citizen towards his erring fellows: he should divert their desires and compel them towards improving activities. Now although the context here is not overtly penological, the mention of restraint picks up earlier discussions. Here, therefore, the same duality appears, in the combination of the restraint of the desires and encouragement towards right action. A new element, however, is added to the intellectualist overtones of persuasive encouragement, for now the good citizen, or the legislator, may have recourse to coercion. Consequently, restraint comes closer to the forceful operation of straightforward conditioning. Yet still Plato supposes that conditioning and education should work in harness.

The clearest formulation of the theory of punishment in the *Gorgias* appears in the eschatological myth at the end of the dialogue. The context creates some difficulties, particularly the retributive slant that can be observed at the beginning of the myth.[22] At 525b, however, Socrates offers an account of what he sees to be the proper function of punishment. The offender is either to be improved (*beltiōn gignesthai*) and thus to benefit, or he is to serve as an example to others who may be frightened by his suffering and be themselves improved thereby. Those who benefit by punishment, whether it be human or divine, are those who have committed curable crimes; only through pain and suffering can they be helped and rid of their evil. But those who have committed severe crimes are incurable and thus no longer susceptible to benefit. Therefore they serve as examples to others, who see their eternal pain and are better advised (*nouthetēmata*, 525c8). Consequently these others benefit.

The bare bones of this theory are straightforward. Plato offers a bipartite penology, combining reform and deterrence: curable criminals are improved by reform, whereas the incurable, who can no longer benefit by reform, are punished to deter others.

The curable/incurable antithesis obviously has its source in the pervasive body/soul analogy. But what does it mean? Earlier passages (such as 478e) suggest the common-sense position that incurability stems from a resistance in the individual to the process of reform, or from his failure to seek treatment. This notion must certainly be present when Plato distinguishes the two categories of criminal. Here, however, he makes

22. Ch. 13 discusses the eschatology in some detail.

the further claim that the criminal's incurability is derived from the magnitude of his offence, rather than from his insusceptibility to reform. Clearly, therefore, Plato regards some offences, such as tyranny, as so unspeakable that their very commission indicates the recalcitrance of their perpetrator, whereas the unconvinced activities of the petty thief, for example, apparently indicate that he is a good subject for reform.

Thus far, the correlation between crime and the ability to be reformed seems straightforward. We might envisage cases, however, either in which a man's appalling wickedness had not found an outlet in spectacular crimes such as tyranny, although he was nonetheless incurable, or, conversely, in which there were mitigating circumstances attached to another, curable criminal's commission of outrageous crimes. In short, although the crime may in general be a telling symptom of the malleability[23] of a man's disposition, the exigencies of circumstances or opportunity—not to mention Plato's own emphasis on the disposition at the expense of its manifestations—may make it difficult to determine the criminal's fixed intent to be or to stay criminal.

The precise nature of the reformative process in this passage still remains to be determined. The prominence of fear suggests simple conditioning, whereby an aversion is created in the individual, as it is in the observer, from repeating the offensive act. However, the response of the curable or the incurable criminal may vary not only according to his pain threshold, but also according to the level of understanding he may reach of the lesson offered by the legislator. Hence the observer is given advice (*nouthetēmata*, 525c8) not to emulate the incurables. It will follow that his behaviour is a matter of choice rather than habit, and choice is a rational process.

The echoes of earlier passages are insistent. Thus Socrates speaks of "becoming better" (which does not necessarily have the medical overtones it has in English) and of ridding ourselves of injustice. Such phrases abound in the analysis of prudence and virtue which takes up the body of the dialogue.[24] Hence in all these contexts, reform is seen to combine conditioning (in a weak version) and education; the latter must be part of the process if virtue is knowledge.[25] At the same time, the central curable/incurable antithesis derives from the medical analogy: vice is disease, and the purpose of the legislator is to cure (cf. 512a). Consequently, reform will be therapy, at least metaphorically;[26] the

23. Practical considerations, of course, will affect sentencing here.
24. Cf., e.g., 477a.
25. Ch. 10.a.
26. It will be remembered that Plato has difficulties with this metaphor; Ch. 10.c.

metaphor is reinforced by the notion that both punishment and medical treatment inflict pain.[27]

The theory of punishment arises directly from the prudential argument. Curable criminals benefit from punishment, which is justified then as benevolent action; indeed, as such, it hardly needs justification at all. The prudential arguments of the dialogue focus upon the interests of the individual who does wrong, rather than the interests of society at large. Correspondingly, the theory of punishment considers, in the first instance, the best interests of the wretched criminal. He is wicked, but involuntarily so, and the priority of the legislator must be to remove his wickedness at source. This may be done, Plato claims, by reformative punishment. If, however, the criminal is not susceptible to reform, his demands upon our benevolence lapse because he can no longer benefit.[28] Then he may be used as an exemplar to deter others from following him into incurable vice.

Questions of the consistency of the theory still remain. In particular, the complex theory of reform needs explanation and thence justification. It is described metaphorically as therapy. But what is the pharmacology of the mind?[29] Plato also seems to suppose that punishment combines the purposes of conditioning and education to achieve the moral improvement of the criminal. The question still remains whether these two methods of reform, and their description as remedial treatment, are alternative, or whether they are intended to be complementary. If they are complementary, are they compatible?

b. THE *PROTAGORAS*

In his great speech in the *Protagoras*, Protagoras expounds a theory of punishment which "has considerable affinities with Plato's own. . . ."[30] It is introduced to demonstrate the universal belief that virtue is acquired not by nature or by chance but by teaching and practice (*epimeleia*) (323c6). As his evidence, Protagoras adduces the fact that men do not show anger, offer advice, or enforce education or punishment on those who have evils in them by accident.[31] On the contrary, such men, the ugly or weak, are pitiable.[32] But some excellence is acquired by prac-

27. This is never far from Plato's mind when he adduces the medical analogy, cf., e.g., *Prt.* 354b, or the classification of goods at *Rep.* 357.

28. Cf. 512b.

29. Cf. the problems of the "vice is disease" thesis, Ch. 10.c.

30. Taylor, *Plato: Protagoras*, p. 96, offers a somewhat overschematised account of Protagoras' theory of punishment.

31. There is an oddity in the Greek here, but Protagoras seems to mean that these men who have evils in them *are* bad. Cf. *Grg.* 497e.

32. Cf. Ch. 9.a,b.

tice and teaching; when a man is bad in this respect, he is the target for anger, punishment, and advice. Since injustice, impiety, and all 'political' vices[33] are subject to punishment, it is clear that the corresponding virtue may be acquired by practice and learning.

The same conclusion may be reached by consideration of the function of punishment itself (324a4). For no one punishes a wrongdoer with an eye to the offence itself, or merely as a reaction against the offence, unless he is retaliating wildly and without reason.[34] This would be senseless, since the offence cannot be undone. Rational punishment, however, looks to the future by preventing the offender himself from repeating the offence and by deterring others from emulating him. So punishment is meant to turn others from vice (*apotropēs heneka*) and to teach men virtue. This is the function of punishment both publicly and privately. Justice, temperance, and virtue, all of which preserve the state, should be communicated to all men, women, and children by education and punishment until they improve. But the man who resists[35] education and punishment should be treated as incurable, and exiled or put to death.

With hindsight, the similarities with Plato's theory of punishment, as it later appears in the *Gorgias*, are striking. Protagoras advocates reform, as does Plato, on an educational basis and repudiates the immediate considerations of retaliation for the offence. He also suggests that we should discriminate between the curable and the incurable criminal and should treat each class differently. But the *Protagoras* as a whole is presented as an attack on the sophist's ethical views. Why, then, does Plato apparently adopt Protagoras' own penal theory in subsequent dialogues?

It may be that Plato here presents the real opinions of the sophist, which he himself found so attractive that he subsequently adopted them as his own. If this is the case at least at a superficial level, the passage offers two valuable pieces of evidence.

33. By "political" vice, Protagoras seems to mean states of character which endanger the survival of a state.

34. There are several points here. First, this seems to be an attack on the violence and irrationality of straight retributivism, which is characterised precisely by this concentration on the offence. Second, it is an important aspect of Plato's own penology that the offence is not of primary importance (cf. Ch. 9.d). Third, there may be significance in the use of *timōreisthai* at b1 and b3, to mean unthinking retaliation. Thus, unlike Taylor, at b4 I understand the verb to be *kolazei*, in contrast to *timōreitai*, and picked up from *kolazein* at b2. Cf. the contrast between *timōria* and *dikē* at *Laws* 728, discussed below, d. Fourth, the clear suggestion is that Protagoras, and thus Plato after him, will propound a 'thinking man's penology'.

35. Literally, "will not listen to." This phrase emphasises the rational aspect of punishment as Protagoras conceives it.

First, there is an explicit and severe attack on the irrationality of retribution and restitution, to the effect that Protagoras dismisses all traditional thinking about the restoration of damage, for the sake of the new morality of reform. At the same time, Protagoras claims that his attitude towards punishment is in fact universal and that all legislators aim to reform and deter. If Protagoras genuinely held such a view,[36] did he then think that ordinary legislation and punishment, as practised, for example, by the Athenians of his day, actually had the effect of reforming and deterring? Or is he advancing a prescription for the rational penology which should exist in a state? His language suggests the former, but common sense argues that he could not have been so naive. Equally, I have argued that in the Gorgias Plato gives the appearance of discussing conventional punishment. But his discussion is hedged with provisos so that he refers only to "just" punishment, which, quite probably, only exists in the fiction of the ideal state.[37]

Second, this account may be adduced as evidence for what Plato himself believed, providing valuable insight into the affinities between punishment and education. The dialogue is specifically about education and its relation to virtue, and "education" is being used in its strict intellectual sense. Thus, although Protagoras does not exclude the complementary function of habituation in teaching men to be moral, punishment is primarily intended to educate men in the business of being moral.

However, Protagoras' theory is similar to Plato's only in its superficial detail. The dialogue as a whole demonstrates that on three essential issues, which provide the ethical background to the reformative penology, the two men part company:

First, Protagoras presents the theory as a proof of his belief that virtue is teachable. However, his mistake, as Socrates sets out to prove, is twofold: he both imagines virtue to be a motley collection of qualities and fails to see that virtue is knowledge. Consequently, although he claims to teach virtue, he does not know what virtue is. In particular, Socrates complains, he does not realise that, being knowledge, it is preeminently teachable.

Socrates, however, supposes that virtue is knowledge but that (or consequently that) it cannot proceed by sophistic methods. Thus the theory of punishment, by implication, should operate not by the persuasions of the sophists but by the methods of dialectic.[38] Now although the Gorgias

36. Which is, of course, highly dubious since it is an opinion put by Plato into the mouth of Socrates' interlocutor.

37. Cf. above, a.

38. Cf. the exchanges, early in the Gorgias, about knowledge, persuasion, and the inadequacies of sophistic teaching; 453 ff.

does not present so extreme an intellectualist theory as this, it requires more reasoning on the part of the criminal than anything Protagoras has to offer.

Second, although both Protagoras and Plato are interested in the disposition of the criminal rather than exclusively in the crimes committed by him, they consider the effects of criminality in a different light. Plato, responding to the prudential argument, is concerned first and foremost with the effect of criminality on the criminal himself.[39] So he leaves considerations of the interests of the community at large aside (apart from the fact that punishment in general is a public, not private process), until the individual's rights have lapsed (by his becoming incurable). Hence his thinking may be characterised as humanitarian. Protagoras, however, is interested in the effects of criminality on the public good and is hence anxious to create political virtue, which keeps the state together (324e1). Thus although Plato justifies the execution of the incurable criminal primarily on the grounds that he can no longer benefit from living, Protagoras, albeit silent on the justification of capital punishment, would adduce the general importance of the preservation of the state (e.g., 323a3, c1). Consequently, Plato's penal justification is simple; Protagoras' is complicated by the possibly warring demands of the individual and of the group. This passage, therefore, brings out Plato's advocacy of an individualist account, which is at odds with the priority urged by Protagoras—and perhaps by Plato's contemporaries in general—that we should consider the public good.

Third, the first stages of Protagoras' argument run directly counter to one of the major tenets of Socratism. For Protagoras supposes that men are culpably vicious and that therefore anger towards them is appropriate (323d). Socrates, however, claims that no one does wrong willingly; consequently, as Plato will claim (e.g., at *Laws* 731c), we should pity the criminals.

Implicitly, therefore, these three areas represent Plato's analysis of the true underpinnings of his philosophy of punishment. They may be summed up by the two Socratic paradoxes, "Virtue is knowledge" and "No one does wrong willingly" (which the rest of the dialogue is designed to explain), combined with the further Socratic tenet, central to the *Gorgias*, that virtue is in the interests of the individual. Thus if we understand what virtue is, as Protagoras fails to do, we will understand the function of punishment. Equally, if we understand that virtue is in our interests and not merely in the interests of the group to which we belong, then we will have an effective justification for the reformative system, which provides us with the means of achieving happiness.

---

39. As I have argued, Ch. 9.a,b,c, and witness the individualist cast of the *Gorgias*.

c. THE *REPUBLIC*

The theory of punishment looms but small in the *Republic* and is presented in a fragmented way. This might be a consequence of the idealism of its political theory.[40] Plato is reluctant to admit that the perfect citizens of the perfect state will ever be in a position to need the process of reform. But, more significantly, the prudential account given here is meant to replace the reasoning of the *Gorgias* by offering a sensitive investigation of moral psychology, rather than of our moral language. Consequently, the air of paradox has dissipated, and one function of punishment in the prudential paradoxes of the *Gorgias* disappears. However, in the three passages where the theory of punishment figures at all, the mature doctrines of the *Republic* offer illumination—and complication—of some important issues.

At 409 Socrates compares the judiciary of the ideal state to the medical profession.[41] Judges and doctors will perform the same task: they will treat the bodies and the souls of those citizens who have good constitutions, but they will allow the unhealthy to die, whereas those who are actively malevolent they will put to death because they are incurable.

At 444, Socrates adduces the analogy between health and psychic excellence. Thus he obtains Glaucon's agreement to the proposal that the just man is happy, regardless of appearances (445a1), on the grounds that health is in our interests. However, the unjust man, who does not pay the penalty[42] and is not improved by punishment, is wretched. For that very thing for which he lives is confused and destroyed, and his life is not worth living.

The tripartite psychology is recapitulated in Book 9 to demonstrate the intrinsic benefit of the life of virtue. The argument from 580 contains passing reference to the function of punishment, although again this is not the central issue. When we are assessing the lives of the just man who is not rewarded for his justice, or of the unjust man who escapes punishment, it is absurd to suppose that the latter is happy; for by escaping notice he becomes even more wicked (591b1). But the spirited

40. Cf. Havelock, *The Greek Concept of Justice*, p. 321, who explains this, oddly, as Plato being "unwilling to accept the fact of individuation."

41. He stipulates, however, that although the doctor should have personal experience of the disease he treats, the judge should be unacquainted with vice.

42. I argued, above, a, that Plato's talk of "penalties" in *Grg.* does not show that he is advancing a retributive theory. The same, surely, is true here, in a context wherein the consequential relation of crime and retribution has been officially shelved. However, "payment" is again well suited to the notion of disposing of the evil from the soul, whereas the participle *kolazomenos*, "being punished," suggests the gradual improvement of the offender under punishment. The combination of both active and passive versions is perhaps intended to convince us that reform can indeed be effective, when carried out under ideal conditions.

part of the man who encounters punishment is calmed and his reason freed (591b3). His soul is organised for the best (the prudential argument again), and he possesses temperance, justice and intelligence—by far more honourable than bodily health. Thus a sensible man will direct his life towards the proper respect of such education (*mathēmata*)[43] for his soul will thereby become virtuous, and he will obey the principle of harmony in all his affairs.

The *Gorgias* offered the curable/incurable antithesis as a central feature of the reformative theory. But in the earlier dialogue, the distinction between the categories of criminal appeared to rest on the gravity of the crimes they had committed. This, I argued, was not only allusively presented, but it was also an implausible criterion for deciding whether a particular criminal was susceptible to the reformative process.[44]

The *Republic*, however, drops the idea that a man's crimes are the only indicators of the malleability of his disposition. As we have seen, it is a mark of the moral psychology of the *Republic* that being has priority over doing, which fades into insignificance.[45] Accordingly, it would be incongruous here to find behaviour the only telling symptom of the disposition. Rather, at 410a, the curable criminal and his malevolent counterpart are differentiated by the bad condition of their souls. The detailed psychology of Book IV offers further enlightenment: the criminal's soul is somehow disordered, and in some criminals, who have certain types of disorder, this may amount to intransigence.

For example, the curable criminal, like the timocratic man (549 ff.), may have a reasoning part which has never developed properly but which may well be susceptible to education. The incurable criminal, however, may suffer irreversibly from a hydra-headed appetite (like the democratic man, 558ff.), the greed of which can never be cut off. The tripartite psychology leaves room for various explanations of curability and incurability. But, whatever the specifications, such an account would have the merit of sense—the sensible practicality of excluding from the penal process him who is dispositionally incapable of being reformed.

There remains the question of whether punishment is the only, or the best, way of achieving this end. Liability to punishment is determined according to what the criminal is, not what he does. But is the treatment of a disposition a punishment at all? In the *Republic* there is

43. It is perhaps significant that no distinction in kind is offered, or need be made, between the education appropriate to make the sensible man virtuous, and the punishment appropriate to free the reason of the unjust man. In both cases, I suggest, Plato would argue for an educative process, rather than begging a retributive system for the case of the less virtuous man alone.

44. Cf. above, a.

45. This, of course, is a problem; cf. Ch. 9.d.

no Polus, to whose notions of punishment the theory must conform. Plato cannot be accused, therefore, of changing the subject. He is still vulnerable, however, to the charge of begging the institution.

Reformative punishment, from the evidence of the *Gorgias*, should involve a complex system of conditioning, encouragement and education, and in this work it is metaphorically described as therapy. The medical metaphor remains unchanged in the *Republic* (409a ff.; 445a).[46] But whereas the inchoate moral psychologising of the *Gorgias*[47] offered no systematic explanation of the workings of the various methods of reform, the theories of *Republic* Book IV suggest a direct correlation. The criminal is to be completely converted (445b3). Now repression or conditioning is suitable treatment for the epithumetic part of the soul;[48] encouragement is appropriate for the *thumoeides*;[49] and education, of course, is proper for the intellect. Accordingly, the complex psychology ties in neatly with—and even provides an explanation of—the complex penology. What is more, the *Republic* even suggests the order in which these elements of reform should be employed. For education is of no use until, as in the child growing up, the monster is tamed and the lion trained to fight on the side of reason. Only then can reason rule.[50]

At times, however, Book IV tells a slightly different story. As healthy activities promote and preserve health, so just acts promote and preserve justice in the soul (444e ff.). The habit of just behaviour, therefore, leads to the actualisation of justice in the soul.[51] This account of the creation of virtue in the soul is not necessarily at odds with the reformative system. For in order to perform just acts, and as a prelude to acquiring the habit of justice, the appetites must be forcibly repressed and the spirit encouraged. This treatment of the lower elements of the soul, therefore, is the condition of habituative justice which, in time, leads to order and true justice, both internal and external, as a matter of rational choice.

Clearly these allusions to the theory of punishment represent no radical change from the penology of the *Gorgias*. Plato still insists that the man who escapes punishment is worse off than the one who suffers it (the converse of Gyges' ring) (445a; 591b), and he still represents punishment as a benefit to the criminal. Punishment is a member of the

---

46. Cf. *Sophist* 229a, where punishment as education is described as analogous to medical therapy.

47. Cf. Ch. 10.a.

48. Cf. the enslavement of appetite, 554a7.

49. Cf. the training of the soldier class, 468 ff.

50. Cf. Ch. 10.b. Cf. 444d8 ff.

51. But cf. Ch. 9.d. for an analysis of the logical problems here.

third category of goods, like gymnastic and medicine,[52] which are good not in themselves but in their consequences. Reform, recommended still on the basis of the body/soul analogy, aims to remove moral evil from the souls of incurable criminals, by whatever means will be effective, whether repressive, permissive or educational.

However, a few changes are evident. The deterrent arm of the theory is barely mentioned (410a1), and the execution of the incurable criminals is urged as much for reasons of utility as humanity (410a5). Considerations of the public good, then, are given greater prominence.[53] But in a work with the political interest of the *Republic* is such a shift of emphasis surprising?

d. THE *LAWS*

An obvious source for evidence of Plato's penological views is the late work, the *Laws*. This is a discussion about the proper legislation of the imaginary state of Magnesia. It consists of a detailed penal code, accompanied by a theoretical account of how legislation should be effected. This structure makes two particular demands on the content of the work. First, dealing with the *minutiae* of legislation causes Plato to consider the practicalities of punishment from the point of view not only of the criminal but also of the legislator and of the victim of a crime. This, as we shall see, leads him away from the individualist approach to criminality suggested in the *Gorgias* and towards considerations of the public good.[54] Second, because he is here explicitly offering and justifying a penal code, we may expect greater clarity and further detail than we found in earlier contexts where punishment was a side issue.

Two long passages are of particular interest: the first appears in Book 5, and the second in Book 9. Both are complex, and considerably vexed in interpretation. I hope to show that it is in the detail, not in the theoretical basis, that Plato's views have changed.

Book 5 presents a general introduction to the penal code by offering recommendations to right behaviour. The question of punishment is again introduced by the prudential argument (726 ff.). A man's soul is his most divine possession. But we tend, giving in to the blandishments of pleasure, to harm our souls, not to honour them. Thus a man may deny responsibility for his misdeeds, considering wrongdoing to be beneficial, whereas in fact it is harmful.[55] Therefore, disobedience to

52. Again, echoes of the *Gorgias*, 464 ff.
53. So the plague of drones is described as *nosēma poleōs*, at 552c4, and it is their anti-social effect that is thus emphasised.
54. I suggested above, c, that hints of this shift are to be found in the *Republic*.
55. 727b ff. The echoes of the *Gorgias* are unmistakeable here.

the injunctions of the legislator actively militates against our interests.

But[56] no one calculates the greatest so-called[57] justice for bad behaviour,[58] namely, that the offender will be assimilated to bad men[59] and, like them, will flee the company and the conversation of the good. Consequently he will behave to others as bad men naturally do, and suffer as they do at the hands of others.[60] Eventually he will become most wretched, either failing to find a cure for his evil, or perishing in order that others may be saved. But his execution should not be called justice (for justice is a fine thing)[61] but *timōria*, the unpleasant consequence of wrongdoing.[62]

The process described here has several stages. First the subject ne-

56. The following passage, 728b2–c8, is difficult to interpret; cf. Saunders' recent discussion, *Notes on the* Laws *of Plato*, pp. 18 ff. *Theaetetus* 176d ff. offers a similar sentiment.

57. "So-called" either because it is not just, in Plato's view, or, more likely, because it is an effect of wrongdoing which follows without the interference of an external judicial agency; cf. Ch.1.c. To describe it as 'justice', therefore, is to take liberties with the traditional meaning of *dikē*. This "justice" should be distinguished from "punishment", *timōria*, described later in the passage.

58. 'Bad behaviour' here seems to mean bad treatment of the soul. Compare 728c6.

59. Cf. the advice to avoid the company of bad men at 854.

60. This sentence is condensed. The phrase *Poiein kai legein* at c1–2 seems to refer back to *poiein* at b7 and to parody the beneficial effects of the company and conversation of good men, b5. I have translated 'behave'. *Paschein*, however, must look forward to the repetitions *pathos* at c2 and *pathē* at c4. What the criminals suffer, therefore, is *timōria* which, as I shall argue, is the contemporary practice of capital punishment.

61. We need not infer, as Saunders does, that *timōria* is therefore positively ignoble, but merely that it is morally neutral.

62. The difficulty here lies in disentangling who suffers *timōria*—the man who is not cured, or the man who is executed. The vexed passage is 728c 4–5: "Both the man who suffers it, and the man who avoids it, are wretched; one because he is not cured, the other because he dies that many others may be saved." Saunders supposes that since *timōria* is not like Platonic reform (e.g., because it is not noble) then it is the man who is not cured who suffers it; whereas the man who avoids it becomes incorrigible and is then executed by the state.

On this interpretation, however, both men are wretched because they are not cured. The second is even more wretched than the first because he is executed as well, whereas the balance of the passage suggests that they are equally wretched. An additional disadvantage of this version is that it tells us nothing at all about what *timōria* actually is, but only that the man who fails to be cured suffers it.

It seems preferable to suppose that *timōria* does refer to some penal activity, and the most likely candidate with which to identify it would thus be the capital punishment of the second man. Thus the first man is wretched, since he fails to find a cure, and his sickness becomes chronic. This happens, of course, when the Platonic system is not in force. The second man, however, has no chance to become wretched, as an incurable, because he is first made wretched by being killed, under the provisions of *timōria*. Thus each man is wretched, but in a different way. There are clear echoes of the *Gorgias* and the equivocation between actual and ideal punishment that appears there.

glects his soul. This leads him into the company of bad men, which, in turn, causes him to emulate them. Then he lays himself open to the traditional consequence of wrongdoing, namely, execution for the preservation of the state. But even if he survives, he is wretched, for he never finds a cure for the evil in his soul, and this evil, as the preceding passage argued, is in his worst interests. Wrongdoing therefore is doubly imprudent, for he risks either a chronic disease of the soul or summary execution.

The purpose of this passage is clearly not to describe the familiar Platonic penal programme, nor even to introduce a new one. Rather, it is intended to amplify the prudential argument. Previously, Plato concentrated on the intrinsic disadvantage of vice, in terms of its effect on the soul. He advances a similar argument here. But in addition he offers the deterrent effect of conventional capital punishment, which is inflicted as a result of wrongdoing and is equally undesirable.

Now although so far *timōria* is not a part of his own theory but rather a feature of contemporary penal systems adduced in support of the prudential argument, it is, for present purposes, undeniably useful. That Plato considers it at all suggests perhaps that he is losing confidence in the main argumentation of the *Gorgias* and the *Republic*, where he claimed that virtue is happiness, vice is misery. And from here it is but a short step to incorporating into his penology deterrent provisions, beyond the execution of the incurables (for the man who is subject to capital punishment here is not incurable, although he is wretched), in support of the appeal to prudence. It will, of course, follow that the Platonic system of reform, which pre-empts execution, is to be recommended.

At 728c, therefore, Plato advises us to pursue the better (*ta ameinona*)[63] with a view to honouring the soul or at least to improve, as best we can, our worse impulses. Such is the rationale behind the reformative theory, which claims that moral activity is in the best interests of our souls and hence of ourselves.

At 731b Plato turns to a new topic, the problem of how the innocent may escape the evil effects of the crimes of others. Those who have committed incurable crimes should be resisted by unrestrained punishment. However, in dealing with those who commit curable crimes, we should remember that every unjust man is so against his will, for who would voluntarily incur the greatest evil in his soul? A man who does so is therefore to be pitied, and our anger towards the curable criminal should be restrained.

This passage reintroduces a familiar element of the original theory

63. Moral rather than prudential.

of punishment: the curable/incurable antithesis, which is now explicitly combined with the Socratic paradox "No one does wrong willingly."[64] The distinction between curable and incurable is now once more made on the basis of the crime each man has committed, and we seem, despite the promise of the *Republic*, to be back with the *Gorgias* picture of recidivism.[65] But here the reformative system is not called into play at all. It is true that the prudential approach of the passage will suggest that reformative punishment should be advocated. The Stranger's present purpose, however, is to outlaw retribution.[66] To this effect he insists that we curb our emotional response to the criminal who has committed curable crimes.

The absence of a reformative penology here may well be the consequence of a new interest in the problems of victim and legislator. The original question (at 731b) is how to avoid the effects of the crimes of others, and the curable/incurable antithesis applies not to criminals but to their crimes.[67] Similarly, the description of the way we should behave towards the criminal offers a new insight into the reaction of both the observer and the legislator to involuntary wickedness.

Plato's primary concern in earlier works such as the *Gorgias* and *Protagoras*[68] was for the criminal. Hence he came to advocate reform as a corollary to the prudential argument, since reform provided the means whereby the vicious man could achieve happiness. However, the penal codification on which Plato is engaged here has suggested to him that there are other problems involved in dealing with criminals, notably, the prudence, for the potential victim, of avoiding the wrongdoer, and the emotional response that the sight of wrongdoing provokes in both observer and legislator.

Again at 735b the Stranger addresses himself to the problems confronting the legislator. The community is a flock from which the unhealthy stock must be removed. This culling will, first, preserve the legislator from the excessive trouble of treating the chronically wicked and, second, protect the rest of the citizen body from infection. The medicine to achieve this end is punishment (*kolazein*) by *dikē* with *timōria*;[69] *timōria* will be continued up to the point of death or banishment. Those who have committed the greatest crimes are incurable[70] and constitute a

64. Cf. Ch. 9.b,c. Plato thus has a dual reason to exculpate the criminal.

65. Cf. also 735e3, cf. n. 70 below.

66. Cf. Protagoras' attack on retributivism, above, b.

67. I take it, however, that this is not simply a matter of the crime's being irreversible, but of its reflecting curability in the criminal. Cf. below, n. 70, and above, a and c.

68. Cf. above a and b. The individualistic approach is argued for in Ch. 9, e.g., at c.

69. The force of *meta* is to subordinate *timōria* to *dikē*, suggesting that it is not the synonym, but the instrument, of *dikē*.

70. This suggests that at 731b "incurable" is meant to describe the criminal's disposi-

source of great harm to the state; they must therefore be removed. Alternatively, those who show themselves unwilling to cooperate in the organisation of the state should be transferred to a colony.

Plato's priority seems to have changed from the early period. He considers the problem of the incurable criminal now from the point of view of the state as a whole: if the person is a danger, that is sufficient reason for his removal.[71] The means to his removal are described as *timōria*. At 728 this meant conventional punishment as it occurs in states which are looking for self-preservation, though Plato was not, in this earlier context, himself committed to such an institution. At 735, however, he advocates the use of *timōria* for the public ends of the purging of the body politic.

Thus the execution of the incurables, urged in the *Gorgias* primarily as a matter of prudence for the criminals themselves, is advocated here for the sake of the safety of others.[72] At the same time, we may infer from the *Gorgias* that the sight of the suffering of the incurables will deter others. And we may infer from *Laws* 728b that the possibility of such punishment is to be adduced as a part of the prudential argument against wrongdoing.[73]

This harsher view predominates, but reform has not entirely disappeared. The medical metaphor prevails in this passage,[74] which strongly suggests that during the process of justice effected by *timōria* the curable criminal might be saved. If there are incurable criminals, those who have committed lesser crimes may indeed be curable. Similarly, the bad candidates for admission to the state should be given every opportunity to be persuaded and converted in favour of the organisation of the state (736c2). Implicitly, therefore, the Stranger admits the possibility that the bad men might be converted and thus reformed and made into virtuous members of the community.

Book 9 is, in its detail, reminiscent of the bleak outlook of Book 5. For example, from the outset of the book, the Stranger is concerned

---

tion, not the possibilities of restoring the damage of the crime. Cf. also the criminal at 853d, who is so hardened that he fails to respond to the admonitions of the legislator. Nevertheless, Plato still seems to suppose that the crime is an adequate measure of the criminal's disposition.

71. I have argued that Socrates would not endorse Protagoras' exposition of this view, above, b, since it does not coordinate readily with the individualist approach.

72. Cf. *politophthora* at 854c7.

73. The two arguments—of the *Gorgias* and of the *Laws*—differ slightly, inasmuch as the *Gorgias* uses the otherwise hopeless incurable to influence others. The details of the argument defend against charges of victimisation. Here, however, there is no such security, since Plato might be tempted to threaten, and even to carry out, wildly excessive punishment to secure deterrence. Cf. Ch. 12.b.

74. Cf. also 853d8.

about the inevitable occurrence of crime in the new state (853c2)[75] and proposes stringent measures to ensure, first, that the potential criminal will be deterred by the threat of punishment and, second, that, when he does offend, he suffers for it. Thus the prudential argument is supported by the deterrent effects of the penal code.

Nevertheless, the intrinsic disadvantage of wrongdoing, which is aggravated by association with bad men (854c, cf. 728b), is still urged, on the individualistic grounds that death is preferable to continued life with a diseased soul. And this hint of a humanitarian approach is followed up. In Book 9 the theory of reform and deterrence is presented formally, making its first appearance in the legislation against sacrilege. Here the Stranger claims that the offender, by paying the penalty proposed,[76] may perhaps become temperate and so improve. For the function of all lawful *dikē* (justice or punishment) is to make the offender either more virtuous or less wicked (854d). But if a man who has received the proper upbringing is nevertheless guilty of sacrilege, he should be executed as incurable. To him his death will be the least of evils, whereas it will be of positive benefit to those who witness his removal.

From 857c the problems and methods of the legislator again form the central topic.[77] The relation between the man who practises *ad hoc* medicine, but knows nothing, and the man who practises medicine with reason and skill illustrates the distinction between haphazard lawmaking and the informed legislation which the Stranger offers. The true doctor does not treat his patient; he educates him. Equally, the true legislator does not coerce; he teaches, providing advice about what is right and just and explaining how that is in our interests.[78] Thus Plato reinforces the medical analogy by suggesting that the educative process of punishment does in fact find an echo in the treatment provided by the doctor. At the same time, he insinuates that neither medicine nor punishment are as they are conventionally conceived.

The Socratic paradox "No one does wrong willingly" has already been adduced in a penological context (731c). But here (860c) the Stranger realises that the voluntary/involuntary antithesis, as it had been

---

75. Contrast the idealistic view of the *Republic* which explained (as I argued above, c) the exiguous penological evidence of that work.

76. Here there is no doubt that the Stranger assumes that harsh punishment will in fact have a reformative effect. We should remember, however, with reference to the earlier discussions of 'paying the penalty', that this is the ideal situation, not the effect of contemporary institutions.

77. Cf. also *Grg.* 464a ff.; *Rep.* II and onwards. The position of the legislator will be discussed in Ch. 12.d.

78. 858d6, discussed in Ch. 10.b.

redefined by Socrates, causes some difficulty. For traditional legislation demands that some acts be described as voluntary and others as involuntary, because some acts, whether they benefit or injure, are done on purpose and others by accident. In contrast, the Socratic paradox claims that all just men are so voluntarily, and all unjust men are so involuntarily.[79] If, therefore, an unjust man commits a deliberate injury, we have the anomalous situation of the involuntary agent (in the Socratic sense) doing an act that is, in the legal sense, voluntary. Alternatively, if a just man accidentally injures someone, he may be described as a voluntary man doing an involuntary act.

The difficulty clearly lies in the ambiguity of the term 'voluntary'. This term may be used in the Socratic sense to refer exclusively to the just man who is voluntarily so ('voluntarily' because, first, everyone wants to be just and, second, such a man has the knowledge and control to be what he wants to be).[80] Alternatively, it may be used in the normal legal sense to refer to an action done deliberately.

As a solution, the Stranger observes that the criteria for determining the Socratic usage of the antithesis should be distinguished from those used to determine the legal usage (861c3). He proposes, therefore, a complex classification of injuries (*blabai*). Injuries may take place either by accident or by deliberation. Accidental injuries should not be evaluated as injustices, inasmuch as they are accidents. Only deliberate injuries may be classified as unjust. Accidents may be done by anyone, whether he be just or unjust. But deliberate actions may qualify as injustices, and, as such, they are committed by unjust men only. Nevertheless, these men will still be acting involuntarily in the Socratic sense. Thus when a man does an injury (which is not an injustice), the law will be called upon to restore the damage but not to proceed against the agent himself. In contrast, if he injures deliberately, he will be punished for his injustice, since he acted with intent. Therefore he will be subjected to reform.

As for the just man, when he acts with deliberation, his action will necessarily be called just, since an act is just only if the intent is just (862b). This does not mean that his moral character predetermines our evaluation of his actions (as just or unjust) irrespective of his intentions in the individual case.[81] Rather, it means that his just disposition leads inevitably to just intentions; thus what he does will predictably be just. Any acts which he does that turn out injurious must be the product of

79. It is a curiosity of Greek that the Stranger can say that they are "bad involuntary," using two adjectives in harness. Cf. Ch. 9.d, on the emphasis on dispositions.

80. Cf. Ch. 9.a,b; Ch. 10.a,b.

81. Cf. the problems of the "good conscience," discussed above in Ch. 10.b, and below in Appendix II.

mistake or accident, therefore at odds with his general moral intent, and therefore involuntary.

Thus we may expect just acts from the just man and unjust acts from the unjust man, when each is acting with intent. In terms of the new definition, the just man under these circumstances will be acting both deliberately and voluntarily, in that he is pursuing his true interests. The unjust man will, however, be acting deliberately but not, in terms of the paradox, voluntarily,[82] since he is in fact failing to follow his own true interests.

The new distinction between crimes and injuries calls for a modification of the penology, rendered even more urgent by the concern, exhibited as early as Book 5, with the interests of the victim. For if damage is done, although it happens by accident,[83] the victim suffers; the legislator's task is to alleviate his suffering by providing for recompense. Thus at 862b6 the Stranger declares that the function of the law, in cases of damage done by accident, is to heal the wound, restoring what has been lost and correcting what has gone wrong. So, by providing restitution, the judge restores the disputants to friendship.[84] Effectively, then, considerations of injury are divorced from those of injustice.

Finally, the Stranger offers a schema of his "cure for injustice" (862d1 ff.). Whenever a man commits an offence, the law will exact restitution for the harm done. Then it will teach and compel him never to repeat his crime voluntarily, or at least to be far less inclined to do so. This may be accomplished by word or by deed, by pleasure or by pain, by restraint or encouragement—in short, by whatever means will be effective to make the offender hate vice and love virtue. But whoever is incurably disposed towards crime no longer has any benefit in life, yet by his death he may confer a double benefit on others, first, by the example of his suffering (which will deter them from criminality) and, second, by ridding the state of his evil presence. Only when these conditions are filled (i.e., the interests of the offender have lapsed *and* the potential benefit to others is certain) is capital punishment justified.

In outline, therefore, the theory of punishment has not changed

82. Cf. the analysis of responsibility and culpability, Ch. 9.a,b. The Socratically voluntary man alone could be culpable (although he is not, but rather laudable, being just); whereas the legally voluntary criminal is not culpable but is still responsible.

83. Accidents had been excluded from consideration in the moral psychology. Cf., e.g., *Prot.* 352a7, the akratic must be *able* to pursue either of the courses of action in question (*exon autōi*).

84. Similar provisions for restitution precede the theoretical account of the legislation for theft at 857a, where it is hardly surprising that the thief is required to restore what he has taken. Cf. also, e.g., 878c8.

from the *Gorgias* to the *Laws*: reform is combined with the execution of incurable criminals to deter the rest. Earlier works described reform as therapy and supposed it to combine conditioning and education. But in the *Laws*, the medical metaphor is even more prominent, and punishment is explicitly described as cure (e.g., at 862c8). Yet a short argument at 857c-e seems designed to show that the true legislator educates rather than coerces, although the provisions for the deterrence of the potential criminal (e.g. at 853) closely resemble the harshest form of conditioning. At 862d the Stranger declares that the means to achieve the reform of the criminal should be subordinated to the end, and thus persuasion should be combined with force, intellectual with habituative means.

Consequently the theory of reform now formally amalgamates the different elements discerned in the early argumentation to establish the penology. And the source of this complexity is now firmly located in the moral psychology, for the Stranger proceeds immediately to outline the tripartite account of the causes of vice.[85]

The innovation of the *Laws* appears in the subsidiary provisions surrounding the theory of punishment proper. First, the new analysis of the distinction between injustice and accidental injury leads the Stranger to formulate a theory of restitution which, when the damage is done by an unjust man, will accompany reform, but which will operate in isolation for cases of accidental damage. This theory, however, remains a side issue, which does not affect the core of the reformative account.

Second, there is the more problematic institution of legal measures to support the appeal to the imprudence of wrongdoing (*timōria*). This was foreshadowed in Protagoras' theory of punishment, but Plato himself had never advocated it before. It differs from, and supplements, the deterrent arm of the theory in that it is not practised solely on the incurable criminal. Also, its power lies largely in the threat, rather than in the exemplar.

The justification of such a theory is difficult on independent grounds. It has, for example, no built-in guarantee against victimisation. What is more, there are problems about its justification and its operation in harness with reform. Although the presentation of the 'official' theory suggests that reformative considerations would take precedence in deciding the particular punishment to be imposed on any individual, it could be argued that in some cases the interests of reform and the interests of deterrence will actively conflict. Plato would presumably argue, however, that if a man can be reformed he will stand in no need of deterrence. If this is so, then the deterrent function will always take second

85. Cf. Ch. 10.b, and Appendix II.

place. Consequently this innovation, which may be seen to be the product of increased pessimism about the security of the prudential argument, is also, like restitution, peripheral to the central theory of reform.

e. SUMMARY

The prominence of penological issues in the four dialogues discussed here varies, as we have seen. Both the *Gorgias* and the *Laws* devote a fair amount of space to the penology, which is hardly surprising. For the *Gorgias* exploits the conventional view of punishment as an evil, to arrive at a paradox in keeping with the Socratic presentation of the other arguments, and in the *Laws*, the Stranger feels it incumbent upon himself to offer a philosophical basis for the penal measures he proposes. In the *Protagoras*, by contrast, the theory is presented not by Socrates but by Protagoras, and it demonstrates the superficial excellence, but basic unsoundness, of the sophist's moral and political views. From this we may deduce where Plato believes the true foundations of his penology to lie. But in the *Republic*, where we would expect a discussion of social institutions such as punishment, there is a minimum of evidence for the penology. This seems to be primarily a consequence of the powerful presentation, in the *Republic*, of the wretchedness of injustice. For the paradoxes and sophistical devices of the *Gorgias* are no longer necessary in the light of the rich moral psychology of Plato's middle period. At the same time, the *Republic*, in contrast with the more pessimistic or prosaic account of the *Laws*, is the product of an idealist outlook, wherein Plato supposes that the citizens of his ideal state will not commit the crimes which will render them subject to punishment. In these terms, therefore, its institution might be seen as an admission of defeat and, therefore, as far as possible something to be excluded.

Despite such differences, the penal theory to be found in these four dialogues remains constant. It centres upon the institution of reform, whose objective is to make the criminal virtuous, for his own benefit. The means employed by reform may be described as therapy, as conditioning (restraint and encouragement), or as education. But, however punishment is characterised, it is determined by whatever means are suitable to the case. Thus not only will it repress, persuade, or educate (depending on which part of the soul needs treatment), but also it will use all kinds of inducements, both painful and pleasurable. For Plato's theory is not an adaptation of current or even ideal retributive penal systems, even though the details of his argument sometimes suggest too strong a reliance upon the language of justice to remove the suspicion of retributivism altogether. No, the innovation of his theory of reform is that the means will be totally subordinated to the end, namely, that the disposition of the unfortunate criminal should be completely converted.

Next Plato proposes a supplementary system of the execution, or severe punishment, of the incurable criminal, with the intention of deterring others from becoming criminal. In addition, in the *Laws* he follows up his contention that virtue is in the interests of its practitioner, by claiming that vice, though intrinsically imprudent, is also subject to punishment and is therefore doubly to one's disadvantage. This kind of punishment, *timōria*, is also deterrent but should be distinguished from the suffering of the incurables. Finally, the *Laws* also provides for the exaction of restitutive payment from the offender; restitution will operate irrespective of the offender's intentions to damage or injure his victim.

Deterrence, in the Platonic system, is often explained by appeal to considerations of the public good. These more or less utilitarian prescriptions arise directly from the political contexts in which they appear, where the benefit of the community, set against the interests of the individual, must have some importance. Likewise restitution appears in the strongly political context of the *Laws*, where Plato's interest in the suffering of the victim arises from the discussion of a community rather than from an ethical analysis.

But the central humanitarian theory is firmly rooted in Plato's ethics and his moral psychology. To begin with, the individualistic ethic, combined with the Socratic exculpation of the criminal, will lead Plato towards a reformative penology. Plato's objective will be to remove the criminal's evil disposition, because such a disposition is inherently to the criminal's disadvantage. And, once Plato has adopted a general policy of reform, its description and its various methods are directly determined by his moral psychology. On the one hand, the idea that vice is caused by ignorance and by the disorder of the lower parts of the soul will suggest education combined with conditioning as the proper methods of *completing* the treatment.[86] On the other hand, the metaphorical conception of vice as disease will encourage Plato to speak of reform as therapy. In general, the process of reform may be described as acquiring the habit of virtuous behaviour that will eventually lead to possession of justice, in full rationality. Thus the combined theory of reform is explained by the moral psychology and protected from conflict by the supposition that conditioning precedes reform.

The only problem that arises here is Plato's equivocation about the focus of punishment. In contexts where the individual and his psycho-

---

86. That the criminal should end up *completely* virtuous must be the objective, if virtue is happiness, and any falling short of virtue is undesirable. Cf. Ch. 9.a,c.

logical makeup are prominent, it is clear that Plato considers that all and only the disordered should be liable to punishment. But in other, more political, contexts, he suggests that the crimes such men commit, caused by the disposition they possess (itself a controversial and logically problematic claim), should be the criterion of liability to punishment. Consequently, not only does Plato need to clarify what constitutes liability to punishment, but he needs to justify his supposition that punishment is the proper vehicle for reform. For if criminality, not crimes, is the focus of the legislator's activity, maybe he should aim not at punishment but truly at therapy.

Finally, the justification of punishment will rest upon the contention that virtue is happiness. If it is so, then reform, the means to virtue, will unquestionably be a benefit. Consequently, it will need no justification at all. Or will it? The humanitarian approach contains many pitfalls, and the following chapter will hope to discover how surefooted is Plato's theory of punishment.

CHAPTER

12

JUSTIFICATIONS, OBJECTIONS AND DEFENCES

Plato's account of punishment covers three functions—in ascending order of priority: restitution; deterrence, either by the execution of the
incurables or generally, to support the prudential argument (*timōria*);
and reform. It is a theory which has many strengths and one fundamental weakness, which this chapter and the one that follows will explore.

a. RESTITUTION

The principle of restitution advocated in the *Laws* supposes that it is
offensive to damage another man or his property, and it demands compensation from the offender. It is justified, therefore, in general by the
benevolence that it activates *towards the victim*. The requirements of ordinary commerce and the traditional response of the Greeks to an injury will prompt Plato to suggest such a procedure. Thus he appeals
(e.g., at *Laws* 862b) for the restoration of what has been damaged, the
cure of what is sick, and the reconciliation of the injured and the injurer.
Damage is inherently undesirable (it is 'sick', imbalanced, or distorted),
and therefore its rectification is justified.

Thus there are two separate elements in the justification of restitution. On the one hand, it expresses benevolence towards the victim of a
crime; on the other, it removes the damage caused by the crime, damage
which itself—aside from considerations of the victim—is to be deplored.

The restitutive procedure, however, seems to be presented as a preliminary to punishment proper (862d4). This stipulation has two important effects:

1. Damage will have been restored before the reformative process
begins, and the judge need make no attempt at restitutive provisions

within a sentence designed to reform its recipient. Therefore, the tension between different objectives, which is the danger of a complex penal theory, is obviated by the position of restitution as a preliminary.

2. If restitution is the theory of punishment entire, several dangers are to be discerned:[1] First, the concentration upon the crime, rather than its perpetrator, renders notions of responsibility vacuous, and this, it might be supposed, is counter-intuitive. Second, the *quid pro quo* principle might encourage the criminal to think of the punishment as the means to earn the proceeds of crime, and, from the point of view of prevention, this is to be avoided. Third, there are difficulties attached to the idea that all crimes are determinable, are commensurable with punishments that can be exacted, and are restorable by the exaction of that punishment. Fourth, there is the question of institution-begging. If restitution is the theory of punishment to be adopted, is it a theory of punishment at all? If not, are there reasons why the institution of punishment is needed?

All these objections may be rebutted, or at least modified, by the response that restitution is merely a rectificatory process preliminary to punishment. The problem of responsibility is left for the theory proper, where Plato promises to deal not with damage but with injustice (*Laws* 862b ff.). The criminal will not view crime as commerce, simply because restitution is not the whole story. His attitudes towards crime will be affected not by the preliminaries but by his actual punishment, which, as the central theory declares, sets out precisely to alter those attitudes. The problem of commensurability is also lessened by the fact that restitution is not the complete process: it may take place where it can without inhibiting our fundamental benevolence towards the offender. Finally, the criticism of institution-begging is appropriate only to the theory of punishment proper. Restitution is not punishment at all,[2] but rectification, concentrating on the crime and taking no consideration of the criminal, his intentions, his disposition, or his future. If the treatment of criminals were limited to this, it would be seriously deficient. But Plato has included restitutive provisions in the best way possible: to deal with the effects of crime without damaging our central intuitions about the penal procedure itself.

b. DETERRENCE

Types of Deterrence

The appearance of deterrent measures in Plato's penology is complex, and their justification is accordingly multiform. The early version

1. Cf. Ch. 2.   2. Cf. Ch. 1.c, and Ch. 2.

of the deterrence theory, the execution of the incurables, appears in harness with reform and has two elements in its justification:

1. Either the criminal is no longer able to benefit from life (*Grg.* 525c3; *Laws* 862c3), or, more positively, he is harmed by continued existence (*Grg.* 512a, by implication from the positive wretchedness of the physical incurable, and *Laws* 854c4,d7).

2. By his suffering he may benefit others, primarily by deterring them from emulating him, and additionally by removing his own evil influence from them.[3]

Thus his punishment either benefits both himself and others, or it is no harm to him and a benefit to others. Plato is careful to stipulate, however, that only when the criminal is deemed incurable, and no longer open to the benefit of reform (*Laws* 863a2), may he be used for deterrent purposes.

This account of deterrence is, *prima facie*, humanitarian. *1*, however, is complex. Its positive form, that the criminal is better off dead, is indeed humanitarian, and the general benevolence urged by *2* is superfluous. If, however, the criminal neither benefits nor suffers from his punishment, which the first argument also allows, then the second does the justificatory work. But the second is a principle of general benevolence, and the account of deterrence will thus tend to be utilitarian.

The alternative version of deterrence is the system of *timōria* in the *Laws*.[4] This is introduced to supplement the prudential argument that the life of virtue is in every way preferable to the life of vice. Vice is against the interests of the criminal either because it becomes chronic, or because it renders him subject to punishment. But this threat of punishment may not be effective without some executions. In these cases, therefore, the few will be punished in the interests of the many (*Laws* 728c5) and a utilitarian line of justification takes over (*Laws* 735e).

The ostensible justification of *timōria* is utilitarian. But the context in which it first appears is humanitarian. Plato's argument at *Laws* 728 is directed against the individual and unfortunate criminal, for whom a continued life of crime is the worst disadvantage. The individualistic approach to the disadvantage of vice will in general provoke humanitarian reasoning. Here, as *timōria* appears as part of the prudential argument, so it will be prompted by the same individualistic bias.

This complexity in the two systems of deterrence suggests that there will be at least some conflict.[5] If a particular punishment is urged for

---

3. *Laws*, 735–6.
4. It should be remembered that *timōria* is not introduced as part of Plato's own penology, but that it becomes incorporated later. Cf. Ch. 11.d.
5. Cf. Ch. 1.d; Ch. 5.i.

both humanitarian and utilitarian reasons, will the same sentence serve both purposes?

Humanitarian Deterrence

For humanitarian deterrence, Plato has solved this difficulty. The individual criminal should be given priority as long as he has any interests left. But the contention that his execution positively serves his interests encounters several difficulties, which will prove to be crucial to Plato's penological account:

1. If the interests of the individual are served by the threat or the execution of capital punishment, then the humanitarian appeals to benevolence *towards the criminal*.[6] This benevolence, however, amounts to the paternalistic argument that this apparently drastic and even final treatment is for his own good. But is paternalism justified?

2. There is some ambiguity about the curable/incurable antithesis, upon which the deterrent provisions rest. As we have seen, at times the distinction between the curable and the incurable criminal seems to be a matter of the crimes committed, whereas at other times it seems to be a matter of the dispositions of each. For reform, the most plausible account of curability is dispositional.[7] But when it comes to the execution of the incurable criminal, the two accounts of the antithesis raise and settle quite different justificatory problems:

   a. If the criminal is rendered incurable by the crime that he commits, we may understand him to have become liable to punishment in the normal legal way (*legal liability*). By committing a serious crime he becomes liable to punishment, surrenders his rights to benevolence, and has no longer any claims upon the humanitarian judge. Consequently he is described as incurable, and utilitarian considerations may enter. Plato's thesis that all wrongdoing is involuntary, however, suggests that such a man, far from surrendering it, has a greater claim on benevolence than any other, for his misfortune is the greatest of all. This version of incurability, therefore, will not do.

   b. If the criminal is dispositionally incurable (*psychological liability*), it is his interests, not his rights, that have become redundant, since he is no longer able to be reformed. The crime that he commits is merely the symptom of his disease.[8]

If *a*, can incurability be a matter of rights and liability in the common legal sense? If *b*, does the criminal have any rights that do not run

---

6. Cf. Irwin, *Plato's Moral Theory*, p. 342, n. 28.

7. Cf. below, e, on the justification for reform rather than repression; cf. Ch. 5.b.

8. Cf. Ch. 10.c. Plato must suppose, I argue below, e, that the crime is the inevitable and infallible symptom of the disease.

straight with his interests? Does he have any rights to be protected against the benevolent despot?

3. The drastic treatment that is advocated by humanitarian deterrence raises a persistent problem. If we are to execute men as soon as they become incurable, then a great deal rests upon the precision of the curable/incurable distinction. But how secure can we (or the legislator or the judge) be in our diagnosis? The judge *must* know what he is doing, but it is probable that he is as ignorant as the next man. Does Plato have any defence against this objection?

4. There is a logical difficulty attached to the consequential justification of the prudential argument. The system of *timōria*, we may suppose, embodies reasoning such as this: "Criminality does not pay; witness the fact that you are punished for it. The punishment that is exacted from you for the crimes you commit is justified on the grounds that it will teach you (humanitarian reasoning) that criminality does not pay." The circularity of this argument is evident. For if the interests of the criminal are prior, and if criminality does not in itself pay, then that is sufficient for the prudential argument. But if criminality does not pay just because it is liable to punishment, then the humanitarian is not justified in exacting that punishment. He should instead abolish punishment altogether—or else admit his utilitarian proclivities.

Utilitarian Deterrence

The alternative justification of deterrence exhibits benevolence *towards the majority* and is, roughly speaking, utilitarian. The function of punishment determined by this philosophy is indeed complex. For it combines the purposes of deterrence with protection of the community at large (*Laws* 862e5–6), not only from the depredations of the criminal[9] but also from the influence of his presence, itself an evil.[10] Such a theory, being utilitarian, confronts those difficulties to which a utilitarian penology is prone,[11] in addition to the problems of resolving the humanitarian and the utilitarian priorities.

Utilitarian punishment, in its bleakest form, excludes neither victimisations of the innocent nor exploitations of the guilty.[12] It cares too little for the interests of the individual, which are the excessive concern of

9. Ch. 4.a. I have described this as prevention.

10. Cf., e.g., *Laws*, 728b: we need to be protected from the evil influence of the company of bad men; 736a1: the incurables are like a sickness of the state (*nosēma poleōs*), and hence we need to quarantine them or remove them altogether.

11. Cf. Ch. 4.

12. That is, the excessive punishment of the man who is guilty of a minor crime; cf. Ch. 4.e.

the paternalist. Three responses are open to the utilitarian when confronted by the victimisation objection:[13] he may argue that victimisations are precluded by the fact that they are indirectly a disutility; he may, on strict utilitarian lines, agree to victimise where necessary; or he may try to put a brake on victimisation by adding to the principle of utility a second principle of just distribution.

Plato's humanitarian *persona* suggests yet a fourth response, for the application of utilitarian principles is permitted only after the interests of the criminal have lapsed. Consequently, punishments that appear to be victimisations are indeed no such thing: either the victim has no interests left, or his execution positively serves them. Hence the harnessing of humanity to utility—potentially embarrassing—has saved Plato from the utilitarian's great vice of riding roughshod over individuals for the sake of the group.

Alternatively, proponents of utilitarian deterrence could construct a defence against the charge of victimisation that would be based on the rights of the criminal. If the criminal is incurable simply because he has committed a severe crime, he might be thought to surrender, by his crime, his rights to protection. Therefore, it would be argued, he may be exploited by the judge at will.

From a humanitarian perspective, as I shall argue further, this account of liability is problematic.[14] However, as a utilitarian, Plato can derive the following indirect defence of victimisation from the legal version of liability: only those who have surrendered their rights in this way can usefully be punished. Or he might have recourse to the definitional stop,[15] and claim that punishments are, by definition, only of those who have become legally liable: they have no rights and thus cannot, by definition, be victimised or exploited.

The institution of *timōria*, however, will prove to be a thorn in Plato's side. For *timōria* contains no safeguards against victimisation, no stipulation that the criminal must be incurable. Although *timōria* derives from humanitarian arguments,[16] there is no guarantee that one inhumanity might not be permitted to benefit many. And so, in the *Laws*, *timōria* is essentially incorporated into Plato's own theory, along utilitarian lines of justification. Even the nod in the direction of the curable/incurable antithesis (*Laws* 735e3) is presented as a problem for the utilitarian legislator and not as a protection for the criminal against being victimised.

Now Plato's use of the prudential argument to supply a teleological account of virtue suggests that he would be reluctant to accept the com-

13. Ch. 4.f,g,h; i.e., indirect, strict and mild utilitarianism, respectively.
14. Cf. below, e.
15. This, I have argued, is a mild utilitarian device. Ch. 4.g.
16. Cf. Ch. 11.d. It is incorporated in the individualist prudential argument.

promise of mild utilitarianism to explain *timōria*. For if all values are to be reduced into a single principle of the good,[17] then the diversification offered by mild utilitarianism will be out of place. No, it appears instead that Plato would prefer the strict utilitarian answer, and argue that the maximisation of good would be the justification for victimisations; after all, the same principle governs the enforced return of the philosophers into the speluncar world of politics (*Rep.* 519d).[18]

Victimisation is likely to occur in any legal system, fraught as it must be with the human failings and ignorance of those who execute sentence and punishment. Plato must guard not only against the deliberate exploitation of the guilty, but against the unwitting execution of the innocent or mildly guilty. And he must explain how to make the calculus of what action is best overall. To these difficulties, Plato alone among penologists has a secure, if expensive, answer, as we shall see shortly.

Plato assumes that the fear of punishment will deter people from becoming criminal, but to this assumption there are two important objections.

1. I have argued that, in the works dating from the *Protagoras* to the *Laws*, Plato believes that a man does not choose to be criminal. But such a man, surely, will not be deterred by fear. The counter to this must lie in the complexities of the moral theory. On the intellectualist version of moral behaviour, a man may fail to realise where his true interests lie and so do wrong. But realising where his true interests lie is no easy matter. To be told is not enough; he must be taught. Thus he will learn, from frightening examples, to avoid vice and seek virtue, and he will realise from the consequences of each what are their intrinsic values. Deterrence will work on criminals, even though they are criminal involuntarily, because their involuntariness is not a matter of complete inability to follow a course of action, but rather of their failure to evaluate courses of action properly. Or, on the habituative account of moral behaviour,[19] the legislator will aim, by the institution of deterrence, to turn men's activity in the right direction, hoping that they will eventually become able truly to choose. The only problem that remains for the legislator is judging the correct fear quotient.

2. Although the objective is to wean the criminal away from his behaviour or his disposition, exploiting his fearfulness is not necessarily the best means to this end. Plato and modern theorists alike suppose

17. Not, of course, a hedonistic account, but *Prot.* 350 ff. provides an object lesson in the reduction of value to a single currency.

18. Although there are some distributive oddities here; cf. below d. This is an example of the difficulties into which non-deontological moral theories may stumble.

19. Cf. Ch. 11.c. Plato concedes at *Rep.* 444d that just behaviour will shape the just disposition.

that the most effective way to alter the criminal is to exploit a penal system. But both would derive stronger support from a radical approach to the institution of punishment,[20] and from a willingness to believe that the same ends might be better achieved by different means.[21]

The deterrent arm of Plato's penology thus reveals both humanitarian and utilitarian characteristics. It is justified either by benevolence displayed towards the individual criminal, or by benevolence displayed towards the majority, towards society at large. Consequently, it faces a series of complementary objections. On the humanitarian front, is paternalism justified? On the utilitarian, is victimisation or gross exploitation likely and if so is that justified? In both cases there are problems of institution-begging: is fear of punishment the best way to create the desired responses in the criminal himself or in society at large? And in both cases there are problems of ignorance: how do we know and how can we minimise the punishments that will effect the desired end? Finally, any deterrent institution raises problems of the rights and the interests of those upon whom it is practised. For Plato, the interests of the criminal are apparently served, so long as he has any. But how do these interests relate to any rights that he may have?

c. REFORM

The institution of reform is the core of Plato's penology. Reform is the primary consideration, which may be ignored only when it cannot be effective. It is to be justified on individualistic, humanitarian grounds; that is, it exhibits benevolence *towards the individual criminal*. Given that Plato does not ignore the interests of the society as a whole, why does he concentrate thus upon the interests of a small and guilty group? The answer to this central question clearly lies in his account of the prudence of virtue, the stupidity of vice. Virtue, the very disposition of the soul which will issue in virtuous activity, is in itself a good, whereas its opposite, criminality, is intrinsically evil. But those who pursue this evil do so involuntarily and so are not to be blamed, but pitied, since they are actively involved in the greatest misfortune *despite themselves*.

In this analysis of the supreme happiness and misery of us all, and the distribution of both, the benevolent penologist must focus, as his first priority, upon the least advantaged.[22] The others—potential crimi-

20. This objection, framed in utilitarian terms, is that Plato slides into rule-utilitarianism and is committed to justifying an institution, rather than treating each case on its needs as the act-utilitarian would. Cf. below, f on institution-begging.

21. Although reform may tell a different story; cf. below, d, and Ch. 11.d.

22. Cf. the benevolent legislator of Rawls' system—or is he benevolent? Rawls' thesis of the original position requires that the group of legislators be not benevolent but egoistic

nal, victim, and potential victim—are, by definition, more fortunate than the criminal himself. So their interests may be deferred until his are served or lapse; thereafter considerations of the majority may enter the legislator's calculations. So, from the individualism and the exculpation that are central to Plato's moral theory, there arises a complex humanitarian penology which has, within that theory, considerable scope for justification.

Even this penology, however, confronts several objections. These may be classified according as they are problems, both moral and procedural, that confront the legislator or the judge (see objections 1 to 4 below); as they are complaints that may be advanced by the criminal who is subject to reform (objections 5 and 6); or as they are residual anxieties that will be displayed by those whom Plato wishes to convince (objections 7 to 9).

1. *The normative criticism.*[23] How are Plato's legislators and judges justified in making all members of society conform to the legislators' and judges' own norms of right and wrong? How do the legislators and judges know what is right and what is wrong?

2. *Moral psychology.*[24] In general, how does the legislator know what constitutes criminality or what, in general, is the appropriate treatment for psychological disorder?[25]

3. *Problems of ignorance.*[26] In particular, how does the judge know what is suitable procedure in individual cases; how does he diagnose the criminality of the man before him?

4. *Why should the legislator be benevolent?*[27] The argument that criminality does not pay was based upon an egoistic account of what is in the individual's interests. Consequently, the individual, egoistic criminal may expect benevolence from others. However, why should the egoism of those others lead them to be benevolent to him? (Cf. 9.)

5. *Liability.* We have seen that Plato equivocates[28] over what constitutes liability both to reform and to deterrent punishment. For at times criminal liability appears to be legal; at other times psychological. What criterion of liability does operate, and is it unexceptionable?

6. *Rights.* The theory is paternalistic,[29] particularly when the talk turns to therapy and away from education, as I have argued.[30] Against the benevolent despot, however, does the criminal have any autonomy? Or, when his interests are served, has he no countervailing rights?[31]

---

and risk-aversive. On the basis of these characteristics their original choice is made, and thus Rawls derives his moral imperatives from teleological considerations. Cf. *A Theory of Justice*, Part I.

23. Ch. 5.e.
24. Ch. 5.f.
25. Ch. 5.g.
26. Ch. 5.g.
27. Ch. 4.d.

28. Ch. 11, passim.
29. Chs. 9 and 10, passim.
30. Cf. also Morris, "Persons and Punishment."
31. Ch. 5.g.

7. *Institution-begging*.[32] The objection that Plato is institution-begging is complex. Either he is assuming that there must be an institution such as punishment and then justifying it as humanitarian, in which case he is failing to adopt a critical approach to the institution; or he is proposing a system which only happens to be called punishment and which is really a non-penal institution of reform. In the latter case, is Plato neglecting some important function of the institution of punishment?

8. *Exculpation*. Is the thesis that all criminals should be exculpated tolerable?

9. *Justice*. Although benevolence towards the criminal may be justified in terms of justice, how does Plato fit the appeal to justice into an apparently non-deontological theory of punishment?

d. THE LEGISLATOR AND THE JUDGE (Objections 1 to 4)

Many of the difficulties to which this complex theory of punishment is prone are founded upon the idea that some things are immeasurable or inaccessible—the problems of "how do we know. . . ?" Plato, uniquely, has a complete response to these problems.

What the virtuous man is like, who needs reform, how much is needed, and how reform is to be accomplished are questions that, in the Platonic system, confront the legislator or—in any particular instance—the individual judge. Equally, the moral issues of why benevolence and why not victimisation lie first before the legislator and then before the judge. On the one hand, then, legislators must know what they are doing, and, on the other hand, they must be virtuous while they do it, to avoid falling into the traps set for the humanitarian.

In the *Gorgias*, Plato explains the virtue of justice, which is a moral skill leading necessarily to right action.[33] However, there is some ambiguity in the dialogue about who is the exponent of this skill. By the end, Plato clearly intends us to understand that the individual moral agent has *dikaiosunē*. At the same time, however, this virtue is possessed, it appears, by the legislator or the judge. Thus at 464b, Plato speaks of lawgiving and correction (*dikaiosunē*) as virtues belonging respectively to legislator and judge.

Justice, therefore, according to the first part of the *Gorgias*, will be a skill practised without mistakes by its exponents; because it is also a virtue, its practice will be morally exemplary.[34] Similarly, towards the end of the dialogue, the just orator (legislator or judge?) is said to instil justice and remove injustice from the souls of the citizens. Thus the soul of

32. Ch. 2, n. 7; Ch. 4.c; Ch. 5.h.
33. Ch. 10.a.
34. Cf. Santas, *Socrates*, p. 152 on justice and intentional incompetence.

the good man is ordered by skill (506d7), because it is the product of the virtuous skill of the legislator. For (to steal a leaf from the *Symposium*) the legislator will be anxious to propagate the good wherever he can (cf. *Grg.* 504d5 ff.), and he will do so in the souls of his citizens.

In the *Republic*, the legislator is the philosopher-king who, having emerged from the shadowy world of opinion into the light of truth (*Rep.* 517b), will return to political life where, guided by his knowledge, he will act wisely (*emphronōs* 517c5).[35] He will be able to know what, in the world of politics, is good and just and right (520c3), and his opinions will not roll around between truth and falsehood (cf. 479a ff.). Consequently, the philosopher-king, as he navigates the ship of state,[36] will know what is the best means to happiness (488a ff.), and he will use his knowledge with virtue (492a). In short, the philosopher-king will be a good man and a wise one, and both his general legislation and his individual decisions will, infallibly, be for the best. In the same way, the just judge will make the right decisions in court and always cleave to justice (433e).

The *Laws* has often been considered pessimistic in its approach to the problems of legislation, and indeed at times in this work Plato seems more sceptical than he did before. However, as I have argued, the penology does not change radically between the *Republic* and the *Laws*, and, equally, the moral psychology retains its intellectualist bias. Consequently, the legislator, ideally wise and virtuous, will always make the right decisions. Thus at 727c2, the advice of the legislator is spurned by the akratic, so the advice is, *ex hypothesi*, good. Similarly, at 858d5 ff. the legislator is the man who gets moral evaluations right and who has command of the prudential argument. He is, in terms of the *Gorgias* and the *Republic*, both skilled and virtuous.

If, in the ideal state where the right theory of punishment is practised, the legislator and the judge are both skilled and virtuous, then several of the problems attached to the theory of punishment disappear. There will be no procedural difficulties in general legislation, or in sentencing. For, because they are knowers, neither the legislator nor the judge will make mistakes (cf. *Rep.* 477e6). They will know what is right and what is wrong, they will know the truth about moral psychology, and they will know what is the correct decision in a particular case.[37]

35. From the point of view of Plato's epistemology, it should be observed that on this account the knower can be right and wise about matters in the perceptible world, which suggests that knowledge and belief are not to be distinguished by their objects, or by their objects alone. Contrast Furth, "Elements in Eleatic Ontology," in Mourelatos, ed. *Pre-Socratics*, with Gosling, "*Doxa* and *Dunamis* in Plato's *Republic*," *Phronesis* (1968):119–130.

36. Navigation is a skill, so the legislator possesses a skill. But his skill is moral, both in the *Republic* and in the *Gorgias*. So I disagree with Irwin (*Plato's Moral Theory*, Ch. 7) that Plato has totally abandoned the craft analogy by the time of the *Republic*.

37. Cf. Ch. 5.g.

Plato's judges are ideally suited to make procedural decisions, whether humanitarian or utilitarian.[38] The wise man will recognise who is curable and who is not, and he will know what type or sequence[39] of treatment will be effective[40] to the reform of the curable and the deterrence of the hitherto non-criminal by executing the incurable. Moreover, he will not face a quandary in deciding when a criminal has reached virtue, for he will recognise the instantiation of the good.[41] On a Platonic account, even the normative criticism is therefore inappropriate, since what is right and what is wrong is a determinable matter of fact, and known by the knowers.

With such infallible men in charge of establishing the law and carrying it out, Plato apparently need have no fear of malpractice. For the wise man is also the good man, and he will not victimise, exploit, or defraud,[42] unless doing so is in the best interests of those whom he is supposed to serve. The benevolence that a humanitarian theory proposes, therefore, is genuine, and not liable to be perverted by the vice of him who practises it.

Such, at least, is the short answer to the fourth objection. The legislator will be benevolent because benevolence is virtue and he is virtuous. At this point, however, Plato's own argumentation gets doubly in his way. First, in both the *Gorgias* and the *Republic* he argues for a new definition of justice—as skill or knowledge (*Grg.* 460) or as psychological order (*Rep.* IV). However, he fails to establish a necessary connection between justice as he defines it and just behaviour as we understand it.[43] Consequently, there is some doubt as to whether the wise legislator will in fact be virtuous (in our sense) and thus benevolent. Second, I have suggested that the core of Plato's moral theory is egoistic: he argues that virtue is in our interests. Given such egoistic reasoning,[44] and a strange definition of justice, how can he argue that benevolence is in fact a virtue? Upon what moral principle could he base such an argument?

To the objection that the wise legislator need not be virtuous, Plato has two possible answers, quite different in kind. First, he may offer a logical principle, the principle of univocity,[45] to rebut the claim that

38. Cf. Ch. 4.b.

39. Ch. 11.c.

40. Cf. Ch. 11.d,e.

41. As, equally, he will recognise other qualities; cf. the problems of verification and accurate predication solved by the theory of *anamnēsis*, *Meno* 80d ff, *Phaedo* 74a ff.; or the accuracy of the returning philosopher, *Rep.* 517c ff.

42. Cf. *Rep.* 442e ff.

43. Cf. Ch. 9.d.

44. It is the egoistic foundations of Plato's theory that make him so vulnerable to the immoralist, whom he tries to refute on matters of fact (what is in our interests) rather than matters of morals. Cf. *Rep.* passim.

45. Cf. Ch. 9.d.

'just'—psychological or social, Platonic or vulgar—is ambiguous. If for each word there is a single form, then the usages of the word must be identical.[46] Therefore if a man is just Platonically, he will also be just vulgarly.

To supplement this linguistic argument, and insufficient without it, Plato has a second defence,[47] which assimilates the doctrines of the *Republic* to the account, given in the *Symposium*, of the ascent of love. The philosopher-king, inasmuch as he is motivated to pursue the good,[48] must be a lover of justice. As such, he will also want to propagate justice wherever he can, not only in himself but also in others. Consequently, his self-appointed task will be to make others virtuous, and this will have the effect of making them happy.

Such a defence, clearly, does not rely so heavily upon the notion of benevolence, but rather upon the *Symposium* account of the self-interest of the lover. As such it coheres more readily with the general prudential argument. Its disadvantage is that the *Symposium* account nowhere appears in the penological texts of the *Gorgias*, the *Republic* or the *Laws*.

To the objection that, on an egoistic account, benevolence is not protected by any moral principle, Plato might construct a different defence. At *Rep.* 514–520e, he offers the allegory of the cave and describes the ascent of the philosopher to the light of truth, and his subsequent return to the darkness of the cave to help his fellows with his knowledge (520c). But Glaucon objects that to compel the philosopher to abandon his own interests and practise benevolence towards others is to do him an injustice. However, Socrates replies this is just—to ask the philosopher that he repay the city's early care of him by now caring for the citizens (520a). This is a just request, and philosophers are just men; therefore they will accede to it.

This argument for benevolence has, I suggest, two flaws. The first is the old problem of ambiguity: has Plato not so redefined justice, that this distributive appeal no longer has any substance? To this his reply might, of course, be that 'just' is univocal. But the second difficulty is more insidious. Plato's analysis of justice has the effect of internalising it (433d1) and suggesting that achieving internal order is the primary objective in doing just actions. But by this move, Plato has devalued the imperative of the distributivist—that to do just actions is to promote the external just state of affairs, which is, in itself, desirable. Nevertheless, the return to the cave is demanded by a distributive, external notion of

46. Santas, *Socrates*, pp. 59 ff. provides an excellent analysis of the Socratic method, with an evolution of the uniqueness thesis to be discerned therein, especially pp. 87 ff.

47. Cf. Ch. 9.d.

48. But see the *Meno*'s quite different analysis of the motivation of philosophical inquiry, 80d ff.

justice. This is the defence of benevolence. But what power, within Platonism, is left to a distributive moral imperative?

e. LIABILITY, RIGHTS AND INTERESTS (Objections 5 and 6)

All Plato's discussions of the curable/incurable antithesis and its relation to punishment raise the interpretative problem of what constitutes liability to punishment, or what criteria operate to explain curability and its converse. Two possible criteria presented themselves in the texts: either Plato thinks that the criminal is liable because he commits a particular crime (legal liability), or he thinks that it is the criminal's disordered soul that renders him a suitable candidate for reform (psychological liability). Common sense suggests that the latter is the most plausible account of who should be reformed, whereas the emphasis in the texts is upon legal liability.

If the criminal becomes liable legally, a question of justification arises. Suppose that the action of the legislator is justified if and only if the criminal has committed a certain crime. Is it plausible to suppose that the criminal's act renders him liable not merely to the future repression of such activity but, further, to the restructuring of his psyche, which is the cause of that activity? Intuitively, the legal notion of liability suggests a repressive, rather than reformative, penology.[49] Parallel questions—of the autonomy of the reformee—arise with psychological liability. For it is difficult to acknowledge that even our unexpressed thoughts render us victim to the activities of the judge.

Several counters are available to Plato:

First, in response to the interpretative difficulties suggested, he might argue that the connection between the criminal disposition and criminal behaviour is neither random nor merely probable. The disposition is the cause of the behaviour,[50] and therefore only the disposition will manifest itself in the action; furthermore, it will always do so. If we find this account of criminality insufficient, or if there are interpretative difficulties attached (particularly, in the *Republic*, with regards to the relation between being and doing), these charges should be levelled at Plato's moral theory as a whole, and not specifically at his penology, which, after all, stands or falls with its ethical foundations.

Second, Plato might argue that the talk of liability is out of place. His system of reform is closer to therapy than to punishment. Indeed, he might say that it is called punishment only because it operates within a legislative context. In this case, questions of how liability arises are in-

49. Cf. Ch. 5.b.
50. Indeed, the Socratic questions about virtue are exactly questions about cause. Cf. Santas, *Socrates*, pp. 87 ff.

appropriate; we should rather consider the criminal ready for punishment as soon as we know that he is disordered. This response is effective against our quibblings about liability. Accordingly, reform is not punishment at all, or only so by analogy. However, if this is the case, objection 7 (institution-begging) becomes formidable.

Third, to the question of the criminal's rights against invasion, Plato will argue that the invasion is benevolent, even paternalistic. The activity of the reformer will necessarily (because he knows what he is doing) result in improved happiness for the criminal. Therefore, it is always in the criminal's interests. How, then, can he complain, if his interests are always served? The complaint rests on the notion that rights and interests do not go hand in hand, not even when the interests are known.[51] Not only may I insist on my rights although my interests will be damaged by my actions (consider the unselfish activity of some civil rights agitators), but I may deny that, because others would derive a benefit from some action that I am reluctant to take, they automatically have rights over me. Indeed, the whole question of criminal activity within a society is a question of rights of some militating against interests of others. Plato must explain, therefore, why the criminal should acknowledge that the benevolent despot's reform of him is justified.

Does Plato have either any notion of rights separate from interests or any defence against the view that he ignores the rights of unfortunates?

The argument to persuade the philosopher to return to the cave, based as it is upon distributive principles, appeals to his duty to repay the state for its care of him; or, conversely, it invokes the state's right to reciprocity from its members. The language of justice is the language of rights and duties, and their distribution.[52] However, although in this isolated instance in the *Republic* Plato uses such notions to dictate the behaviour of his philosophers, the internalisation of the theory of justice in general precludes his appeal to the rights of the individual vis-à-vis his fellows. Instead, as we have seen, Plato argues that punishment serves the individual's interests and supposes that this claim is sufficient to justify the penology.

Discussion of rights, however, concerns not only distributive justice. To argue that I have a right to be free from paternalistic interference (and it matters not by which distributive principle I acquired that right) is to make a claim about my autonomy[53] and thence about the freedom

51. There is a connection here with the problem of *akrasia*. Will the akratic, if he knows what is best, allow us to force him to do it? The answer must be no, so long as we suppose that there is such a thing as *akrasia*.

52. Cf. Vlastos, "Justice and Equality," in R. Brandt, ed., *Social Justice* (Englewood Cliffs: Prentice-Hall, 1962), pp. 31–72.

53. Cf. Morris, "Persons and Punishment."

that I think I should have to make my own choices. In this context, however, Plato's moral theory provides a powerful rebuttal to the objector. Two factors in that theory bear on the question of autonomy. The first is the analysis of choice[54] and is closely bound up with the second, which concerns the intellectualism not only of the moral theory in general[55] but of the penology in particular.[56]

Plato's account of choice is that if I know something is in my best interests, then I will pursue it. The problem for the criminal, however, is that—among other things maybe[57]—he is ignorant.[58] The process of punishment, then, is designed to reform him completely. Hence it is complex, ultimately, not only to condition him into right behaviour but to teach him to know what is right and to realise that the right is in his interests. The educated ex-criminal will learn that virtue is in his interests and he will be in a position to complete the generalised statement that he desires happiness with the particular statement that he wants virtue (that is, wants to be virtuous) because virtue is happiness. It follows that, although in committing his crime he appeared to choose the life of vice, his true choice is the life of virtue. Thus, after the event, he may consent to his own punishment, and his autonomy, on this account, is in no way impaired.

Within the intellectualism both of his account of choice and of the provisions of his penology,[59] Plato has access to a reformative theory of unique strength. *If we grant him his moral theory* and, in particular, his account of *akrasia*, we must allow this defence against the threat that reform poses to the autonomy of the individual. If we do have rights against the benevolent despot, those rights are not infringed by his reforming us; rather they are held in abeyance until such time as we are able to make a true, informed choice. At that time we will give our retrospective consent to all that has happened in the interests of making us happy.

f. BEGGING THE INSTITUTION (Objection 7)

The objection that Plato begs the institution may be framed as a dilemma. Either he is assuming that punishment is a necessary social institution and then, as such, characterising it as reformative, or he is denying that reform is a punishment. In the first case we may ask whether punishment is indeed a necessary institution, and in the second case we

---

54. Cf. Ch. 9.a.   56. Cf. Ch. 11.
55. Cf. Ch. 10.a,b.   57. Ch. 10.a,b.
58. At least in the sense that he does not know.
59. Such that, for complete reform, education *must* be a part of the process. Cf. Ch. 11.e; cf. also Ch. 5.g.

may alter the emphasis of that same question and ask whether the institution of punishment does in fact fill some need that will remain unsatisfied without it.

The arguments of the *Gorgias* rely largely upon paradox and linguistic manipulation. The topic of punishment is introduced to shock the conventionalism of Polus and his like about what is in fact a good for us. In order to achieve this effect, Plato must beg the institution, for he wants to exploit the unquestionable undesirability of penal institutions as they are commonly conceived. Thus when he speaks of punishment, he must, for the argument to work, be speaking of the traditional institution.[60] This procedure opened him to Dodds' objection[61] that he is begging the institution and, at this juncture, this does indeed appear to be the case. If so, the argument is unsatisfactory, because he fails to explore the radical possibility that punishment is in fact an unjustifiable institution which should not be bolstered by humanitarian reasoning but, rather, be abolished.

However, the evidence of the *Laws* suggests that reform is not punishment at all, but only so called by analogy.[62] In that work, Plato suggested that any means whatsoever that would accomplish the reform of the criminal should be considered by his judge.[63] Yet punishments are painful by definition[64] and do not allow the pleasant means that the Stranger suggests at 862a5. In this case, Plato is not begging the institution, but properly questioning its propriety. Thus he calls the reformative procedure punishment, I suggest, in much the same way that he calls the bad man a criminal.[65] Punishment is a procedure to which the criminal is liable, and it is carried out in a public context. But there the similarity to traditional penal systems ends.

Even at this deeper level, however, trouble awaits the radical penologist. Unquestioningly to assume punishments is certainly a mistake. But does the institution serve a real need in the community which would not be served by its reformative analogue—where reform does not necessarily impose suffering? My final chapter will argue that if Plato does not beg the institution, he does fall into this deeper trap.

---

60. Although there is some equivocation as to whether he conceives the institution as actual, or as ideal. Cf. Ch. 11.a. Cf. also the derivation, in the *Laws*, of *timōria* from contemporary institutions.

61. Quoted in Ch. 11.a.

62. Cf. Ch. 1.c. For three major reasons: (a) liability may be psychological, not legal; (b) the criminal is exculpated; (c) the punishment need not impose suffering.

63. *Laws* 862d, discussed in Ch. 11.d.

64. Cf. Ch. 1.c.

65. Cf. Ch. 9.b. The bad man is bad inasmuch as he is liable to punishment, but he is not blameworthy.

g. EXCULPATION AND JUSTICE (Objections 8 and 9)

The theory of reform is based upon a moral theory which exculpates the criminal. From a rational perspective, this may well be the right attitude to adopt towards all those who commit crimes. For in every case we can offer extenuating circumstances, whether social, physical or psychological, as to why this criminal committed that crime. This account of practical causation causes difficulties in formulating a theory of full intentionality and leads us to sympathise with an exculpatory moral psychology.

This, at least, is the rational perspective. From the emotional point of view, however, we tend to be less charitable. Suppose a youth were to come up to you in the street and kick you on the shin. Rationality may tell you that he is maladjusted and should be excused on that basis; resentment, however, will urge you to kick back, while your shin continues to smart. Maybe that emotional response can, in time, be overcome by rationality, but maybe not, and, if not, then an exculpatory theory of punishment will be unsatisfactory.

Similarly, we may object to our own actions' being affected by the determinism of an exculpatory account. This, as Morris argues, erodes our vital sense of ourselves as persons:

The primary reason for preferring the system of punishment as against the system of therapy might have been expressed in terms of the one system treating one as a person, and the other not.[66]

The same problem arises with questions of justice. I have argued that Plato's account of punishment in particular and his moral theory in general presents an internalised view of justice. As a result, external justice—the just state of affairs—is devalued, and it forms no part of the theory of punishment. For, of course, Plato's penology is not retributive, but humanitarian. He urges us to look to the least-advantaged and to count ourselves lucky if we are virtuous, even if we suffer injustice at the hands of others who are unfortunate enough to possess the illusory advantage of Gyges' ring.

The interests of the suffering victim are secondary compared to the more pressing claim of his wretched injurer. And the rights of the many are sacrificed to the rights of the criminal few by the benevolence of the judge. The counter-intuitive aspect of this argument is its strength and at the same time its weakness. It is strong because it is striking and forces us to reconsider our moral intuitions. But it is weak because in the end Plato ignores those moral intuitions—as the final chapter will show, to his cost.

66. "Persons and Punishment," p. 490.

CHAPTER
13

PLATO'S ESCHATOLOGY

Plato's formal theory of punishment combines reform of curable criminals with the exploitation of incurables to deter others. The eschatological myths, however, offer some odd passages.

a. THE EVIDENCE

In the *Republic* Plato's main case is for the intrinsic desirability of virtue. However, he also makes the secondary claim that it is good in its
consequences; it is beneficial. To this end he moves on from his test-case
of the just man who appears to be unjust, to consider the just man who
is acknowledged by both gods and men to be so (612b ff.). Such a man
will be loved by the gods and respected by his fellows, whereas his opposite will be hated by the gods and scorned and punished (613e) by
men. We should not be deceived, therefore, by the apparent ill-fortune
of a just man or the apparent prosperity of his opposite, for the gods
see to it that everything is ordered to the ultimate benefit of the good
man and the ultimate harm of the bad.

This preliminary account of the consequences of virtue presents the
common man's attitude toward punishment. But such an attitude is altogether different from the reformative policies that Plato advocates
earlier in the work.[1] Consider, for example, how this type of punishment fits into the classification of goods. Reformative punishment is in
the third category of those things which contribute to our benefit. The
punishment mentioned here, however, is not a good at all, whereas its
converse, the rewards of virtue, must belong to the first category, as

1. Ch. 11.c.

things which are good in themselves. The punishments which are suffered by the unjust man and the rewards which accrue to the just are
supposed to be the consequences of virtue, in contrast to reform, which
is a means to the happiness that is virtue.

There follows an eschatological myth about the fortunes of the souls
in the underworld. The souls come to judgement when they die, and
they receive rewards and punishment according as they have lived. The
just are sent to Elysium, whereas the unjust suffer in Tartarus. The
wicked suffer tenfold what they inflicted on others and thus pay the
penalty tenfold[2] for their crimes (615b). If they are incurably wicked
they are not released at all, nor are they set free otherwise, until sufficient penalty has been paid for their crimes (615e). Those who have
been just and holy in their incarnate lives, however, are rewarded tenfold for their virtue, according as they deserve (615c1).

When they come to be reincarnated, all these souls, whether good or
bad, are fully responsible for their choice of reincarnated life and for
their subsequent fortunes. The god is not to blame, we are told; the
responsibility lies with the chooser. Thus, for example, the man who
made an impulsive and wrong choice of life blamed everyone else, but
he was wrong to forget that he had no one to blame but himself (619c).

At *Gorgias* 523a ff., Socrates illustrates the judicial administration of
the underworld. The souls of those who have lived a just and holy life
go to the isles of the blest, where they live in happiness. But the souls of
the wicked are thrown into Tartarus, the place of reparation and justice
(*tisis kai dikē*). In previous times, this juridical exercise was hampered by
the fact that both the judges and the judged were still incarnate. So Zeus
decreed that judgement should take place after death, on naked souls,
and should be delivered by discarnate judges. This would be done in
order that the decision might be just, *dikaios*. Now the injustices of the
previous system, whereby the souls were going to Tartarus or Elysium
undeservedly (*anaxioi*), would be avoided.

A just sentence, we must infer, requires that the desert, *axia*, of the
soul be properly determined, which can be done when the soul is free
of the trappings of earthly existence. Then it will be rewarded or punished in a manner appropriate to the life it has led, and this will be
justice.[3]

2. Contrast this approach to 'paying the penalty', where the emphasis is on the penalty
and its size, with the use of 'paying the penalty' at *Grg.* 476 ff. Cf. Ch. 11.a, where I argued
that the emphasis was on the payment, and then on *giving up* the evil in the soul. The
vocabulary of the present passage recalls the restitutive/retributive approach of early literature. Hence Plato uses the verb *ektinein*, derived from the Homeric idea of *apotisis*. Cf.
Ch. 6.

3. Cf. the cognates of *dikaios* at 523b6; 523e6; 524a6.

The myth of the *Phaedo* is introduced by the claim that the life of vice is intrinsically harmful, whereas virtue is in our interests (107c ff.). The effect of our previous lives is felt as our souls journey to the place of judgement and thence to the underworld. There they "experience the things that they must, and stay for the time required."[4] But Socrates strikingly fails to say that they must stay as long as is needed to improve them and restricts himself instead to the bleak remark that they stay as long as they must. What determines how long they *must* stay?

The bad soul, one which is unduly influenced by its appetites, has no easy journey to the underworld. Suffering, it lingers around the sensible world, paying many penalties (*polla antiteinasa*). Eventually, it is compelled to go beneath the earth, where it is steadfastly avoided by the other souls. Ultimately, it is forced away to its appropriate place (*tēn prepousan oikēsin*). Meanwhile the good and temperate soul lives in the place it deserves (*ton autēi prosēkonta topon*).

The life of wickedness is wretched for many reasons. First, it is intrinsically miserable; second, when the wicked die they pay the penalty for their misdeeds, even before the descent to the underworld, by remaining in an unhappy limbo. Thereafter, not only are they shunned by their companion souls in the underworld (an unpleasant consequence of their turpitude) but they are actively punished as they deserve for the life they have led. Their just counterpart, however, is rewarded appropriately. Inevitable punishment at the hands of the nether gods therefore follows upon wrongdoing and is a further factor to recommend virtue to us.

There follows a long cosmological account until, at 113d, Socrates returns to the fate of the soul. After judgement the souls go off to various places appropriate to their characters. The average souls, neither outstandingly good nor overwhelmingly bad, are sent to Acheron, where they are purified and pay the penalty for their misdeeds, whereupon they are absolved from guilt (113d7). Again, they receive rewards apportioned *kata tēn axian*, according to their deserts.[5] But the souls' re-

---

4. Courtesy of D. Gallop, *Plato: Phaedo* (Oxford: Clarendon, 1975), p. 62, reading *dei* at 107e2.

5. This passage is characterised by Gallop, *Phaedo*, p. 233, as purgatorial, and he explains this by referring to Dodds' comments on *Grg.* 525 (*Gorgias*, p. 381): "Divine punishment is never vindictive . . . as it is in Judaeo-Christian theory; it is either remedial (Purgatory) or deterrent (Hell)."

Obviously, this allusion is to the formal structure of the penology at *Grg.* 525. But there seem to be two problems attached to such a description of *Phaedo* 113. First, there is no mention of the theory that punishment should combine reform with deterrence; rather, as I have suggested, the force of this passage seems to be to demonstrate the consequences that follow on virtuous and vicious behaviour when the soul comes to divine judgement after death. Second, the force of 'purgatory' seems to me to be dubious in both contexts.

.prieve will come only when they have obtained the forgiveness of their victims; until this has been done, and their release can be assured, they must return again and again to Tartarus. One measure of the deserved punishment, therefore, is the satisfaction demanded by the victim for the offence he has suffered—a matter for the victim himself to determine, and not a question that should be settled by the expert, whether he be a legislator, a doctor or a trainer.

Similar accounts of punishment are given in eschatological contexts in the *Phaedrus* and the *Laws*. The *Phaedrus* myth classifies the various lives a man may live in ascending order according to the soul's greater grasp of the truth. But before reincarnation, a man receives the portion (*moiras metalambanei*) appropriate to the justice or the injustice of his previous life (248e). Thus the reward and the punishment of the soul are determined by a man's previous conduct; the way in which he led his incarnate life dictates a man's desert (249a8). The soul of the philosopher wins release from the cycle after three incarnations, as is just (249a1; c4), but the other souls come to judgement at the end of their lives, whereupon some pay the penalty in the places of punishment beneath the earth, and others are allowed by justice to rise heavenwards for their reward.

In the *Laws*, 870e, the Stranger threatens that payment is exacted in Hades for wrongdoing. But, what is more, the reincarnated soul will be compelled to pay the natural (appropriate?) penalty (*tēn kata phusin dikēn ekteisai*) in its next life. For it will suffer at the hands of others what it inflicted on its victims; this will be its portion (*moira*) throughout its life.

The invocation of the *lex talionis* at 872e is made in the same terms. Here the Stranger speaks in oracular mood: avenging justice guards against the murder of relatives; thus of necessity the man who commits a crime of this kind will himself suffer a like fate. A parricide will himself be murdered by his children in a future incarnation; a matricide will be reincarnated as a woman and suffer likewise. There is no other possibility of purification from a crime of this kind[6] than the payment of a life for a life by the criminal, who thereby satisfies the grievance of the entire family of his victim. By fear of such punishment at the hands of the gods, the Stranger supposes, men will be restrained from committing such dreadful crimes.

Finally, in the teleological account of the universe the draughts-player

---

For such a notion is, like purification (113d; cf. Orestes' purification in the *Eumenides*—a religious, not a reformative, requirement since he claims to stand in no need of reform), better fitted to ideas of expiation by paying the penalty than of moral improvement or reform. And that reform is not the principal concern of this passage is suggested by the reparative conditions for the release of the soul from this 'purgatory'.

6. This recalls the reference to purification at *Phaedo* 113.

awards a new life to the soul, according to its deserts, that it may achieve the appropriate portion. Once more Plato uses the now familiar vocabulary of desert (*prosēkousa moira, kata to prepon*).

These passages share several characteristics, which suggest that the process of punishment is differently conceived from the reformative theory to be discerned elsewhere.[7]

1. Rewards and punishments will be determined by considerations of what the offender *deserves*. As *Laws* 872e makes clear, the offender's desert is dictated by the crime he has committed, and the penalty is either correlated directly with the crime or, as the *Republic* suggests, is a multiple thereof. Although reform should consider whether the punishment effectively achieves the moral rehabilitation of the offender,[8] here Plato refers to the propriety of the punishment—its justice or dueness (*prepon, prosēkon, moira, axios* and the cognates of *dikaios*). There is no suggestion that the primary object of punishment is reform.

2. The exculpation of the offender and the pity felt towards him, which were argued for in the dialogues, have been dropped. In their place, Plato emphasises the *personal responsibility* of the souls—for what happens to them both after death (inasmuch as they are paying for what they did when alive) and when they are reincarnated (the choice of lives in the *Republic*).

3. Any positive utility to be derived from punishment seems to be the *satisfaction of the grievance of the victim* (*Phaedo, Laws*) or the fulfilment of the requirements of justice. But justice is not reached by the offender's paying restitution to the victim for what he has suffered. On the contrary, the victim is an onlooker, if he is involved at all, and he is recompensed simply by witnessing the wretchedness of the man who originally made him suffer.

4. There are also frequent references to the payment of a *penalty with no recipient* at all—in the *Phaedrus* myth or at *Laws* 870e, for example.

5. Purification is mentioned in both the *Gorgias* and the *Phaedo*, but it is at least arguable whether this is viewed as positively remedial or whether, as had been the situation in earlier literature, it is viewed as expiation. In both cases, the soul would be rid of a burden of guilt, but in one case this is effected by reform, in the other by retribution.

6. It is striking that these passages combine the institution of punishment with *reward*, so that the souls are benefited for the good they have done as well as harmed for the evil.

7. Such benefits or harms are seen, as the *Republic* suggests, as *the consequence of virtue and vice.*

---

7. Although the evidence of the *Gorgias* myth is comparatively weak.
8. Ch. 5.g.

8. Eschatological punishment and reward should be distinguished from reform. Reform is the means to virtue and happiness, but this punishment is the *end of a process*.

b. CHARACTERISATION OF THE EVIDENCE

Exculpation has been dropped, and the humanitarian approach has lapsed. Punishment in the eschatology is certainly not reformative. Nor is it deterrent in the Platonic mould, since the restriction of punishment to the incurables is lifted. However, it is clearly intended to fill some deterrent purpose. Thus the introduction to some of the myths is prudential (*Phaedo*, *Republic*), and the Stranger in the *Laws* makes some play with the deterrent effect of fear.

Restitution also plays a part: the victims of crimes are considered on one or two occasions. Both deterrence and restitution may be determined by considerations of desert, but, as such, they are parasitic on retributive ideas.[9] And neither deterrence nor restitution can explain the complex of characteristics that has been observed: this notion of desert; the insistence on personal responsibility; expiation or penalisation in general without regard for the effect on others; the complementing of punishment with reward; and, above all, the anxiety to satisfy the requirements of justice.

Retribution, fundamentally, is just or fair:

The deep-seated sense of fairness which revolts against punishment of the innocent revolts also against any treatment of the guilty which appears to confound guilt and innocence. It is felt to be unfair that a man's grievous fault should make no difference to the treatment he receives and that he should be treated just as favourably as if he had done no wrong. It is reasonable that we should do unto others as we would wish them to do unto us. But, conversely, it is fitting and proper that what others do to us should be affected for better or worse by the quality of what we have done to them. It may be claimed that this makes sense, and any other principle makes non-sense.[10]

The retributivist claims that the just state of affairs is desirable and important and that it comes about when each man has his desert.[11] Such a claim reflects the hope that virtue will not go unrewarded or, alternatively, the distress that is felt when it does. In general, it is distressing to witness manifest unfairness, that is, any obvious failure to correlate receipt and desert. The justice of retribution prevents this distress, because justice is, simply, the converse of manifest unfairness.

Retributive punishment is an end, not a means (characteristic *8*

9. Ch. 3.c; Ch. 7.f.
10. W. Moberley, *The Ethics of Punishment* (London: Faber, 1968), p. 80.
11. Ch. 3.a,b.

above). It consists in giving a man what he deserves (*1*), as a consequence of what he has done (*7*). Giving a man what he deserves is itself held to be a generally desirable objective. The exact measure of desert may require specification by the penologist, but however it is specified, it is a different penal criterion from both utility and humanitarian expediency. So different is it that punishment according to need or to utility may be diametrically opposed to punishment according to desert (see *4*). For example, the juvenile hooligan might need a compulsory course of socialisation; we might be better off if he restored the damage done; although what he deserves is a punch on the nose.

The notion of desert demands not only that we punish decried behaviour but also that we reward (*6*) recommended behaviour. Reward, indeed, is an important aspect and even distinguishing mark of retributive practice. It bears the same characteristics as its correlate: it is seen as the end, not the means; it is awarded according to desert; and it aims to promote a just state of affairs.

Furthermore, whether reward or punishment is involved, retributivism cannot have a comprehensive theory of exculpation (*2*), since a man's desert is dictated by what he does with deliberation and intent; his actions cannot be 'involuntary' in any fundamentally important way. For example, it makes little sense to say that the rich miser who is coerced into feeding the poor deserves a reward for what he has done. Desert, therefore, involves blame and praise, and rules out the attitude towards intention typified by the Socratic paradoxes.

A further, instrumental approach to retribution argues that the purpose of the infliction of pain on the offender is to relieve the grievance of the victim (*3*). This is often held to be an aspect of desert: the criminal deserves the punishment and correspondingly the victim deserves the recompense.[12] And sometimes the retributivist advances a utilitarian reinforcement of retribution, saying that punishment of this kind promotes the greatest good of the greatest number. This defence protects the deterrent aspect of retribution, rather than its central 'fairness' tenet, and tends to see the punishment again as a means to the maximisation of benefit (a prudential argument).

But under these conditions one of two things holds. Either this is a fully fledged utilitarian doctrine with, consequently, no right of appeal to 'justice' at all, or else this kind of deterrence is parasitic on retribution. If the latter is true, the punishment is supposed to demonstrate that it is unwise to act in a manner to provoke punishment. At the same

12. Cf. Feinberg, "Justice and Personal Desert." The present argument adduces the claims of restitution to be an instrument of fairness, and implies that retribution is the means to achieving emotional restitution. As a crypto-restitutive theory, this version of retribution runs the risk of conflicting directives in sentencing. Cf. Ch. 3.c.

time, the priority of retribution demands that in cases where what is just is seen to have no deterrent effect, utility must still give way to desert. By parity of reasoning, the satisfaction of the victim is but a side effect of the central demands of justice.

Against teleological theories of punishment, retribution has deontological strength.[13] To all the arguments of the rehabilitator, the behaviourist, or the utilitarian, the retributivist replies that we do have some deep-rooted commitment to fairness, and that his system will perpetuate or restore the just state of affairs.

Whenever we recommend justice or complain against injustice, we appear to assume some basic standard of distribution, whether this be egalitarian or otherwise. The operation of retribution (reward or punishment) centres upon the distributive notion of desert.[14] Retribution and distribution are not converses, and the basis of the original distribution is not retribution. Rather, the purpose of retribution is to promote or restore the original distribution, however that may be constituted. Thus retribution focuses on distribution. Desert then measures the extent to which any given agent aims to maintain, or threatens to destroy, the distributive *status quo*. And retribution is the return to the just balance, considered in terms of what happens to the agent, rather than in terms of restitution to the victim.

From this connection between distribution and retribution two things do not follow. First, it does not follow that we are all committed to some theory of justice—for example, Marx and the strict utilitarians deny distributivism altogether. Second, it does not follow that all distributivists are necessarily retributivist. However, the adoption of a distributivist ethic does tend to recommend retribution, whereas the denial of distributivism diminishes the attractions of a retributive penology.

Undoubtedly, punishment is retributive in Plato's eschatology, although hitherto this has gone unnoticed. All the factors are present: the aim towards fairness, an interest in desert and the implication that the

13. Cf. Ch. 3.c, Ch. 4.d, Ch. 5.c, where I have argued that all penologists worry, at the least, about justice.

14. Rawls, *Theory of Justice*, p. 314, argues that retribution is not the converse of distribution, on the grounds that his version of the latter is made not on the basis of moral worth (whence desert) and retribution, but from the position of ignorance which is part of the technical substructure of his theory. But (a) this technical substructure has more of a deontology than Rawls admits. Cf. Ch. 3, n. 43 and Rawls' own adumbration of the principles of self- and mutual-respect, and the origin of moral principles (*Theory of Justice*, Part III), where the teleological appearance is derived from the technique of describing moral sentiments by their growth, and not as they are, fully-fledged. (b) Even though retribution and distribution are not converses, they are related, focally; cf. Owen, "Logic and Metaphysics." Hence both retribution and distribution are spoken of as *just*.

offender is culpable, the proposal to reward, and the two secondary justifications of deterrence and the satisfaction of the victim.

c. PROBLEMS OF A RETRIBUTIVE ESCHATOLOGY

Both restitution and deterrence fit into the reformative theory. However, they need not conflict with retributivism either, provided that they are subordinated to the central aim of bringing about the just state of affairs. Thus if deterrence may only be achieved by exceeding the deserved penalty, then, on strict retributivist lines, the deterrent objective must be abandoned. If this is granted, there is nothing to prevent restitution and deterrence from being the subsidiary effects of the retributive procedure.

Likewise, it is possible to reconcile retribution and reform, by regarding any additional retributive effects of reform as a bonus, or by allowing that retribution may sometimes have reformative impact: the criminal "sees that he did wrong." Nevertheless the two principles are different. If each is held to be of equal value, the demands of one will at some point conflict with the demands of the other.[15]

We have already seen the opposition of need and desert, two key concepts of reform and retribution. Thus reform may require that punishment be diminished or increased, at the same time as retribution forbids it. The objectives of the two practices are similarly divergent: reform aims to make the criminal just (or virtuous), whereas retribution is directed towards 'doing the just' on him. Clearly, to be treated justly may not make a man just; nor is the process of making a man just necessarily a just one. Reform must forsake the doing of justice for the instilling of it should the crisis arise, whereas retribution will not ultimately care for the disposition of the criminal, provided that he pays the penalty for his crime. So reform and retribution cannot be held simultaneously as first-priority principles of punishment. Yet this appears to be what Plato wants—consider the myth of the *Gorgias* in which the official theory of reform is preceded by a story of retribution.[16]

d. A SOLUTION—REJECTED

Can we explain away the retributive eschatology? To begin with, the context in which retribution occurs is itself problematic. Both the lan-

---

15. Cf. Ch. 5.i.

16. I have suggested that the evidence of the *Gorgias* is the weakest for retributivism. However, the myths as a whole offer a strong retributive account, thus strengthening the *Gorgias* presentation where, alone of all these passages, reform and retribution appear together, thus provoking the problems of conflict.

guage and the style of the myths are in direct contrast with the hard arguments that precede them. For example, Plato moves from the dialectical style of the last argument of the *Phaedo* (100 ff.) to an extended speech in which he expatiates on the way the world is constituted (from 107). At the same time, the subject matter shifts from the detailed analysis of essential predication to a high-flown description of the soul's journey in the underworld. Therefore, the contrast between the argumentative sections and the myths is superficially striking.

The same disjunction, at a more serious level, is exemplified in the various accounts and descriptions of the soul. The task of reconciling the psychology of the dialogues in their entirety is beset by a series of problems.

The *Phaedo* identifies the soul with the intellect and ascribes the lower impulses to the body (94b-d). The immortality of the soul is argued for by the consideration (among others) that it is simple and incomposite and thus more likely to survive than the complex of body and soul together (78c ff.). In the *Republic*, the lower impulses come to be ascribed to the soul rather than the body; thus the tripartite theory is formulated. But the immortal part of the soul must be simple (611); this is the part which is closest to truth and reality, and therefore it is the intellect. Similarly, the *Timaeus*, which relocates the emotions in the body,[17] declares the immortality of the intellect. But in the *Phaedrus*, however, where the account of the soul appears in the myth, it is described as a complex (the charioteer and his two horses) even when it is discarnate. Equally, the souls of the gods, which must be discarnate, have three parts. The account of immortality here, therefore, is at odds with the evidence of other dialogues, and it demands reconciliation.

In the *Gorgias* and in the *Republic*, *akrasia* was accounted for by the new tripartite psychology,[18] so that the lower parts of the soul explain the causes of vice. Thus it is the complexity of the soul which is responsible for its moral character. Individuation, therefore, is of the complex, not the simple, soul, and the personality of a man thus resides in all the parts, not in his reason alone. But if the reason alone survives, then the personality of the soul will lapse on separation from the body. Yet in the myths the souls are not only spoken of as if they were embodied (having physical faculties, such as sight and the ability to walk) but they are unequivocally endowed with personality; witness the man who bewails his unwise choice, or the gossiping reunion of the souls as they return to the judges, in the *Republic*. Moreover, as we have seen, the

17. Cf. the physiological account of criminality at *Tim.* 86-7; Ch. 10.c.
18. Cf. Ch. 10.b.

eschatology places strong emphasis on personal responsibility and on the notion that the souls as they appear before the nether judges are infected by their incarnate behaviour. So the soul does not escape the contamination of the body, according to the doctrines of the myths, although the argumentative claim that the surviving soul is simple would suggest the opposite.

In short, therefore, there is asymmetry between the soul as it is argued for in the body of a dialogue, and the soul as it is presented in the myth. How may the gap be narrowed?

To begin with, the very existence of this problem indicates that we should not take the detail of the myths seriously but that we must, in some way, interpret. Indeed it is a matter, I suppose, of common sense that Plato did not believe that there was such a man as Er and that he did not intend these passages, presented as stories, to be taken as literal truth.

At the opposite extreme, it could be argued that the myths are only stories, whose function is largely decorative; therefore Plato is not committed to any of the doctrines that may be elicited from them.

Maybe we could deposit them in the rag-bag of Orphism[19] or Pythagoreanism[20] and avoid having to explain them at all. This interpretation supposes that the myths pay lip-service to contemporary religious ideas and contain no Platonism at all. But Socrates explicitly claims, at *Grg.* 523a2, that the myth is true. The dismissive interpretation, by denying Plato's commitment to the myths, seems as absurd as its literalist converse. For it attributes to Plato the strategical and philosophical blunder of ending important pieces of argument with the damp squib of eschatological myths which he did not invent and does not believe.

19. W.K.C. Guthrie's explanation of the changing nature of the soul, "Plato's views on the Nature of the Soul," in Vlastos, *Plato: II*, pp. 230–243. Guthrie suggests on the one hand that the truly complex soul is only activated on association with the body (thus accommodating the views of the *Phaedo* and the *Republic*) but that the discarnate soul still contains three "streams of energy directed towards objects of different sorts."

On the other hand the philosophic soul, which in the *Phaedrus* wins release from the cycle of reincarnation, is simple, having rid itself of the lower impulses which are responsible for its fall. In this way, Guthrie suggests, the two strands of thought can be more or less reconciled. The 'less' may further be accounted for, he suggests, by the influence of Orphic thinking on Plato's attitudes.

20. Dodds, *Gorgias*, p. 373: "It is presented as something which Socrates has heard from an unnamed informant . . . a device to avoid making Socrates responsible for opinions he did not hold." The "unnamed informant" is identified as Pythagorean in *The Greeks and the Irrational*, pp. 207–235, where the myths are explained as the effect of the 'inherited conglomerate,' notably Pythagoreanism.

e. INTERPRETATION

Tate[21] suggests that we distinguish two underlying meanings beyond the surface detail of the stories Plato tells. The first is the "moral," which is the distillation or message of each myth, a general principle that the story instantiates. The second, more slippery function is the "undersense" or allegory which, in Hackforth's words, is "a description in symbolic terms which can readily be translated into what they stand for."[22] The disadvantage of the allegory, as Tate points out, is that it may not be a true one, since Plato allows that a moral may be contained in a story which is false, as long as it is plausible and convincing.[23] Thus, of these two positive interpretations, we may expect a moral from the myths, but we cannot count on an allegory.

The *Gorgias* myth is presented to complete (*peranein*, 522e7) the argument that wrongdoing is the supreme evil, which is worst of all, Socrates points out, if we enter the underworld laden with vice (522e). The myth is intended, therefore, to expand the prudential argument with which the whole dialogue is taken up, even though by this time Callicles is already convinced. The same is true of the myth of Er in the *Republic*. As we have seen, it finalises the proof that not only is virtue happiness but it receives its due rewards at the hands of gods and men. In the *Phaedo* Socrates protests against the risk of neglecting our souls, particularly since they are immortal (107c). The *Phaedrus* claims simply to present the nature and fortunes of the soul (246a), whereas the *Laws* lays emphasis again on the eternal imprudence of wrongdoing.

The function of the eschatological myths, therefore, is to support, by a consequential account, the arguments asserting the prudence of virtue. The moral is that virtue is both agreeable and beneficial, vice disagreeable and harmful. But, says the voice of reconciliation, this moral is only a moral. Plato is not committed to divine punishment, or to retribution, or to the suggestion that the exculpation urged by the Socratic paradox lapses when the soul separates from the body. These are simply devices to render the vehicle of the moral more convincing.

Maybe. But the moral is established by means of a deterrent penology which, as I have argued, is parasitic on retribution. If, then, we are to extend the moral to an allegorical interpretation, the eschatologies cannot be collapsed into the general prudential argument but must retain their retributive impact. And for two reasons we should, I think, look for allegory. First, the various myths are similar, which argues that they

21. "Plato and Allegorical Interpretation," *C. Q.* (1929):145, arguing from *Rep.* 378.
22. *Plato's Phaedrus*, p. 72.
23. The noble lie, 414b ff.

are, in Plato's eyes, true—at least at the points of similarity. Second, there are strong elements in the myths which cannot be explained away as inherited detail—in particular, the emphasis on personal responsibility and the anxiety to arrive at a just settlement for virtuous and vicious alike.

The tradition attributed great importance to theodicy. It could be argued that Plato, who is after all within the tradition of Hesiod and Theognis, felt the need to offer a theodicy also. He offers one in a mythical framework, but he nevertheless believes that it holds good not merely as the moral of the works in which it appears but as an allegory of what does actually happen to the soul after death. However, if this is a theodicy, the tension between reform and retribution is at its most severe. On the one hand, Plato is saying that legislators, whether human or divine,²⁴ should be concerned not with vindictive punishment but with the improvement of the wretched criminal. On the other hand, he is declaring that the gods should operate a retributive system on discarnate souls. Therefore he is indeed claiming both that the gods ought to reform and that they ought to exact retribution. But the two prescriptions are incompatible. If then, Plato's sole purpose is to institute such a theodicy, he is to be criticised, at best for failing to reconcile retributivism with reform, and at worst for dishonesty.

However, this retributive eschatology should not be viewed as mere artifice, and therefore Plato should not be accused of dishonesty. The impulse towards retributivism, I shall argue, is felt deeply in the moral fabric of Greek thought, and, indeed, in our own.

f. JUSTICE

Two problems in Plato's moral theory bear on this issue.

1. Plato urges exculpation on the grounds either that the criminal is unable to control the conditions that make him commit crimes or that he is mistaken in his objective.²⁵ Within the argumentation of the moral psychology, this view, if striking, is not untenable. However, it has inherent difficulties. In a recent discussion on the nature of moral luck, Williams and Nagel²⁶ focus upon the notion of our behaviour being, more or less, out of our control. As Nagel points out, the disadvantage of the view that all our moral actions are caused by factors beyond our control in one way or another is that it leaves us with no moral judgments at all. But, in consequence,

24. Cf. *Rep.* 380b.
25. Cf. Ch. 9, Ch. 10, Ch. 12.g.
26. "Moral Luck," *Proc. Ar. Soc.* Supplement (1976):115–135; 138–151.

The self which acts and is the object of moral judgement is threatened with dissolution by the absorption of its acts and impulses into the class of events. . . . The effect of concentrating on the influence of what is not under his control is to make this responsible self seem to disappear, swallowed up by the order of events.[27]

Our response to this difficulty is to insist, despite our moral logic, that our actions[28] may be assessed and our selves regarded as culpable. This reaction is not a matter of reason, but of emotion: we cannot accept a view of moral judgements whereby our selves are 'swallowed up'. Similarly, Strawson argues that we *cannot* permanently suspend moral judgements about our fellows, or adopt an 'objective' stance towards them, although this is what universal exculpation, and the thesis of determinism, requires.[29]

It follows that we must and do make moral judgements about ourselves and our fellows. These judgements carry, and sometimes even consist in, an assessment of desert; for example, "He deserves better than that" is itself a compliment, not a dispassionate evaluation of the subject's desert. It is futile, therefore, to disallow moral judgements but this is what Plato tries to do.

2. Plato suggests a view of justice which concentrates on the nature and structure of the individual soul, analogous to the structure of the state.[30] This explanation of what it means to be just, recommended for the prudential reasons outlined in the *Republic*, has the effect of etiolating a value which is a fundamental aspect of the thinking of Plato's predecessors,[31] for the prudential argument of the *Republic* is presented on an egoistic basis which leads to an internalised account of justice as psychic harmony. This, Plato declares, is the central significance of 'justice' (443d). But a major purpose of the term 'just', as it appears in the tradition, was, rather, to describe the state of affairs in which not only we ourselves but also our fellows—friends or enemies—are seen to receive their just deserts.[32] Thus some behaviour could be recommended beyond appeal to our immediate or even ultimate interests,[33] and it was possible to decry an action on the grounds not only that it was harmful but that it was unjust.

The just state of affairs, therefore, is the basis upon which all our

27. *Ibid.*, p. 148.
28. Cf. Morris, "Persons and Punishment," on our acts intolerably becoming events on the therapeutic account of punishment.
29. "Freedom and Resentment."
30. Cf. Ch. 9.d; Ch. 12.d,g.
31. Cf. Chs. 7 and 8.
32. Cf. Ch. 7.c.
33. Recall, here, Plato's difficulty with the return of the philosopher to the cave; Ch. 12.d.

assessments of just men are built, and justice in the individual is logically derivative from justice in the organisation. Justice in retribution similarly acquires its meaning from its focus, the just distribution.

Consider this problem in another way. Plato's theory of justice is an account of a virtue. His theory is not distributive, except in the artificial sense that the harmony of the soul is distributively organised. So the basic application of 'just' has been shifted to apply no longer to the state of affairs but to the virtue, which was hitherto held to be derivative from the state of affairs. This theory of justice leads readily to a reformative penology.

But from the reformulation of 'just' there arises a difficulty which, I suggest, is the source of the retributive elements in the eschatology. I have argued that the acceptance of distributivism will probably, though not necessarily, bring retributivism in its wake. Equally, I have maintained that the denial of distributivism will tend to cut off the impulse towards retribution. But neither firm acceptance nor complete denial is open to Plato, for he has so remodeled the idea of justice as to leave it with a distributivist appearance, while denying the fundamental priority of the just state of affairs by saying that it has no distributive function. In the confusion distributivism leaves him a legacy, which is the attraction exercised upon him by an account of retribution.

What is more, interest in justice is not only a modern preoccupation. In tragedy,[34] the tragic effect was derived from the moral distress we suffer when we see men failing to receive their just deserts. But our assessment of their deserts depends upon our moral judgement of them as good, bad, or indifferent. Distress at the unjust state of affairs arises when the good suffer or the bad flourish. The entire phenomenon I have called manifest unfairness. It is based on distributive notions of what is fair, and it may be resolved only by a system of justice wherein punishment operates retributively and rewards are apportioned on the same basis.

So even Plato responds to the problem of manifest unfairness and to the anxiety provoked by a system in which the culpability of the criminal is disallowed. He is not presenting us with two theories of punishment. The theory of reform still stands as his answer to the questions of penology. In the retributivist eschatology he offers (under pressure from his antecedents) not a theory but a belief that justice does indeed prevail for all. His retributivism, therefore, is genuine. As such it still conflicts with reform. But it is not introduced dishonestly, as an alternative analysis of the way human or divine legislators ought to punish. On the contrary, it is his observation that, in fact and at last, there is such a thing as justice.

34. Ch. 7.c.

APPENDIX

I

THE REFUTATION OF POLUS: *GORGIAS* 474B3 FF.

The argument from *Grg.* 474b is supposed to demonstrate, against Polus, that all men believe that doing wrong is worse than suffering it. The proof that overturns Polus' position is outlined in the text (Ch. 9.b). But it depends upon a dubious principle (*E*):

Of two fine things, that one is finer which exceeds the other in pleasure or benefit or both. Similarly, of two shameful things, that one is more shameful which exceeds the other in pain or harm or both.

Socrates fails to specify who it is who derives the benefit or suffers the harm, or who experiences the pleasure or the pain. Thus Dodds claims that Polus' concession that doing wrong is worse than suffering it "clearly meant that it was less *ōphelimon* for the community, and from this it does not follow that it is less *ōphelimon* for the agent . . . " (Plato: *Gorgias*, p. 249). (Cf. Santas, *Socrates*, p. 239.) Consequently, it has been thought, the principle becomes suspect, and its exploitation ("There is no pain involved in doing wrong," [*G*]) invalid.

Vlastos, "Was Polus Refuted?" (and see Santas, *Socrates*, pp. 233 ff.) argues that the induction of *E* relies upon a series of examples which are not symmetrical. In some cases the pleasure of what is fine is experienced by the observer (colours, shapes, etc.), in others by the perpetrator (learning, etc.), and in still others by the subject (institutions). Plato is not entitled, on this basis, therefore, to a general principle which supposes that the shameful is defined in terms of what is painful or harmful *to the perpetrator and to him alone*. Consequently, Vlastos argues, that there is no pain involved in doing wrong cannot be inferred from the earlier moves. For from the point of view of the observer there may indeed be pain involved in doing wrong—we may find it morally distressing, for example.

Now, certainly both commentators are right that Plato does not specify in the principle who enjoys the benefit or the pleasure, and he does derive the principle from asymmetrical examples. But let us consider what the principle is meant to tell us. It is intended to fill out some sense of *kalon* which will enable us to analyse its meaning in its various occurrences. To this end, Plato takes a series of examples—to give him the benefit of the doubt, random examples—of things that are vulgarly called *kalon*. From these examples, he argues that there are two common factors that appear when we speak of a thing's being *kalon*: either it is useful or it is pleasant, or both. The examples make it clear, however, that the principle thus derived is not so specific as to designate *who* (i.e., observers, perpetrators, etc.) finds these *kala* useful or pleasant. Of a *kalon* picture, it will probably be the observer who exclaims "I find that *kalon*." On being asked to explain why he finds it *kalon*, he will reply that it gives him pleasure. Of a *kalon* political institution, however, we might expect the exclamation to come from someone subject to it, and he will explain that he finds it *kalon* because it benefits him.

The restriction, therefore, upon the principle thus derived will be that it must be the person who finds a thing *kalon* who will enjoy the pleasure or receive the benefit. We may cavil at this notion that evaluative terms can be atomised in this way. This, I suspect, is the fundamental intuitive objection to the present passage. But we cannot, yet, criticise Plato on the grounds of his logic. Quite properly, he refuses to specify, in the generalised principle, that the pleasure or benefit should be enjoyed only by the observer, or only by the perpetrator, or only by the subject.

How then is the principle exploited? Polus agrees that doing wrong is more shameful than suffering it. This, we may suppose (cf. *tous allous anthropous*, 474b3) is the universal opinion. This view of wrongdoing, therefore, will be shared by those who observe it, those who suffer it, and those who do it. In each case, they will say "This action is *aischron*." *Aischron*, according to the principle, is to be cashed in terms of harm or pain, or both. So who suffers? The observer of wrongdoing might well agree with Vlastos that he finds wrongdoing shameful because it causes him pain (the pain of seeing others victimised). The victim will agree, for he directly suffers the pain, and he might add that suffering wrong is bad for him, into the bargain. But the wrongdoer himself, when he, conventional man that he is, admits that his action is shameful, will disagree. "How can you suppose that for me it is painful?" he will demand; "Why should I do it if it were?" Plato then asks him why he still concedes that his action is shameful, and the wrongdoer, to his consternation, will realise that it is shameful for him because it is harmful for him.

Now, this conclusion rests upon two assumptions. First, it relies upon the principle that something, called *aischron* by someone, will be so called as a reflection of the pain or the harm they are liable to suffer from it. This principle may be simplistic, but it does follow without outrageous logic, from the examples that Plato offers. Second, it rests upon the assumption (conceded by Polus) that the wrongdoer will subscribe to the universal opinion that his wrongdoing is shameful; it also rests upon the understanding that such a man neither suffers now nor anticipates suffering pain from his action—such as the pain of subsequent remorse.

Thus far, therefore, the objections of the two commentators are seen to be groundless. Plato's failure to specify who suffers the pain or the harm is quite proper in view of the fact that many people, occupying different roles, may call something *aischron*: they may observe, do, or suffer (cf. Rawls, *Theory of Justice*, p. 404). However, there is a proviso: this reference, once established, should not be tampered with. It must be the person who speaks of *aischra* and *kala* who enjoys or suffers. So, although the specification may vary from instance to instance, it should not be shifted within a particular example. In other words, it does not follow, from the fact that I find something *aischron*, that it is harmful *for you*.

The first argument, to show that wrongdoing is worse than suffering wrong, can be understood without accusing Plato of shifting the specification. However, trouble looms when he attempts to combine this principle with the "interconnexion of the modalities of correlates," as Dodds calls it—the principle that as an action is done, so is it suffered. From this, combined with the analysis of *kalon* and *aischron*, Plato attempts to show that punishment is a benefit to him who suffers it. (This argument is discussed in the text, Ch. 11.a.) But to reach this conclusion, he shifts the specification of who enjoys the benefit. The argument runs thus:

If a man punishes justly, then the patient is punished justly.
If justly, then *kalōs*.
Therefore the man who is punished suffers *kala*.
Therefore he "suffers" pleasures, or benefits, or both.
But not pleasures.
Therefore he enjoys a benefit.

The modal principle allows the shift from punishing justly to being punished justly. In this case, the punisher will declare "I am doing a *kalon* thing." He may explicate this in terms of the pleasure just actions give him, and we will acknowledge his account of why he finds his action *kalon*. But then the shift to the passive, to be legitimate, must carry this specification with it. Thus the punishee will be punished justly and so *kalōs, inasmuch as* his punishment will give pleasure *to his judge*. It does not follow from this that he himself will benefit. We could only draw that conclusion if he too said "This action (my being punished) is *kalon*, and I judge it so because it will give me (pleasure or) benefit."

Now, Plato could derive this conclusion in the same way that he terminated the first argument, by relying upon vulgar opinion (which includes the opinion of the wrongdoers themselves) to subscribe to the evaluation in question. Thus were he able to say that the punishee, like the rest of us, calls his punishment *kalon*, then, on grounds of logic, even if counter-intuitively, we could argue that punishment benefits the criminal.

However, Plato does not do this, but instead feels the need to call upon the modal principle. He does so because he rightly doubts that the punishee too would describe what he suffers as *kalon*. In order that the punishment should be described as *kalon* at all, and for the argument to get under way, Plato must appeal to the opinion of the judge and must settle the issue by means of the shift to the passive.

Here, then, is at last the illegitimacy of the argument. The combination of the analysis of *kalon* with the modal principle will only produce a valid argument if the reference of *kalon* is preserved in the shift from active to passive. *Kalon* relates, on the account I have offered, to whoever says the thing is *kalon* and therefore considers himself to enjoy the pleasure or the benefit. But Plato fails to preserve the specification. Therefore he does not show that the wrongdoer who escapes punishment is more wretched than he who does not.

NOTE: I am indebted here to a discussion with Melanie Johnson and William Jordan.

APPENDIX

II

THE CAUSES OF VICE: LAWS 863A3-864C1

This controversial passage has been variously interpreted, e.g., by Saunders, "The Socratic Paradoxes in Plato's *Laws*"; O'Brien, "Plato and the 'Good Conscience'," and *The Socratic Paradoxes and the Greek Mind*, pp. 190 ff.; Görgemanns, *Beiträge zür Interpretation von Platons Nomoi*, pp. 134 ff.; and Gould, *The Development of Plato's Ethics*, pp. 125 ff.

The passage is introduced at 863a5−6, where Cleinias asks the Stranger to clarify the distinction between injustice and injury and "the business of voluntary and involuntary acts" (Saunders, "Socratic Paradoxes," p. 425). I take these remarks to be programmatic. Consequently, what follows should explain the nature of injustice, and the relation between injustice and damage, the nature of damage having already been dealt with.

A. *Anger is a part or affect of the soul which subverts it by unreasoned violence* (863b3).

Despite the use of the word *meros* ("part or affect"), the subsequent discussion indicates that Plato is not referring directly to the tripartite psychology here, but rather to the distortions or vices of different parts of the soul.

B. *Pleasure is a different part or affect of the soul, which deceitfully persuades it to abandon its purposes and to do what pleasure wants* (863b6 ff.).

That the soul "abandon its purposes" seems to be in the sense of its being persuaded to do what pleasure wants. Saunders points out ("Socratic Paradoxes," p. 426) the intellectualist contrast between the unreasoned (*alogistos*) influence of anger and the deceitful reasoning of pleasure. We might contrast the doctrine of the *Republic* that the spirited part generally fights on the side of reason.

We may infer from *B*, and the argument will eventually claim, that by the diversion of the soul's purposes pleasure or anger make a man unjust; whereas the programme (863a) and the earlier argument at 860d allow the further conclusion that such a man is also involuntary in the Socratic sense.

   C. *The third part or affect is ignorance, which could correctly be described as a cause of crime* (863c1 ff.).

The Greek here is very compressed and interpretation is required. *Triton* does not agree with *agnoian*, so we must import *pathos kai meros* from *A* and *B*. It is not clear whether Plato supposes there to be more than three parts or affects, but the tripartite theory, supported by his reference to the parts of the soul, suggests the definite rather than the indefinite article to introduce *C*. Moreover, the Greek does not make it clear whether ignorance explains all crime or only a third of it. However, the reference to the three types of crime at 864b1 suggests the latter.

There are further problems about the interpretation of *hamartēmata*, which may mean 'mistakes' rather than the more loaded 'crimes'. However, 864a1 suggests that the whole passage is primarily a discussion of injustice, rather than accident, as does the list of the causes of *hamartēma* at 864b1. An alternative possibility, according to which this passage represents a radical departure from Socratism, is that Plato is suggesting that anger and pleasure are the causes of injustice, whereas ignorance is the cause of mistake. This fits readily with the programme of discussing both injustice and injury and with the abrupt remarks at 863d-e (cf. Görgemanns' interpretation, *Beiträge*, pp. 138–139). It ignores, however, the conclusive evidence of 864b1 that anger, pleasure and ignorance are *equally* the causes of crime.

Ignorance, the Stranger goes on, may be subdivided into simple and complex; the latter, which is more vicious, occurs when a man is ignorant but believes he knows. This recalls remarks at 732a and also at *Soph.* 229c, about the arrogant but ignorant man who, traditionally, was Socrates' major target. Thus far the analysis seems to follow the tripartite psychology of the *Republic*, in that there are three distinct but parallel causes of vice which may operate in turn. Next, however, ignorance is contrasted with anger and pleasure:

   D. *We speak of anger and pleasure either overwhelming us or being overcome by us* (863d6).

   E. *But ignorance is never said to overcome us or to be overcome by us* (863d10).

These two moves have caused a great deal of the difficulty surrounding the passage. Saunders ("Socratic Paradoxes," p. 427, n. 1) explains the disjunction with the suggestion that anger and pleasure can be resisted, whereas ignorance cannot. But *E* also denies that ignorance overcomes us, in which case it is not a question of resistance.

The distinction between the three causes of vice is, I suggest, of a different kind. Anger and pleasure are impulses that may be repressed or not, but ignorance is not an impulse at all; it is a lack. As knowledge is the power that enables us to resist anger and pleasure (cf. 864a3, on my interpretation), so ignorance is the absence of that power, which leaves us at the mercy of our emotions. (Ignorance is ambiguous, in the passage as a whole, between the contrary and the contradictory of knowledge.)

> *F. But all three (anger, pleasure, ignorance) are the same in that they turn a man from his real purpose to its opposite* (863e2).

To refer back to the programme, this explains how men act involuntarily. Their desire is perverted by the power of anger or pleasure, or by the debilitating effect (or the tendency to failure) of ignorance, and thus what they actually achieve they do not really want. Here we recall the discussion of choice, *Grg.* 466e ff.

> *G. The tyranny of emotions (anger, fear, pleasure, etc.) in the soul we describe as injustice, whether any damage is done or not* (863e6 ff.)

The concessive clause reintroduces the issue of damage and fulfills the promise of 863a5 to deal with injury. *G* distinguishes the damage done in a crime from the criminality of its agent. The preceding argument has established that injustice, occurring when the emotions overwhelm the agent's true purposes, is involuntary, even when the unjust acts are deliberately perpetrated. These compressed lines, therefore, fill the programme, by giving an account both of injustice and injury, and of the twofold voluntary/involuntary antithesis (861e ff., discussed in Ch. 11.d).

> *H. The belief in the best, in control in a man's soul, orders his life, even if a mistake occurs; and everything that he does must be called just* (864a1).

G contained no mention of the third affliction of the soul, ignorance. Are we to assume, therefore, that *H* follows the antithetical format of *D* and *E*, with an account of the type of injustice which is provoked by ignorance? But the belief in *to ariston* apparently results in justice, not in injustice. *H*, then, must be an account of the opposite state of soul from ignorance.

It still remains, however, to determine the strength of the intellectualist thesis presented in *H*. Two opposed interpretations are available. The first is the 'good conscience' version, to which Adkins, for example, adheres: "If a man's reason and desires are not in conflict, *whatever his basic view of life*, he is to be termed *dikaios*, providing that his actions are based on reason, not passion or desire" (*Merit and Responsibility*, p. 308, his emphasis). Thus belief in the best may fail, but it is well-intentioned and therefore just. The alternative is propounded by O'Brien ("Plato and the 'Good Conscience'"), who supposes that the belief in the best is simply equivalent to knowledge, and that the phrase *kan sphallētai ti* means "even if some damage be done."

Against the first position, there is considerable evidence. First, if Plato is now supposing that a 'good conscience' is sufficient to ensure that a man's actions be declared to be just, he has moved considerably away from the original prudential line, where virtue was correlated with success. Second, as Saunders points out, the 'just atheist' is well-intentioned (908b ff.), yet his actions are nevertheless bad and subject to correction. Third, although the exponents of this view might cite the weakness of *doxa*, belief, against the intellectualist possibilities of *epistēmē*, on several occasions Plato interchanges or associates belief with knowledge (at *Laws* 688b3, 689a-b, and at *Rep.* 585b14). On this evidence, belief in the best must be not merely well-intentioned, but also true and therefore effective for right action. And finally, the vexed text of the summarising remarks (864b1) describes the causes of crime, and instances, as the third, the *ephesis* of true belief about the best. This is taken, by the "good conscience" adherents, to refer to good intentions which go astray. Saunders ("Socratic Paradoxes," p. 429) suggests "an unsuccessful shot at the truth," arguing that here the Stranger is referring to ignorance, not to the belief in the best (on the grounds previously adduced, that it is ignorance which is a cause of crime). Perhaps most attractive of all is Diès' emendation of *ephesis* to *aphesis*, which allows him to translate: 'L'abandon des espérances et de l'opinion vraie en ce qui concerne le meilleur" (*Platon: Les Lois*, vol. 3 [Paris: Belles Lettres, 1956], p. 114).

From this it will appear that I prefer O'Brien's version of *H*. The difficulty here, however, is the translation of the phrase *kan sphallētai ti*. On the 'good conscience' line, these men with true belief can in fact make intellectual mistakes, but their reason is generally in the right direction. Of such men, we might say "He is right except when he makes a mistake," which is banal; or "He is generally right, so we will ignore the occasions when he is wrong," which begs the question. O'Brien, in my opinion rightly, rejects this view on the grounds that it devalues the intellectualist thesis to a useless level. It appears, however, that the vexed phrase cannot refer straightforwardly to 'damage', but that it must refer to 'mistake' of some kind (cf. Saunders, "Socratic Paradoxes," p. 431, *Grg.* 461d1, *Rep.* 361b1).

The difficulty then is to produce some sense of 'mistake' which does not violate the intellectualist thesis. At the same time, the structure of this sentence and that of the one before, compared with the programmatic remarks at 863b, suggests that the phrase in some way parallels "whether any damage is done or not" at G, and accounts for the accidents to which the man with true belief is prone. He makes, then, some kind of mistake, not in his moral grasp—for this is, according to my interpretation of the intellectualist thesis, complete—but in his practical assessments.

BIBLIOGRAPHY

TEXTS

Texts used have been Oxford Classical Texts with two exceptions:

Diels, H., and Kranz, W. *Die Fragmente der Vorsokratiker*. 6th edition. Zurich: Wiedmann, 1968 (the text for Pre-Socratics and Sophists, cited as DK, followed by the specific reference).

Edmonds, J.M. *Elegy and Iambus*. London: Heinemann, 1968 (the text for Solon, Theognis, Tyrtaeus).

Other editions, commentaries, and translations are included in the bibliography.

BIBLIOGRAPHY

This bibliography contains references to all the works cited in the notes and to additional books or articles that may be of value. I have given references to collections of articles and, where appropriate, to articles within such collections, when they are mentioned in the notes.

Acton, H.B., ed. *The Philosophy of Punishment*. London: Macmillan, 1969.

Adam, J., ed. *The Republic of Plato*. Cambridge: Cambridge University Press, 1965.

Adkins, A.W.H. "Honour and Punishment in the Homeric Poems." *B.I.C.S.* (1960):23–32.

————. "Friendship and Self-sufficiency in Homer and Aristotle." *C.Q.* (1963):30–45.

————. *Merit and Responsibility*. Oxford: Clarendon Press, 1965.

————. "Homeric Values and Homeric Society." *J.H.S.* (1971):1–14.

————. *Moral Values and Political Behaviour in Ancient Greece*. London: Chatto and Windus, 1972.

Allen, R.E. "The Socratic Paradox." *J.H.I.* (1960):256–265.

Anscombe, G.E.M. *Intention*. Ithaca: Cornell University Press, 1976.

Anton, J.P., and Kustas, G.L., eds. *Essays in Greek Philosophy*. Albany: State University of New York Press, 1971.

Austin, J.L. "Three Ways of Spilling Ink." *Ph.Rev.* (1966):427–440.

———. "A Plea for Excuses." In *The Philosophy of Action*, edited by A.R. White, pp. 19–42. Oxford: Oxford University Press, 1968.

Bambrough, R. "The Socratic Paradox." *Ph.Q.* (1960):229–300.

———. *New Essays on Plato and Aristotle*. London: Routledge, Kegan Paul, 1965.

———. "Plato's Political Analogies." In *Plato: II*, edited by G. Vlastos, pp. 187–205. London: Macmillan, 1971.

Barrow, R. *Plato, Utilitarianism and Education*. London: Routledge, Kegan Paul, 1975.

Benn, S.I. "An Approach to the Problems of Punishment." *Philosophy* (1958):325–341.

Berlin, I. "Equality." In *Concepts and Categories*, edited by Berlin, pp. 81–102. London: Hogarth, 1978.

Bonner, R.J. "The Administration of Justice in the Age of Homer." *C.Ph.* (1911):12–36.

———. "The Administration of Justice in the Age of Hesiod." *C.Ph.* (1912):17–23.

Bonner, R.J., and Smith, G. *The Administration of Justice from Homer to Aristotle*. Chicago: University of Chicago Press, 1930.

Burnyeat, M.F. "Virtues in Action." In *The Philosophy of Socrates*, edited by G. Vlastos, pp. 209–234.

Church, R.M. "The Varied Effects of Punishment on Behaviour." In *Punishment*, edited by R.H. Walters, J.A. Cheyne, and R.K. Banks, pp. 19–22, 34–39. London: Penguin, 1972.

Claus, D.B. "*Aidōs* in the Language of Achilles." *T.A.P.A.* (1975):13–28.

Creed, J.L. "Moral Values in the Age of Thucydides." *C.Q.* (1973):213–231.

Crombie, I.M. *An Examination of Plato's Doctrines*. 2 vols. London: Routledge, Kegan Paul, 1962.

Cross, R.C. and Woozley, A.D. *Plato's Republic: A Philosophical Commentary*. London: Macmillan, 1964.

Davidson, D. "How is Weakness of the Will Possible?" In *Moral Concepts*, edited by J. Feinberg, pp. 93–113. Oxford: Oxford University Press, 1969.

———. "Actions, Reasons and Causes." In *The Philosophy of Action*, edited by A.R. White, pp. 79–94. Oxford: Oxford University Press, 1968.

Demos, R. "A Fallacy in Plato's *Republic*?" In Vlastos, *Plato: II*, pp. 52–56.

Denniston, J.D., and Page, D., eds. *Aeschylus: Agamemnon*. Oxford: Clarendon Press, 1960.

Détienne, M., and Vernant, J.-P. *Cunning Intelligence in Greek Culture and Society*. Sussex: Harvester Press, 1978.

Dickie, M.W. "*Dikē* as a Moral Term in Homer and Hesiod." *C.Ph.* (1978):91–102.

Diès, A., ed. *Platon: Les Lois VII–XII*. Paris: Belles Lettres, 1956.

Dodds, E.R. "Plato and the Irrational." *J.H.S.* (1945):16–25.

———, ed. *Plato: Gorgias*. Oxford: Clarendon Press, 1959.

———. "Notes on the *Oresteia*." *C.Q.* (1953):11–21.

————, ed. *Euripides: Bacchae*. Oxford: Clarendon Press, 1960.

————. "Morals and Politics in the *Oresteia*." *P.C.P.S.* (1960):19–31.

————. *The Greeks and the Irrational*. Berkeley: University of California Press, 1966.

Dover, K.J. "The Political Aspect of Aeschylus' *Eumenides*." *J.H.S.* (1957):230–237.

————. "Some Neglected Aspects of Agamemnon's Dilemma." *J.H.S.* (1973):58–69.

————. *Greek Popular Morality in the Time of Plato and Aristotle*. Oxford: Blackwell, 1974.

Dworkin, R. *Taking Rights Seriously*. London: Duckworth, 1977.

————. "Taking Rights Seriously." In Dworkin, *Taking Rights Seriously*, pp. 184–205.

England, E.B., ed. *The Laws of Plato*. Manchester: Manchester University Press, 1921.

Ewing, A.C. *The Morality of Punishment*. London: Kegan Paul, 1929.

Feinberg, J., ed. *Moral Concepts*. Oxford: Oxford University Press, 1969.

————. *Doing and Deserving: Essays in the Theory of Responsibility*. Princeton: Princeton University Press, 1970.

————. "Justice and Personal Desert." In Feinberg, *Doing and Deserving*, pp. 55–94.

————. "The Expressive Function of Punishment." In Feinberg, *Doing and Deserving*, pp. 95–118.

————. "Action and Responsibility." In Feinberg, *Doing and Deserving*, pp. 119–151.

————. "Crime, Clutchability and Individuated Treatment." In Feinberg, *Doing and Deserving*, pp. 252–271.

————. "What's so Special about Mental Illness?" In Feinberg, *Doing and Deserving*, pp. 272–292.

————. "Rawls and Intuitionism." In N. Daniels, ed., *Reading Rawls* (Oxford: Blackwell, 1975), pp. 108–123.

Finley, M.I. *The World of Odysseus*. London: Chatto and Windus, 1964.

Flew, A.G.N. "Crime or Disease." *B.J.S.* (1954):49–62.

————. "The Justification of Punishment." In Acton, *The Philosophy of Punishment*, pp. 83–104.

Fontenrose, J. "Work, Justice and Hesiod's *Works and Days*." *C.Ph.* (1974):1–16.

Foot, P., ed. *Theories of Ethics*. Oxford: Oxford University Press, 1967.

————. "Moral Beliefs." In Foot, *Theories of Ethics*, pp. 83–100.

Forrester, J.W. "Some Perils of Paulinity." *Phronesis* (1975):11–21.

Foster, M.B. "A Mistake in Plato's *Republic*." *Mind* (1937):386–393.

————. "A Rejoinder to Mr. Mabbott." *Mind* (1938):226–232.

Frankena, W.K. "The Naturalistic Fallacy." In Foot, *Theories of Ethics*, pp. 50–63.

————. *Ethics*. Englewood Cliffs: Prentice-Hall, 1963.

Frankfurt, H. "Freedom of the Will and the Concept of a Person." *J. Ph.* (1971):5–20.

Furley, D.J. "Aristotle on the Voluntary." In *Articles on Aristotle*, edited by J. Barnes, M. Schofield and R. Sorabji. Vol 2, pp. 47–60. London: Duckworth, 1977.

Furth, M. "Elements of Eleatic Ontology." In *The Pre-Socratics*, edited by A. Mourelatos, pp. 241–270. New York: Doubleday, 1974.

Gagarin, M. "*Dikē* in the *Works and Days*." *C.Ph.* (1973):81–94.

———. "*Dikē* in Archaic Greek Thought." *C.Ph.* (1974):186–197.

———. "The Vote of Athena." *A.J.Ph.* (1975):121–127.

———. *Aeschylean Drama*. Berkeley: University of California Press, 1976.

Gallop, D. "Justice and Holiness in *Prot.* 330–1." *Phronesis* (1961):86–93.

———. "The Socratic Paradox in the *Protagoras*." *Phronesis* (1964):117–129.

———, ed. and trans. *Plato: Phaedo*. Oxford: Clarendon Press, 1975.

Geach, P.T. "Ascriptivism." *Ph.Rev.* (1960):221–225.

Gellie, G.H. "Motivation in Sophocles." *B.I.C.S.* (1964):1–14.

Gernet, L. *Droit et société dans la Grèce ancienne*. Paris: Sirey, 1955.

Ginsberg, M. *On the Diversity of Morals*. London: Mercury, 1962.

———. "The Nature of Responsibility." In Ginsberg, *On the Diversity of Morals*, pp. 79–96.

Glover, J. *Causing Death and Saving Lives*. London: Penguin, 1977.

Gluckman, M. *Politics, Law and Ritual in Tribal Society*. Oxford: Blackwell, 1965.

Görgemanns, H. *Beiträge zur Interpretation von Platons* Nomoi. Zetemata 25, München: Beck, 1960.

Gosling, J. "*Doxa* and *Dunamis* in Plato's *Republic*." *Phronesis* (1968):119–130.

———. *Plato*. London: Routledge, Kegan Paul, 1973.

Gould, J. *The Development of Plato's Ethics*. Cambridge: Cambridge University Press, 1955.

Gouldner, A.W. *Enter Plato: Classical Greece and the Origins of Social Theory*. New York: Basic Books, 1965.

Gross, H. *A Theory of Criminal Justice*. Oxford: Oxford University Press, 1979.

Gulley, N. "The Interpretation of 'No-one Does Wrong Willingly' in Plato's Dialogues." *Phronesis* (1965):82–96.

———. *The Philosophy of Socrates*. London: Macmillan, 1968.

Guthrie, W.K.C. "Plato's Views on the Nature of the Soul." In Vlastos, *Plato: II*, pp. 230–243.

Hackforth, R. "The Hedonism in Plato's *Protagoras*." *C.Q.* (1928):38–42.

Hall, R.W. *Plato and the Individual*. The Hague: Nijhoff, 1963.

Hare, R.M. *Freedom and Reason*. Oxford: Clarendon Press, 1963.

———. *The Language of Morals*. Oxford: Oxford University Press, 1952.

Hart, H.L.A. "The Ascription of Rights and Responsibility." *Proc.Ar.Soc.* (1948–49):171–194.

———. *The Concept of Law*. Oxford: Oxford University Press, 1961.

———. "Are there any Natural Rights?" In A. Quinton, *Political Philosophy* (Oxford: Oxford University Press, 1967), pp. 53–66.

———. *Punishment and Responsibility*. Oxford: Clarendon Press, 1968.

———. "Prolegomenon to the Principles of Punishment." In Hart, *Punishment and Responsibility*, pp. 1–27.

———. "Legal Responsibility and Excuses." In Hart, *Punishment and Responsibility*, pp. 28–53.

———. "Murder and the Principles of Punishment: England and the United States." In Hart, *Punishment and Responsibility*, pp. 54–89.

Havelock, E.A. *The Liberal Temper in Greek Politics*. London: Cape, 1957.

————. *The Greek Concept of Justice.* Cambridge, Mass.: Harvard University Press, 1978.

Von Hirsch, A. *Doing Justice.* New York: Hill and Wang, 1976.

Honderich, T. *Punishment, its Supposed Justifications.* London: Penguin, 1971.

————, ed. *Essays on Freedom of Action.* London: Routledge, Kegan Paul, 1973.

Hook, S., ed. *Determinism and Freedom.* New York: Collier, 1961.

Hospers, J. "What Means This Freedom?" In Hook, *Determinism and Freedom,* pp. 126–142.

Hourani, G.F. "Thrasymachus' Definition of Justice in Plato's *Republic*." *Phronesis* (1962):110–120.

Irwin, T. "Recollection and Plato's Moral Theory." *Rev. Metaphysics* (1974):752–772.

————. *Plato's Moral Theory: The Early and Middle Dialogues.* Oxford: Clarendon Press, 1977.

Jones, J. *On Aristotle and Greek Tragedy.* London: Chatto and Windus, 1962.

Kahn, C. "Anaximander's Fragment: The Universe Governed by Law." In Mourelatos, ed., *The Presocratics,* pp. 99–117.

————. "The Meaning of 'Justice' and the Theory of Forms." *J.Ph.* (1972):567–579.

Kant, I. *Groundwork of the Metaphysic of Morals.* Trans. H.J. Paton. New York: Harper, 1964.

————. *The Metaphysical Elements of Justice.* Trans. J. Ladd. New York: Library of Liberal Arts, 1965.

Kenny, A.J.P. "Mental Health in Plato's *Republic*." *Proc.Brit.Acad.* (1969):229–253.

Kerferd, G.B. "The Doctrine of Thrasymachus in Plato's *Republic*." *Durham University Journal* (1947):19–27.

————. "Protagoras' Doctrine of Justice and Virtue in the *Protagoras* of Plato." *J.H.S.* (1953):42–45.

————. "Thrasymachus and Justice: A Reply." *Phronesis* (1964):12–17.

Kirk, G.S., and Raven, J. *The Presocratic Philosophers.* Cambridge: Cambridge University Press, 1966.

Kirwan, C. "Glaucon's Challenge." *Phronesis* (1965):162–173.

Kitto, H.D.F. *Sophocles, Dramatist and Philosopher.* London: Oxford University Press, 1958.

Kraut, R. "Egoism, Love and Political Office in Plato." *Ph.Rev.* (1973):330–344.

————. "Reason and Justice in Plato's *Republic*." In *Exegesis and Argument,* edited by E.N. Lee, A. Mourelatos, and R.M. Rorty, pp. 207–224. Assen: Van Gorcum, 1973.

Kristeller, P.O. "History of Philosophy and History of Ideas." *J.H.Ph.* (1964):1–14.

Lee, E.N., Mourelatos, A., and Rorty, R.M., eds. *Exegesis and Argument: Studies Presented to Vlastos.* Assen: Van Gorcum, 1973.

Lesky, A. "Decision and Responsibility in the Tragedy of Aeschylus." *J.H.S.* (1966):78–85.

Liddell, H.G., Scott, R., and Jones, H.S.J. *A Greek-English Lexicon.* 9th ed. (Abbreviated as *LSJ.*) Oxford: Clarendon Press, 1961.

Little, A.M.G. *Myth and Society in Attic Drama.* New York: Columbia University Press, 1942.

Lloyd-Jones, H., trans. and comm. *The Eumenides of Aeschylus.* Englewood Cliffs: Prentice-Hall, 1970.

————. *The Justice of Zeus.* Berkeley: University of California Press, 1973.

Long, A.A. "Morals and Values in Homer." *J.H.S.* (1970):121–139.

Lukes, S. "Moral Weakness." In G. Mortimore, ed., *Weakness of Will*, pp. 147–159. London: Macmillan, 1971.

Mabbott, J.D. "Interpretations of Mill's 'Utilitarianism'," in Foot, ed., *Theories of Ethics*, pp. 137–143.

———. "Punishment." In Acton, *The Philosophy of Punishment*, pp. 39–54.

———. "Is Plato's *Republic* Utilitarian?" In Vlastos, *Plato: II*, pp. 57–65.

McCloskey, H.J. "An Examination of Restricted Utilitarianism." *Ph.Rev.* (1957):466–485.

———. "A Note on Utilitarian Punishment." *Mind* (1963):599.

McGibbon, D. "Metempsychosis in Pindar." *Phronesis* (1964):5–11.

Mackenzie, M.M. "The Tears of Chryses: Retaliation in the *Iliad*." *Philosophy and Literature* (1978):3–22.

Mackie, J.L. *Ethics: Inventing Right and Wrong*. London: Penguin, 1977.

Marx, K. *Critique of the Gotha Program*. In *The Marx-Engels Reader*, edited by R.C. Tucker, pp. 383–398. New York: Norton, 1972.

Melden, A.I., ed. *Essays in Moral Philosophy*. Seattle: University of Washington Press, 1958.

Mill, J.S. *Utilitarianism*. Edited by M. Warnock. Glasgow: Fontana, 1962.

Moberley, W. *The Ethics of Punishment*. London: Faber, 1968.

Morris, H. "Persons and Punishment." *The Monist* (1968):475–501.

Morrow, G. *Plato's Cretan City*. Princeton: Princeton University Press, 1960.

———. "Plato and the Rule of Law." In Vlastos, *Plato: II*, pp. 144–165.

Mourelatos, A. *The Route of Parmenides*. New Haven: Yale University Press, 1970.

———, ed. *The Pre-Socratics*. New York: Doubleday, 1974.

Mundle, C.W.K. "Punishment and Desert." In Acton, *The Philosophy of Punishment*, pp. 65–82.

Müller, C.O. *Dissertations on the Eumenides of Aeschylus*. London: 1853.

Nagel, T. "Moral Luck." *Proc.Ar.Soc.Suppl.* (1976):138–151.

———. *Mortal Questions*. Cambridge: Cambridge University Press, 1979.

Neely, W. "Freedom and Desire." *Ph.Rev.* (1974):32–54.

Nicholson, P.P. "Unravelling Thrasymachus' Arguments in the *Republic*." *Phronesis* (1974):210–232.

North, H. *Sophrosyne: Self-Knowledge and Self-Restraint in Greek Literature*. Ithaca: Cornell University Press, 1966.

Nozick, R. *Anarchy, State and Utopia*. Oxford: Blackwell, 1974.

O'Brien, M.J. "Plato and the 'Good Conscience': *Laws* 863e5–864b7." *T.A.P.A.* (1957):81–87.

———. *The Socratic Paradoxes and the Greek Mind*. Chapel Hill: University of North Carolina Press, 1967.

———. "The 'Fallacy' in *Prot.* 349d–350c." *T.A.P.A.* (1962):408–417.

Ostwald, M. *Nomos and the Beginnings of Athenian Democracy*. Oxford: Clarendon Press, 1969.

———. "Was There a Concept *agraphos nomos* in Classical Greece?" In Lee et al. *Exegesis and Argument*, 70–104.

———. "Ancient Greek Ideas of Law." In *Dictionary of the History of Ideas*, pp. 673–685. New York: Charles Scribner's Sons, 1973.

―――. "Plato on Law and Nature." In *Interpretations of Plato*, edited by H. North. *Mnemosyne* Suppl. (1977):41–63.

Owen, G.E.L. "The Place of the *Timaeus* in Plato's Dialogues." In *Studies in Plato's Metaphysics*, edited by R.E. Allen, pp. 313–338. London: Routledge, Kegan Paul, 1965.

―――. "Plato on Not-being." In Vlastos, *Plato: I*, pp. 223–267.

―――. "Logic and Metaphysics in Some Earlier Works of Aristotle." In *Articles on Aristotle*, edited by J. Barnes, M. Schofield, and R. Sorabji, Vol. 3, pp. 13–32. London: Duckworth, 1979.

Page, D., ed. *Euripides: Medea*. Oxford: Clarendon Press, 1938.

Palmer, L.R. "The Indo-European Origins of Greek Justice." *Trans.Philol.Soc.* (Oxford) (1950):149–68.

Penner, T. "Thought and Desire in Plato." In Vlastos, *Plato: II*, pp. 96–118.

―――. "The Unity of Virtue." *Ph.R.* (1973):35–68.

Des Places, E., ed. *Platon: Les Lois I–VII*. Paris: Belles Lettres, 1956.

Podlecki, A. *The Political Background of Aeschylean Tragedy*. Ann Arbor: University of Michigan Press, 1966.

Popper, K. *The Open Society and its Enemies*. Vol. I: *Plato*. London: Routledge, Kegan Paul, 1966.

Quine, W.V.O. *Ontological Relativity*. New York: Columbia University Press, 1969.

―――. "Reference and Modality." In *Reference and Modality*, edited by L. Linsky, pp. 17–34. Oxford: Oxford University Press, 1971.

Quinton, A.M. "On Punishment." In Acton, *The Philosophy of Punishment*, pp. 55–64.

―――, ed. *Political Philosophy*. Oxford: Oxford University Press, 1967.

Rawls, J. "Two Concepts of Rules." In Foot, *Theories of Ethics*, pp. 144–170.

―――. *A Theory of Justice*. Oxford: Clarendon Press, 1972.

Raz, J., ed. *Practical Reasoning*. Oxford: Oxford University Press, 1978.

Robinson, R. "Plato's Separation of Reason from Desire." *Phronesis* (1971):38–48.

Robinson, T.M. "Soul and Immortality in *Republic* X." *Phronesis* (1967):147–151.

Rodgers, V.A. "Some Thoughts on *Dikē*." *C.Q.* (1971): 289–301.

de Romilly, J. *La Loi dans la Penséé grecque, des origines à Aristote*. Paris: Budé, 1971.

Ryle, G. "On Forgetting the Difference Between Right and Wrong." In Melden, *Essays in Moral Philosophy*. Seattle: Washington Paperbacks, 1966, pp. 147–159.

Sachs, D. "A Fallacy in Plato's *Republic*." In Vlastos, *Plato: II*, pp. 35–51.

Santas, G.X. "Socrates at Work on Virtue and Knowledge in Plato's *Laches*." In Vlastos, ed., *The Philosophy of Socrates*, pp. 177–208.

―――. *Socrates*. London: Routledge, Kegan Paul, 1979.

Saunders, T.J. "Two Points in Plato's Penal Code." *C.Q.* (1963):194–199.

―――. "The Socratic Paradoxes in Plato's *Laws*." *Hermes* (1968):421–434.

―――, trans. *Plato: The Laws*. London: Penguin, 1970.

―――. *Notes on The Laws of Plato*. *B.I.C.S.* Supplement 28 (1972).

―――. "Plato on Killing in Anger: a Reply to Professor Woozley." *Ph.Q.* (1973):350–356.

——. "Penology and Eschatology in Plato's *Timaeus* and *Laws*." *C.Q.* (1973):232–244.

Searle, J. "How to Derive 'Ought' From 'Is'." In Foot, *Theories of Ethics*, pp. 101–114.

Sidgwick, H. *Methods of Ethics*. London: Macmillan, 1907.

Simon, B. *Mind and Madness in Ancient Greece*. Ithaca: Cornell University Press, 1978.

Skemp, J.B. "Individual and Civic Virtue in the Republic." *Phronesis* (1969):107–110.

Skinner, B.F. "Punishment: A Questionable Technique." In Walters, R.H., Cheyne, J.A., and Banks, R.K. *Punishment*, pp. 23–33. London: Penguin, 1972.

——. *About Behaviorism*. New York: Vintage Books, 1976.

Smart, J.J.C. "Extreme and Restricted Utilitarianism." In Foot, *Theories of Ethics*, pp. 171–183.

——, and Williams, B.A.O. *Utilitarianism, For and Against*. Cambridge: Cambridge University Press, 1973.

Snell, B. *The Discovery of the Mind: The Greek Origins of European Thought*. Oxford: Blackwell, 1953.

Sorabji, R. "Aristotle on the Role of Intellect in Virtue." *Proc.Ar.Soc.* (1973–4):107–129.

Stahl, H.P. "Learning Through Suffering? Croesus' Conversations in the History of Herodotus." *Y.C.S.* (1975):1–36.

Strang, C. "Plato and the Third Man." In Vlastos, *Plato: I*, pp. 184–200.

Strawson, P. "Freedom and Resentment." In *Studies in the Philosophy of Thought and Action*, edited by P. Strawson, pp. 71–96. London: Oxford University Press, 1968.

Stroud, R.S. *Dracon's Law of Homicide*. Berkeley: University of California Press, 1968.

Tate, J. "Plato and Allegorical Interpretation." *C.Q.* (1929):142–154; (1930):1–10.

Taylor, A.E. *A Commentary on Plato's Timaeus*. Oxford: Clarendon Press, 1928.

Taylor, C.C.W., ed. and trans. *Plato: Protagoras*. Oxford: Clarendon Press, 1976.

Teichman, J. "Punishment and Remorse." *Philosophy* (1973):335–346.

Thomson, G., ed. *Aeschylus:* Prometheus Vinctus. Cambridge: Cambridge University Press, 1932.

Urmson, J.O. "The Interpretation of the Moral Philosophy of J.S. Mill." In Foot, *Theories of Ethics*, pp. 128–136.

——. "Saints and Heroes." In Melden, *Essays in Moral Responsibility*, pp. 198–216.

Vlastos, G. "Solonian Justice." *C.Ph.* (1946):65–83.

——, ed. *Plato's* Protagoras. New York: Library of Liberal Arts, 1956.

——. "Justice and Equality." In *Social Justice*, edited by R. Brandt, pp. 31–72. Englewood Cliffs: Prentice-Hall, 1962.

——. "Was Polus Refuted?" *A.J.Ph.* (1967): 454–460.

——. "Socrates on *Acrasia*." *Phoenix* (1969):71–88.

——. "Equality and Justice in Early Greek Cosmologies." In *Studies in Presocratic Philosophy*, edited by D. Furley and R.E. Allen, pp. 56–91. London: Routledge, Kegan Paul, 1970.

————, ed. *The Philosophy of Socrates*. London: Macmillan, 1971.

————, ed. *Plato: I*. London: Macmillan, 1971.

————, ed. *Plato: II*. London: Macmillan, 1971.

————. "Justice and Happiness in the *Republic*." In Vlastos, *Plato: II*, pp. 66–95.

————. *Platonic Studies*. Princeton: Princeton University Press, 1973.

————. "The Individual as Object of Love in Plato." In Vlastos, *Platonic Studies*, pp. 3–34.

————. "Reasons and Causes in the *Phaedo*." In Vlastos, *Platonic Studies*, pp. 76–110.

————. "Socratic Knowledge and Platonic Pessimism." In Vlastos, *Platonic Studies*, pp. 204–217.

————. "The Unity of the Virtues in the Protagoras." In Vlastos, *Platonic Studies*, pp. 221–265.

————. *Plato's Universe*. Seattle: University of Washington Press, 1975.

————. "The Theory of Social Justice in the Polis in Plato's *Republic*." In North, *Interpretations of Plato. Mnemosyne* Suppl. (1977):1–40.

Walker, N. Review of von Hirsch, *Doing Justice. B.J.C.* (1978):79–84.

Walsh, J.J. "The Socratic Denial of *Akrasia*." In Vlastos, *Socrates*, pp. 235–263.

Watson, G. "Free Agency." *J. Phil.* (1975):205–220.

Wertheimer, A. "Punishing the Innocent: Unintentionally." *Inquiry* (1977):45–66.

West, M.L., ed. *Hesiod: Theogony*. Oxford: Oxford University Press, 1966.

————, ed. *Hesiod: Works and Days*. Oxford: Oxford University Press, 1978.

White, A.R., ed. *The Philosophy of Action*. Oxford: Oxford University Press, 1968.

Wiggins, D. "Deliberation and Practical Reason." *Proc.Ar.Soc.* (1975–76):29–51.

Williams, B.A.O. "The Analogy of City and Soul in Plato's *Republic*." In Lee *et al.*, *Exegesis and Argument*, pp. 196–206.

————. "Ethical Consistency." In *Problems of the Self*, edited by B.A.O. Williams. Cambridge: Cambridge University Press, 1973.

————. "Moral Luck." *Proc.Ar.Soc.* Suppl. (1976):115–135.

Wootton, B. *Crime and the Criminal Law*. London: Stevens & Sons, 1963.

Woozley, A.D. "Plato on Killing in Anger." *Ph.Q.* (1972):303–317.

————. "Socrates on Disobeying the Law." In Vlastos, *Socrates*, pp. 299–318.

INDEX LOCORUM

PLATO

SUBJECT AND NAME INDEX

Designer:	Sandy Drooker
Compositor:	Graphic Composition
Printer:	Braun-Brumfield
Binder:	Braun-Brumfield
Text:	10/12 VIP Baskerville
Display:	Typositor Weiss Series II
Cloth:	Holliston Roxite B 53544
Paper:	50 lb. P & S Vellum B32

DATE DUE			
FEB 10 '88			

DEMCO 38-297